I0019895

Cyril Onwubiko

Security Framework for Attack Detection in Computer Networks

Cyril Onwubiko

Security Framework for Attack Detection in Computer Networks

VDM Verlag Dr. Müller

Impressum/Imprint (nur für Deutschland/ only for Germany)
Bibliografische Information der Deutschen Nationalbibliothek: Die Deutsche Nationalbibliothek
verzeichnet diese Publikation in der Deutschen Nationalbibliografie; detaillierte bibliografische
Daten sind im Internet über http://dnb.d-nb.de abrufbar.
Alle in diesem Buch genannten Marken und Produktnamen unterliegen warenzeichen-, marken-
oder patentrechtlichem Schutz bzw. sind Warenzeichen oder eingetragene Warenzeichen der
jeweiligen Inhaber. Die Wiedergabe von Marken, Produktnamen, Gebrauchsnamen,
Handelsnamen, Warenbezeichnungen u.s.w. in diesem Werk berechtigt auch ohne besondere
Kennzeichnung nicht zu der Annahme, dass solche Namen im Sinne der Warenzeichen- und
Markenschutzgesetzgebung als frei zu betrachten wären und daher von jedermann benutzt
werden dürften.

Coverbild: www.purestockx.com

Verlag: VDM Verlag Dr. Müller Aktiengesellschaft & Co. KG
Dudweiler Landstr. 99, 66123 Saarbrücken, Deutschland
Telefon +49 681 9100-698, Telefax +49 681 9100-988, Email: info@vdm-verlag.de

Herstellung in Deutschland:
Schaltungsdienst Lange o.H.G., Berlin
Books on Demand GmbH, Norderstedt
Reha GmbH, Saarbrücken
Amazon Distribution GmbH, Leipzig
ISBN: 978-3-639-08934-9

Imprint (only for USA, GB)
Bibliographic information published by the Deutsche Nationalbibliothek: The Deutsche
Nationalbibliothek lists this publication in the Deutsche Nationalbibliografie; detailed
bibliographic data are available in the Internet at http://dnb.d-nb.de.
Any brand names and product names mentioned in this book are subject to trademark, brand or
patent protection and are trademarks or registered trademarks of their respective holders. The use
of brand names, product names, common names, trade names, product descriptions etc. even
without a particular marking in this works is in no way to be construed to mean that such names
may be regarded as unrestricted in respect of trademark and brand protection legislation and
could thus be used by anyone.

Cover image: www.purestockx.com

Publisher:
VDM Verlag Dr. Müller Aktiengesellschaft & Co. KG
Dudweiler Landstr. 99, 66123 Saarbrücken, Germany
Phone +49 681 9100-698, Fax +49 681 9100-988, Email: info@vdm-verlag.de

Printed in the U.S.A.
Printed in the U.K. by (see last page)
ISBN: 978-3-639-08934-9

Previously published materials

1. **C. Onwubiko** (2008), "Multisensor Message Exchange Mechanism", *International Journal of Electronic Security and Digital Forensics (IJESDF)* , ISSN (Online): 1751-9128 - ISSN (Print): 1751-911X, Vol. 2, No. 2, September 2008.

2. **C. Onwubiko** and A. Lenaghan (2007), "Managing Security Threats and Vulnerabilities for Small and Medium Enterprises", *5th IEEE International Conference on Intelligence and Security Informatics, IEEE ISI 2007, IEEE Press, New Jersey, USA*, pp. 244-249, IEEE Catalog Number: 07EX1834, ISBN: 1-4244-1329-X, May 2007.

3. **C. Onwubiko**, A. Lenaghan, and L. Hebbes (2006), "An Integrated Security Framework for Assisting in the Defence of Computer Networks", *Joint IST Workshop on Sensor Networks & Symposium on Trends in Communications Proceedings, IEEE Catalog Number: 06EX1373*, ISBN: 1-4244-0368-5, pp. 52-55, Slovakia, June 2006.

4. **C. Onwubiko** and A. Lenaghan (2006), "An Evolutionary Approach in Threats Detection for Distributed Security Defence Systems", *4th IEEE International Conference on Intelligence and Security Informatics, IEEE ISI 2006, Springer,* ISBN: 3-540-34478-0, May 2006.

5. **C. Onwubiko** and A. Lenaghan (2006), "Response Mechanism for Defending Computer Networks", *International Journal of Computer Science and Network Security, IJCSNS 2006*, **Vol. 6, No. 8A, pp. 36-42,** *Computer Science,* ISBN/ISSN 1738-7906, August 2006.

6. **C. Onwubiko** (2008), "Data Fusion in Security Evidence Analysis", *Proceedings of the 3rd Conference on Advances in Computer Security and Forensics, ACSF 2008, Liverpool John Moores University, Liverpool, UK*, ISBN: 978-1-902560-20-5, pp. 1-7, July 2008.

7. **C. Onwubiko** and A. Lenaghan (2005), "Vulnerability Assessment: Towards an Integrated Security Infrastructure", *International Conference on Computer Science & Information Systems (ICCSIS 2005), Computer Science and Information System, Greece*, pp. 157-172, ISBN: 960-88672-3-1, June 2005.

8. A. Lenaghan, **C. Onwubiko**, L. Hebbes, R. Malyan (2005), "Security Spaces for Protecting Users of Wireless Public Hotspots", *IEEE International Conference, IEEE EUROCON 2005*, **Vol. 1, pp. 648 - 651,** *Serbia & Montenegro, Belgrade,* ISBN: 1-4244-0049-X, November 2005.

9. **C. Onwubiko** and S. Omosule (2005), "An Information Systems Security Infrastructure to address Content Security Threats", *Proceeding of the International Conference on Advances in Information and Communications Engineering, AICEG2005, pp. 47-57, ISBN: 9988643136, August 2005.*

10. **C. Onwubiko** and A. Lenaghan (2006), "Spatio-Temporal Relationships in the Analysis of Threats for Security Monitoring Systems", *Proceeding of 2nd International Conference on Computer Science & Information Systems, Athens, Greece 2006, Current Computing Developments in E-Commerce, Security, HCI, DB, pp. 455-471, ISBN: 960-6672-07-7, June 2006.*

11. **C. Onwubiko**, A. Lenaghan, L. Hebbes, and R. Malyan (2005), "The Representation and use of Relation Information for the Detection of Threats by Security Information Management Systems", *European Conference on Computer Network Defence, EC2ND 2005, Wales, UK, pp. 50-60, ISBN: 1-84628-311-6, December 2005.*

12. **C. Onwubiko** (2006), "Towards a Backup Cipher for the Advanced Encryption Standard (AES)", *Communication Networks and Electronic Security - Journal for ICT Security Synergy in Advanced and Developing Economies, ISSN: 1746-8558, **Vol. 1, Issue 1**, 2006.*

13. **C. Onwubiko**, A. Lenaghan, and L. Hebbes (2005), "An Improved Worm Mitigation Model for Evaluating the Spread of Aggressive Network Worms", *IEEE International Conference, IEEE EUROCON 2005, **Vol. 2, pp. 1710-1713**, Serbia & Montenegro, Belgrade, ISBN: 1-4244-0049-X, November 2005.*

14. **C. Onwubiko** and A. Lenaghan (2009), "Challenges and Complexities of Managing Information Security", *International Journal of Electronic Security and Digital Forensics (IJESDF), ISSN (Online): 1751-9128 - ISSN (Print): 1751-911X, **Vol. 3, No. 1**, 2009.*

Dedication

To my wife *Gloria*, our daughter *Jessica*, and our son *Jason*.

Contents

List of Figures

Acknowledgments

I would like to thank the following people for their various contributions to this book: Dr. Thomas J. Owens in the School of Engineering & Design, Brunel University, London, UK; Dr. Andrew P. Lenaghan of Flawless Money Ltd, Manchester, UK; and Dr. Eckhard Pfluegel in the Faculty of Computing, Information Systems and Mathematics, Kingston University, London, UK.

I would especially like to thank Jane Donovan, who proofread and copy edited this book. Special thanks to Samuel Cecile the acquisition editor, who provided editorial advise and support to ensure that the book was produced in time and of excellent quality.

I give special thanks to my former colleagues at COLT Telecommunications Group, for their support, especially, Andre Van Der Walt and Mark Stevens, who helped critique and provide useful feedback regarding the cover page of the book. I would like to thank friends and family, whose prayers and support were most rewarding.

Finally, I thank God for strength, good health and knowledge to this write this book, with whom all things are possible.

Cyril Onwubiko
Intelligence and Security Assurance
E-Security Group
Research Series
London, UK

Forewords

I recently finished reading *The Naked Sun*, the second novel in Isaac Asimov's classic 1950s science fiction series. In it a shrewd and somber New York detective, plainclothesman Elijah Baley, is sent from earth to a distant utopian world to investigate a murder that puzzles the local authorities. Although the inhabitants of the distant world are descendants of earth, the two cultures have diverged significantly. Both regard the habits and behaviour of the other as a little strange. Much of the interest in the novel lies in the necessity for plainclothesman Baley to reexamine how he applies his detective skills in a new and unfamiliar context. The evidence of the crime is unchallenged, but the means and motives at play are surprising.

In the world of network security, the evidence that individual systems such as firewalls or intrusion detection systems gather is familiar, and the threats that can be detected is well understood. In Cyril's work, the unification of evidence from multiple sources creates a new and unfamiliar context in which to reason about network attacks. This new context promises powerful ways to detect and respond to threats but, as Baley found in his distant world, it forces us to reexamine many of our underlying assumptions and to be prepared to interpret the evidence in new and different ways.

I shared many interesting discussions with Cyril as the research on which this book is based emerged. While we were both members of the network and communication research group, Cyril generously lent his time, expertise and sheer enthusiasm for the network security to enrich the masters programs at Kingston. What I admired throughout was his very pragmatic approach. However philosophical or academic the discussion might be Cyril had a great ability to draw out the crucial point and do something to test it. He knew how to ask the right question. Often within days of a speculating about a new aspect of the theory we would be exchanging code or discussing some fresh data that cut to the core of the matter. As the great physicist Richard Feynman once said, 'What I cannot create, I do not understand.' and Cyril's approach certainty took this to heart. Ideas were there to be implemented, assumptions to be challenged and evidence tested.

I believe this work tackles some timely themes. Threats to networks lie not just in the brute force of distributed attacks or in cunning malware, these risks and the means to mitigate them are well understood. The threat also lies in attacks, where the activities of a patient and stealthy attacker stay well below the radar of any individual sensor. In isolation, no individual event may appear suspicious enough to raise the alarm. The challenge is to detect a pattern unfolding over time and across a whole network that reveals the attack. As in many good whodunits, it is often as much the frame of reference as the evidence that reveals the truth.

Andrew Lenaghan, PhD
Senior Consultant I.T & Network Security
Flawless Money Ltd, UK

I first encountered the material in this book in my role as external examiner of the doctoral thesis from which its contents are taken. As someone who has taught wireless communications security and network security and encryption for many years in the United Kingdom, Germany, and Greece, I recognised at once that this body of work presents a crucial step in a paradigm shift in the way network security is viewed that has been gaining pace in recent years. This paradigm shift is characterised by a move away from the exclusive use of localised systems to protect network security, such as user authentication and firewalls, towards distributed defence approaches such as security information management systems that integrate security events from multiple sources to provide a unified view of the security of the entire network. The crucial step presented in this book is the development of an integrated security framework for detecting enterprise wide network attacks, such as distributed denial of service attacks, accomplished by the application of the Dempster-Shafer theory of evidence. To assist network administrators visualise and mitigate identified distributed attacks graph matching algorithms are employed.

The book is easy to read and develops its core ideas in a consistent and efficient manner. It is a classic research text in that it develops what is essentially one big idea that cannot be effectively presented within the confines of a journal paper. I recommend this book to network security researchers as a rich source of research ideas for basic research with a similar potential for gaining fundamental insights into the security of distributed systems that the application of game theory has delivered in the context of the study of the robustness of wireless ad hoc networks. Finally, I recommend this book to network security practitioners as a way of gaining a better appreciation of the likely practical consequences of the move towards distributed defence approaches that will assist them better appreciate the role, context and potential of distributed defence approaches.

Dr. T.J. Owens CEng
Senior Lecturer Communications
ECE School of Engineering and Design
Brunel University, Uxbridge
Middlesex UB8 3PH, UK

Preface

"The LORD made the earth, using his *wisdom*. He set the sky in place, using his *understanding*. With his *knowledge*, he made springs flow into rivers and the clouds drop rain on the earth" – Prov. 3, 20.

This book provides an introduction to a security framework for detecting widespread attacks targeted on computer networks. It discusses and demonstrates how the framework is used to detect enterprise-wide attacks perceived on computer networks, which would have ordinarily gone undetected with most current network security approaches. The proposed framework consists of three components: *sensor, analysis* and *response*.

Sensor components gather evidence about security attacks perceived in the network, and on individual hosts. Analysis components correlate and combine pieces of attack evidence gathered by the sensors, to accurately identify and detect attacks perceived in the network. Response components execute recommended responses, and can be configured to assist humans in mitigating the attacks.

The various components of the framework communicate with each other through a lightweight signalling mechanism referred to as "*security spaces*". A security space is a type of middleware that is based on "tuple space", which allows sensor, analysis and response components to connect, contribute and communicate security-related information to each other. The application of security spaces to distributed sensor and federated sensor environments is demonstrated.

The detection of enterprise-wide attacks targeting computer networks is accomplished by distributing sensors across the network to collate evidence of perceived attacks. Evidence of attacks gathered by sensors are sent to the analysis component for further investigation. In the analysis component, a novel approach in security visualisation and multisensor data fusion is applied. This approach is underpinned by the *pattern activity graph* and the *Dempster-Shafer theory of evidence*. The Dempster-Shafer theory of evidence is used to collectively combine pieces of independent attack evidence gathered by the sensors. The fusion of multisensor evidence assists to provide accurate identification and detection of attacks perceived in the entire network, most of which are not possible with existing network attack detection approaches.

Security visualisation graphs of attacks perceived in the network are provided. These assist security administrators to visualise and swiftly mitigate attacks perceived in the network. A security visualisation graph is based on a model graph referred to as a *pattern activity graph*. Pattern activity graphs of security incidents are analysed using intelligent and pattern matching techniques, such as graph theory, graph and subgraph isomorphisms.

Finally, the framework is demonstrated through a series of experiments conducted on a testbed network where live network traffic was monitored.

Chapter 1

Cyber security problems and solutions

This chapter provides an introduction to the various problems computer networks face today, such as vulnerabilities in computer networks, threats and attacks. The chapter also provides a survey of the different solutions that organisations employ to protect computer networks.

1.1 Introduction

Computer networks are under constant attacks. These attacks result from both attackers with malicious intents, and also, inadvertently from legitimate users of the system without malicious intents. Cyber attacks such as insider attacks, deliberate software attacks, malware, espionage, phishing, pharming, and denial of service attacks cause harm or predispose assets to harm leading to consequential loss to the organisation. With the growing number of security incidents, computer networks need adequate security protection.

To protect computer networks from security attacks, a current approach is to deploy countermeasures, such as firewalls at the network perimeter, intrusion detection systems (IDSes) within the network, and virus scanners on end user systems. While these countermeasures provide a degree of protection, they struggle to detect emerging security threats [6]. Emerging security attacks appear to be distributed and coordinated [9], while the defences offered by these countermeasures operate in isolation from one another. Each countermeasure possesses only fragments of evidence about the overall state of the network, and consequently its response may be both delayed and limited in scope.

Recent security attacks, for example, distributed denial of service, which can be launched from multiple hosts across the Internet highlight the limitations of a fragmented approach to network security (illustrated in Figure 4.1). In the case of overall network protection, identifying attacks on individual systems is only one part of protecting the network, and a significant issue is identifying threats or attacks targeting the entire network. We investigated an integrated security framework that is able to detect widespread network attacks across the enterprise. An integrated security framework is a unified framework that integrates various security components to accurately identify and detect attacks perceived at different points in the network. The premise is that evidence of attacks gathered on individual hosts or parts of the network are collectively combined to accurately detect attacks targeting the enterprise.

This book provides an introduction to an integrated security framework. It also discusses the various components of the framework, the techniques employed in the framework, the different domains in which the framework can be applied, and finally, it demonstrates the application of the framework using a testbed network where live Internet traffic are captured, in order to accurately detect and identify widespread attacks perceived across a population of computer hosts. Further, the application of the framework to terrorism and organised crime arenas are suggested.

1.2 Motivation

Computer network communication is now likened to a standard utility, such as electricity or telephone access [82]. Hence the *integrity, availability* and *confidentiality* of its offered services become critical. To maintain a *reliable, available* and *confidential* communication requires adequate protection of computer networks. However, two major security issues hinder the provision of adequate protection to computer networks: *vulnerabilities* in computer networks, and *threats* that exploit them.

Managing security threats and vulnerabilities in Computer networks are two fundamental challenges facing small and medium enterprises (SME) [11]. Unfortunately, vulnerabilities exist in most systems; and the concern that vulnerabilities in systems cannot be completely avoided [10] makes the protection of computer networks essential. Vulnerabilities in systems are weaknesses in systems or the absence of security procedures, technical controls, or physical controls that could be exploited by an adversary to harm or predispose systems to harm [1]. Security threats exploit vulnerabilities, or chains of vulnerabilities in systems to harm them, or predispose them to harm. Harm to systems occurs in the form of *interruption, destruction, disclosure, modification* or *denial of service* to information or/and system.

Emerging security threats are blended and aggressive. According to the US-CERT [4], blended threats combine several attack methods (viruses, worms, Trojans) to increase the level of destruction and reach. These threats often result in significant loss of sensitive data, and propagate quickly via multiple attack vectors. An example of this is unsolicited email (spam) that has a malicious attachment or a malicious website from where a Trojan can be downloaded onto the user's computer [4]. These types of threats exploit multiple chains of vulnerabilities to infiltrate computer networks, and act as attack vectors to computer systems [10].

Similarly, emerging attacks have been shown to be coordinated [9], possessing the capability to multiply very quickly and rapidly [7]. For example, *code-driven attacks* use the Internet as a medium to propagate, causing harm to valued assets. According to Ghosh [7], code-driven attacks are evolving Internet threats that quickly propagate, causing harm to hundreds of systems.

Further examples of attacks include the Code Red incident of 2001 that exploited a buffer overflow in a library module of Microsoft Windows' Internet Information Server. This allowed it to infect hundreds of thousands of computers [8], causing damage estimated at millions of dollars [163]. The Slammer [163], MS-Blast [70], and Sasser [68] worms all exploited known vulnerabilities in computer systems, which allowed them to infect hundreds of other systems. Security threats (such as network worms) are now being used as attack agents in denial of service (DoS) [67], and distributed denial of service (DDoS) [69] attacks. These types of attacks affect the *confidentiality*, *integrity* and *availability* of computer network services.

Identifying attributes of emerging threats or attacks is important; however, what has become critical is identifying factors that stimulate their prevalence. According to CERT [71] the following factors contribute to the growing number of attack incidents: i) increasing sophistication of *attack tools*; ii) automation and speed of attack tools; iii) faster discovery of vulnerabilities; iv) increasing permeability of firewalls; and v) increasing threats from infrastructure attacks. Attack tool signatures are difficult to discover through analysis and hard to detect through signature-based systems, such as anti-virus and intrusion detection systems. Attack tools are programs that attackers use to conduct an attack (or attacks). For example, NMAP [140] is an open source attack tool for network exploration, security vulnerability assessment and ethical hacking. DSCAN [141] is an attack tool for distributed port scans. Three important features of attack tools help them to evade detection from traditional defence systems:

◆ The *anti-forensic nature* of recent attack tools means attackers now use techniques that obfuscate their activities (probing and intrusion), making it difficult and time consuming to analyse and evaluate threats they pose.

◆ The *dynamic behaviour* of recent attack tools means they can be automated to vary their patterns and behaviours based on random selection, or through direct intruder management [71].

◆ The *modularity of attack tools* means attack tools can be changed quickly by upgrading or replacing portions of the tool, leading to polymorphic tools that change by themselves.

Ubiquity and coordinated management of attack tools also contributes to the growth in incidents of network attacks. For example, the prevalence of attack tools, especially with most of these tools readily available on the Internet means attacks can be easily launched by any adversary with access to the Internet. With the advent of distributed attack tools, attackers can now manage and coordinate large numbers of attack tools on the Internet.

The impact of security attacks on organisations in terms of financial losses is significant. According to the 11th Annual Computer Crime and Security Survey [72], the estimated total losses caused by various types of attack incidents in 2006 were $52.4 million. This information was obtained from 313 respondents that were willing and able to estimate losses. The four top categories of threats that accounted for nearly 74.3% of the total losses were: i) viruses; ii) unauthorised access; iii) theft of laptop or mobile hardware; and iv) theft of proprietary information. Similarly, in concurrent years, (2001 and 2002) according to the CSI/FBI crime survey, *malicious codes* (viruses and worms) have been the number-one [2], and dominant threats for the past several years [3]. This highlights the growing trend in computer security threats and attacks, especially attacks targeting the SME.

There is evidence that home users are also targets of increasing malicious attacks. For example, there is a marked increase in intruders specifically targeting home users who have cable modems and DSL connections [73]. It is important to note that systems connected to the Internet via cable modem are more susceptible to attacks than those connected via DSL connections. This is because a cable modem service uses a shared cable line to provide service to a neighbourhood. Effectively the neighbourhood is seen as a local area network, and technically, without any security measures in place, anybody that belongs to this logical LAN is able to access any other member. For example, using Windows' network neighbourhood, one cable modem can access another cable modem within the same neighbourhood. This provides the reachability required to launch successful attacks.

To detect and mitigate security attacks, one approach is to deploy firewalls in security monitoring. But it is shown that the increasing permeability of firewalls has left this approach lagging threats that harm valuable assets. Firewalls are often relied upon to provide primary protection from intruders. However, technologies are being designed to bypass typical firewall configurations; such as IPP (the Internet Printing Protocol) and WebDAV (Web-based Distributed Authoring and Versioning) [71].

Another approach to mitigating security attacks is the use of stand-alone defence systems. For example, security scanners are used to detect the presence of system flaws (vulnerabilities in systems), and firewalls are used to block certain traffic, while IDSes are used to detect intrusions. But, these security systems defend in isolation. Each system deals with traffic that passes through it, such that evidence gathered from one system is not made available to the other system when making inferences. Hence, this approach to security defence is insufficient in protecting computer networks, because stand-alone defence systems' responses are often fragmented and uncoordinated.

Stand-alone, uncoordinated countermeasures such as firewalls or IDSes provide fragmented security evidence that is presented in different formats. For example, scanner logs, firewall logs, IDS logs, and sensor logs all exist in different formats. Unfortunately, a mechanism to integrate, analyse, correlate and normalise these logs is not often available. These systems (such as firewall or IDS) are effective on their own, and able to provide independent protection to a section of the network. But the concern that emerging security attacks are evolving, coordinated, and rapidly propagating leaves the defences of stand alone, uncoordinated approaches insufficient.

In order to adequately detect emerging security attacks, a requirement is to combine and integrate the defences offered by stand-alone countermeasures. In this respect, an integrated security framework is proposed. An integrated security framework is a *unified security approach* composed of sensor, analysis and response capabilities, that collectively gather, analyse and counter threats coming from multiple attack sessions.

1.3 Challenges to cyber security

As was seen in section 1.2, to protect computer networks from security attacks, existing approaches use stand-alone, "localised" countermeasure systems such as firewall at points in the network, intrusion detection systems behind the firewall or anti-virus systems on a part of the network, or on end user systems to detect and mitigate perceived attacks.

These stand-alone but localised systems are effective independent defence systems on their own. However, they only offer security protection in isolation. Each security system logs and analyses a session of traffic that passes through it, offering fragmented security evidence and thus provides independent protection to individual hosts in the network. But the concern is how to inspect and collectively analyse attack evidence gathered by these independent defence systems in order to protect the entire network.

According to Yang et al. [5] and Eddaoui and Mezrioui [6], existing stand-alone but localised approaches are insufficient in preventing emerging security attacks, because current attacks are decentralised, automated and intelligent, while existing localised approaches lack network-wide response to current attacks. Similarly, Braynov and Jadiwala [9] have shown that emerging security attacks are widely distributed, and often coordinated in nature. Coordinated attacks are hard to mitigate, not only because they are well crafted to use obfuscating techniques to evade detection, but they are also programmed to use different agents (zombies) to masquerade their attack sessions, to avoid being seen as one cooperating attack, emanating from a single source.

The hypothesis of this book is that security attacks can be represented by a visual model (pattern activity graph). The visual representation assists security administrators to detect, analyse and respond to attacks perceived on networks, as opposed to attacks perceived only on individual hosts. The key problem to be addressed is how to *combine pieces of evidence from various sensors* (stand-alone countermeasures) to accurately detect and identify specific security attacks perceived on the entire network. Note: in this book, a range of sensors are used, from "dumb" sensors, such as ARPWATCH that do minimal processing to sophisticated sensors, such as SNORT, that can be used as an intrusion prevention system.

1.4   A recommended solution approach

The foundation of this book is the theoretical security framework developed to help security administrators to detect security attacks perceived on a population of networked computers. The application of the framework in data fusion, multisensor fusion, federated and distributed LANs is demonstrated, including how security administrators are able to use the framework to accomplish the following tasks:

◆ to detect attacks on a population of computer networks by distributing sensors to gather attack evidence.

◆ to collectively combine and correlate pieces of attack evidence obtained from multiple sensors in order to provide a higher accuracy and understanding of perceived attacks.

◆ to offer expressive visualisation of attacks perceived on the entire network by way of graph representation.

1.5   Scope of the book

This book is about an integrated security framework that assists security administrators to visualise, detect and consequently mitigate security attacks perceived on computer networks. The work focuses fundamentally on providing a sound theoretical underpinning to the realisation of a framework that integrates the defences offered by stand-alone countermeasures to provide enterprise-wide attack detection. It defines three types of components: sensor, analysis, and response. Each component of the framework is defined and explained. Conceptualised models of each component are formalised and discussed. Part of the practical investigation relates to detecting network scans, network worms, and stealthy network scans attacks. These are achieved through a testbed network. The testbed network monitors live Internet traffic containing both normal and attack data.

It is pertinent to note that physical threats, such as theft of a computer hardware, and threats due to natural disasters, such as hurricane or flooding, were not modelled in the experiments. This is because current sensors deployed in the framework were unable to detect attacks resulting from these threats. However, the framework is scalable to incorporate myriads of heterogeneous sensors to detect various types of attacks in its analysis. To detect various types of attacks, the assumptions are that:

◆ specialised sensors able to detect such attacks are available, and

◆ pieces of attack evidence gathered from such sensors can be incorporated in the analysis.

1.6   Research concepts and ideas

A body of practical and theoretical analysis is employed in this study to detect security attacks perceived on computer networks. These include:

◆ Pattern matching techniques, such as *graph theory and graph matching*. Graphs are used to model and describe attacks perceived on computer networks, while graph matching techniques, such as *graph and subgraph isomorphisms* are employed to check similarities in graph descriptions to identify specific attacks perceived on the network.

◆ An evidential reasoning technique, the *Dempster-Shafer theory of evidence,* which combines and analyses pieces of attack evidence obtained from multiple security sensors, to correlate data and provide accurate detection of attacks.

◆ Analysis data (datasets) obtained through a *testbed* to evaluate the research objectives.

Graph representation, graph and subgraph isomorphisms, Dempster-Shafer theory of evidence, tuple space and mathematical analysis are fundamental techniques employed in this research to solve the defined research problem. The use of a testbed network is a conventional practice used to obtain datasets for evaluating the research objectives. The techniques used in this research are well-proven, and have been employed in mainstream areas, such as machine learning, pattern recognition, case-based reasoning and network monitoring to solve both academic and practical research problems. Details of these concepts are explained later when discussing each contribution.

1.7   Structure of the book

This book consists of eleven chapters. The first chapter is *Cyber Security Problems and Solutions*, which discusses the *motivation, problem definition, solution approach, scope, concepts and ideas* employed in the research. The remaining chapters are structured as follows:

- ◆ Computer network security as a discipline is investigated with respect to concepts and terminology used in the field. The need to provide effective security protection to valued assets leads to discussing importance of security and factors affecting security investments in most organisations. This is chapter two: *Computer Network Security.*

- ◆ To identify trends in security protection, a review of security threats, approaches in attack detection, prevention and mitigation is provided. Investigating previously employed techniques and approaches to detect security attacks, it was shown that these approaches could be classified in terms of their functional roles. Hence, a classification of approaches to attack detection is provided. Intrusion detection systems (IDSes) are also investigated, and a new classification based on sensor detection construct is proposed and used in classifying IDS contributions and algorithmic designs. This is chapter three: *Understanding Threats and Attacks to Computer Networks.*

- ◆ To protect computer networks against emerging security attacks, the need for security defence models is investigated. It is identified that current defence approaches are localised, while emerging defence initiatives are distributed. Emerging defence models are reviewed with respect to their protection construct, such as preventive, reactive and retrospective. The usefulness of defence models to security monitoring, distributed defence services and electronic commerce is discussed. This is chapter four: *Defence Approaches for Protecting Computer Networks.*

- ◆ It is shown that current (localised) defence approaches are insufficient in mitigating emerging security attacks. Hence the need to investigate a new approach in security defence. Thus, an integrated security framework, which is underpinned by a *sensor, analysis* and *response* defence paradigm is proposed. The framework helps security administrators in detecting widespread attacks targeting computer networks. A high level description of the framework, and a detailed discussion of each component of the framework are provided. The design requirements of the framework are also highlighted. This is chapter five: *Integrated Security Assistance Framework for Protecting Computer Networks.*

◆ The response component of the framework is discussed, comprising limitations of existing response mechanism. A comprehensive description of the response mechanism is provided, including its design principles and operational requirements. The various components of the response mechanism are explained, comprising generic responders, fuzzy responders, automated instruction, human-assisted instruction, and response action. This is chapter six: *The Response Component of the Framework.*

◆ Security space - the signalling middleware of the framework - is described. The motivation behind security spaces is explained. The operations of security spaces and limitations of existing mechanisms for exchanging security-related information, such as the Syslog protocol and simple network management protocol, are discussed. The design and operational requirements of the signalling mechanism are outlined, while security spaces application to multisensor and federated sensor environments are provided and well discussed. This is chapter seven: *Security Spaces - The Signalling Mechanism of the Framework.*

◆ The analysis component of the framework is discussed, comprising two powerful and novel techniques utilised to analyse security evidence perceived in the network. Because of the depth and coverage of each techniques discussed, separate chapters are used for each technique. Hence, visualisation and pattern matching techniques, such as graph theory, graph representation, pattern activity graph, graph isomorphism and subgraph isomorphism are investigated. This is chapter eight: *Security Visualisation.*

◆ Multisource data fusion is investigated for aggregating pieces of independent attack evidence gathered by myriad heterogeneous sensors deployed in the network. To combine diverse and independent evidence gathered by sensors, the Dempster-Shafer theory of evidence is investigated. The Dempster-Shafer theory of evidence is compared to other contending fusion techniques such as the Bayesian inference technique, Kalman filter, and Probability theory. This is chapter nine: *Multisource Data Fusion.*

◆ The framework design, choice of sensors, experimental setup and demonstration of specific attacks launched in the network are explained. Specific attacks detected on the testbed network include *network scans, network worms, web attacks, policy violations* and *stealthy network scans*. Also discussed are testbed results and datasets obtained from security monitoring. This is chapter ten: *Experimentation*.

◆ Finally, the discussion is concluded, and suggestion to future directions of the work is provided. This is chapter eleven: *Conclusion*.

1.8   Resource centre

A website (**www.research-series.com/securityframework**) is dedicated for teaching, learning and understanding the security framework. This dedicated site is intended to provide additional resource to help readers make the most of the book, such as:

◆ Learning guide, portable and downloadable versions of sample chapters.

◆ Useful comments from various use cases.

◆ Corrections to errata in contents.

◆ Updated content and new information, such as:

  ▷ New ideas and topics that occurred after the book has been completed.

◆ New innovations with the framework, such as:

  ▷ other analysis techniques.

  ▷ new sensors, experiments and toolkits.

◆ Press releases, technical presentations and other documentations.

1.9   Terminology and acronyms

1.9.1   Terminology

Analysers: Software agents (programs) that process sensor data (for example, security evidence gathered by the sensors) to deduce the risk level or outline resultant countermeasures required to mitigate the perceived threat.

Asset: Anything that is of value to the organisation, comprising of systems, software, operating systems, firmware, information, data and people.

Data Graph: A graph generated from security event logs. A data graph is compared with a template graph in order to deduce similarities in graph structures.

Defence: The action of defending, or resisting an attack.

GAISP: Generally accepted information security principles, a principle-based information security management, formerly known as "generally accepted systems security principles" (GASSP) formed in mid-1992 and developed by the Information Systems Security Association (ISSA).

GAPP: Generally accepted principles and practices, a comprehensive process-based information security management framework by NIST, aimed to provide a baseline that organisations can use to establish and review IT security programs.

Entity: A person, system or process. For example, a user/attacker, host, UNIX cron process respectively.

Harm to assets: The interruption, destruction, disclosure, modification or denial of service to information or/and systems.

Network worms: Self-replicating programs that exploit faults on vulnerable system resources, which are classified as operational, external, human-made, software, malicious, deliberate and permanent [20].

Peer-contact ratio: The number of hosts (systems) contacted by a particular host for a specified period of time, in case of an outbreak, perceived threat or attack.

POP: A site where there exist a collection of telecommunications equipment, such as routers, modem banks, leased circuits, computers.

Prevention: The action of stopping something from happening or occurring.

Responders: Software agents that execute recommended countermeasures, for instance, coordinating multiple responses or re-configuring security components to nullify perceived attacks.

Security attacks: Computer network attacks on computing systems, networking infrastructure, information or programs leading to a security breach.

Security policy: A formal statement of the rules that governs entities that are given access to valued corporate assets, what information or data is available to them, and what they can do with the given access (Fraser, 1997).

Security space: An abstract space or middleware. It offers a means through which security components (sensors, analysers and responders) connect, contribute and communicate security related information.

Security threats: Potential actions that could exploit vulnerabilities in systems to harm them or predispose them to harm. Threats help to realise or give rise to attacks.

Sensors: Software agents (programs) that sense, gather and communicate security related information and attack activities to the analysis component (analysers). They range from "dumb", or very basic monitors, such as ARPWATCH, TCPTRACK, to "intelligent" sensors, such as SNORT and Statistical Packet Anomaly Detection Engine (SPADE).

Template graph: A graph representation of *a known security attack* that is used to compare data graphs to detect that attack on the network.

Threat agents: Entities with the capability to introduce (or/and) realise threats to assets, whose adverse actions are performed on assets from which they derive their value [43].

Vulnerabilities in assets: Weaknesses in assets or the absence of security procedures, technical controls, or physical controls that could be exploited to harm or predispose an asset to harm, leading to a security breach [41].

Zombies: Computer agents that are controlled by intruders to launch malicious attacks on computer networks.

1.9.2 Acronyms

AS: autonomous system

AWCC: applied watch command center

BPA: basic probability assignment

BIR: business impact review

BS: British standard

CAIDA: cooperative association of internet data analysis

CEE: common event expression

DoS: denial of service

D-S: Dempster-Shafer

DSL: digital subscriber line

EMERALD: event monitoring enabling responses to anomalous live disturbances

ESM: enterprise security management

FCM: fuzzy cognitive modeling

GASSATA: genetic algorithm for simplified security audit trail analysis

GLB: gramm-leach-bliley

HIPAA: health insurance portability and accountability act

ICMP: internet control message protocol

IDIOT: intrusion detection in our time

IDMEF: intrusion detection message exchange format

IDS: intrusion detection system

IP: internet protocol

IPS: intrusion prevention system

IPSec: internet protocol security

ISAF: integrated security assistance framework

MARS: monitoring, analysis and response system

MCS: maximum common subgraph

NIST: national institute of standards and technology

NSM: network security monitor

OSSIM: open source security information management

PAG: pattern activity graph

PDA: personal digital assistant

POP: point of presence

RFC: request for comments

SCTP: stream control transmission protocol

SD: service delivery

SLA: service level agreement

SPADE: statistical packet anomaly detection

TCL: tool command language

TCP: transmission control protocol

TRS: threat response system

TTL: time to live

UDP: user datagram protocol

UTM: unified threat management

VoIP: voice over IP

Chapter 2

Computer network security

This chapter provides an introduction to the concepts and terminology of computer network security. It also discusses importance of security to organisations. Factors thought to influence security investments in organisations are discussed in detail.

2.1 Introduction

While computer security has been extensively researched, there is still a lack of consensus in the definition of the subject (as noted by both Bishop [22] and Gollman [23]). As a result, different terms are often used to represent the same concept. Conversely, the same term might be used by many people with slightly varying meanings, assumptions or interpretations. One reason for this may be because computer security is still a relatively young discipline, compared with say, chemistry or physics. Andrews and Whittaker [24] and Bishop [22] share this view.

A survey of some of the key definitions in Computer Network Security is provided, and the fundamental aspects of computer security, such as confidentiality, integrity and availability of computer networks and their offered services, are discussed in depth. Finally, the importance of security, and factors affecting security investments in most organisations are investigated. In the next chapter, an elaborate review of security threats, and approaches in threat detection, prevention and mitigation is provided.

2.2 Security in computer networks

Security is a broad term, comprising many aspects, such as *computer security, information security, data security, network security, physical security* and *human or personnel security.* A general discussion on security covering various aspects is presented. However, three specific areas of interest, namely *computer security, network security* and *computer network security* are discussed in detail. Reference materials covering other aspects of security, for interested readers, can be found in Anderson [172], Bishop [100], Gollman [23], Schneier [190] and Stallings [35].

2.2.1 Security in general

According to Helmbrecht [25], "Security is a basic human need. Without security the social order would simply collapse". Security is a conscious human practice since the beginning of time. The need to protect people and their belongings has always been, and will always exist. This is evident as every country in the world has one form of law enforcement agency or another, such as the *national police force* or *the military*. The national police are responsible for maintaining law and order in society, through policing or safeguarding people and their belongings; the military is responsible for protecting the state or country in times of enemy invasion, war or national conflicts.

In computing, for instance, the same set of needs exists. The need to keep communications secret, especially during wars, accounted for the earliest forms of security practices, which the author refers to as 'ancient cryptographic endeavours'. For example, during the 7th century BC, the use of *"scytale"* in cryptographic practices was profound [26]. A *"scytale"* is a tool used to perform a transposition cipher, consisting of a cylinder with a strip of leather wound around it to enable secret messages to be written on it. The ancient Greeks and the Spartans in particular are said to have used this cipher to communicate during military campaigns [26]. From the 7th century BC to the 3rd century BC, a clear description of the operation of *"scytale"* could not be found until 50-120 AD when Mestrius Plutarchus provided a clear description of its operation.

The first known account of modern cryptographic practice was the use of ciphers in *numerical substitution* that is credited to the Greeks (see The Codebreakers, by David Kahn [27]). Writing alphabets onto a grid and then using the grid coordinates to substitute for each letter in a message was how *numerical substitution* operated. According to Ross [28], Julius Caesar was the first to use *simple substitution cipher* to encrypt messages sent to his army commanders. The simple substitution cipher was seen as a significant improvement in cipher development at that time.

This development in message secrecy continued, but was revolutionised by the *Enigma machine* used during World War II (WWII). The *Enigma* was controlled both mechanically and electronically to encrypt and decrypt cipher [29]; and was the first account of a *modern cipher design in electronics*.

The advent of digital computers and development in electronics after WWII made much more complex ciphers possible. Today, cryptography, the science of keeping information secret, is well developed. Modern cryptography includes symmetric key and public key encryption algorithms that assist to preserve both confidentiality and integrity of communications.

2.2.2 Computer security

Early computer security practices were largely based on physical security. That is, physically protecting information (information security) and computing equipment [30]. For example, sensitive documents were kept in metal filing cabinets and secured with a padlock, while computer equipment was kept in the nodes and guardsmen employed to protect it. Bell and LaPadula [31], claim that computer security covering other aspects of security started in the 1970s with the development of the Multics operating system. The aspect of security covered was access control to information held on a localised system, such as a mainframe computer. Corbató and Vyssotsky [32], describe Multics as "a general-purpose time-shared multi-access operating system used to prevent unauthorised access to information held on a system". Note: multics (multiplexed information and computing service) is a mainframe time-sharing operating system begun in 1965 and used until 2000. Multics began as a research project and was an important influence on operating systems development. The system became a commercial product sold by Honeywell to education, government and industry [143].

In the early 1980s, *computer security* was seen as the process of protecting organisations' assets by ensuring the safe, uninterrupted operation of the system, and the safeguarding of computer systems, programs and data files [33]. This protection was offered to organisations' *localised assets*, such as hardware, software, firmware, information and data within the organisation. The focus was to preserve the three fundamental aspects of information systems resources such as *availability, confidentiality and integrity* within the organisation [1].

It was not until the late 1980s with the advent of public communications networks, such as the Internet, was the security of communications networks - information transported across shared or public communications networks - considered to be apparent and important. It is pertinent to note that the connection of computer systems via shared networks was not believed to contribute to major security issues, but rather it provided avenues for more exposure to threats and attackers. According to Brinkley and Schell [34], connection to networks introduces a need for communication security to counter the possibility of an attacker tapping communication lines used by these networks. The networks themselves provided few fundamentally new computer security problems, other than enhanced accessibility of the interconnected systems to potential attackers. It is important to note that at the time Brinkley and Schell were writing, communications security concerns were primarily related to voice or telephone tapping. The use of computers in communications networks, such as in wide area networks, or metropolitan area networks was not common practice at that time.

2.2.3 Network security

Network security is concerned with the protection of data communications networks, and/or information transported across communications lines (telecommunications). According to Stallings [35], "a major change that affected security was the introduction of distributed systems and the use of networks and communications facilities for carrying data between terminal user and computer, and between computer and computer. Hence, network security measures are needed to protect information during their transmission".

Whitson [30] describes network security as the measures required to protect systems and transported data. Onwubiko and Lenaghan [11] define network security as the process of protecting the *confidentiality, integrity* and *availability* of computer networks, their communications and offered services. Evaluating these definitions, a single thread is identified. Network security is concerned with the security of data communications networks, or the security of information transported across shared and/or public networks.

From late 1999, the need to incorporate both *computer security* (meaning security of information in a localised system) and *network security* (meaning, security of communications, and information transported across shared or public networks) gave rise to the terminology *computer network security*.

2.2.4 Computer network security

The term *computer network security* has gained wider acceptance in both the computing and security communities. To demonstrate the relevance and wider use of this terminology; in 2006 alone, there were more than 20 textbooks with the term computer network security as part of their title, and more than 10 top security conferences/workshops with the title computer network security. This excludes security conferences featuring modules or tracks on computer network security, (according to a search return from amazon.com). Although *computer network security* is still relatively new today, each aspect of computer network security, such as cryptography, intrusion detection systems, or firewalls has been extensively researched and studied in its own right.

The task of protecting computer networks, computer systems, information, and/or communications can therefore be referred to as computer network security. By adapting NIST's definition of computer security [1], *computer network security* is defined as the protection afforded to computer networks in order to attain the fundamental objectives of preserving the *confidentiality, integrity* and *availability* of computer networks and their offered services, which include hardware, software, firmware, information and telecommunications. Thus, the primary objectives of security in computer networks are to preserve the:

- *confidentiality* of systems and communications (discussed in section 2.3.1): A requirement to avoid unauthorised disclosure of information and communications infrastructure either intentionally or inadvertently.

- *integrity* of computer networks, data and information (discussed in section 2.3.2): A requirement aimed at ensuring that computer networks and their offered services are *accurate, complete, consistent, authentic and timely*.

- *availability* of computer networks and their offered services (discussed in section 2.3.3): A requirement to ensure systems and their offered services (resources) are available at *acceptable levels* to legitimate entities.

2.3 Computer network security issues

This section provides background knowledge on traditional security issues, such as confidentiality, integrity and availability of computing resource to legitimate owners or users of the system.

2.3.1 Confidentiality

Confidentiality is an essential requirement of computer network security, which guarantees that private or confidential systems, communications, documents, or transactions must not be disclosed inadvertently or intentionally to unauthorised (non-legitimate) entities. In the literature, *confidentiality* is mostly discussed as an information requirement [1, 36], but this is not the case. System and network infrastructure also require protection from unauthorised disclosure. An example is a bank that conceals surveillance cameras at strategic locations in its office, only known lawfully to its bank staff. If a member of the bank unlawfully (inadvertently or intentionally) discloses the location of a camera to a customer, this act is regarded as an attack on the system's confidentiality.

2.3.1.1 Inadvertent disclosure

Inadvertent disclosure of a system or information is the accidental disclosure of the existence of a confidential system or information to unauthorised persons. This can be due to *incompetence* on the part of personnel or due to social engineering. An example of *inadvertent disclosure* is the case of accidental disclosure of a patients medical/health information (records) to an unauthorised person by an incompetent hospital clerk.

2.3.1.2 Intentional disclosure

Intentional disclosure is a deliberate disclosure of the existence of a confidential system or information with the motive of abusing or breaching the confidentiality of that system or information. For example, the deliberate capture and release of corporate email communications by a disgruntled employee is regarded as an intentional disclosure of information.

An attack on confidentiality, can be in the form of disclosure of the existence of a legitimate system or information to unauthorised individuals either electronically or offline. Offline disclosure means verbally or in printed form (copied or faxed).

For example, if a manager shows an employee's bonus letter to another employee who is not authorised to see the letter, this is regarded as an abuse of confidentiality. However, it is not regarded an abuse of confidentiality if the authorised owner's consent is sought. Similarly, using a network sniffer to 'wire-tap' secret communications is regarded as an attack on the confidentiality of that communication; however, it is not an attack on confidentiality if the purpose of sniffing the communication is for authorised network fault-finding or troubleshooting. Confidentiality of computer network systems and communications is synonymous to lawful or authorised disclosure. Thus, unauthorised disclosure of systems, or/and information is regarded as attack on confidentiality.

2.3.2 Integrity

According to NIST [1], information is said to have integrity when it is *timely, accurate, complete* and *consistent*. Pipkin [37], defines integrity as the assurance of *accuracy, completeness* and *performance* according to specifications. But in a survey conducted by Pfleeger and Pfleeger [38], integrity is said to mean different things to different people. Hence the need to re-visit integrity.

Although NIST's specification for evaluating information integrity is seen as the *defacto* specification, but the specification did not include *authentication* as one of its specified criteria when evaluating information integrity. Without authentication it is impossible to validate a system's identity. How can the identity of a system seeking to communicate with another system be validated? Thus, authentication is useful in identifying systems, proving who they are, and validating their identities, which consequently assures that information being transported between these systems is reliable. If the identities of systems seeking to communicate can not be validated, critical information could be sent to an unlawful system, leading to a compromise or an abuse of information. Therefore, it is argued that the criteria used by NIST in evaluating information integrity is incomplete. In this book, a fifth attribute, *authentic*, is added to NIST's integrity criteria.

Thus, when evaluating the integrity of computer networks and their communications, the criteria should be to check if the computer networks and their offered services are: *accurate, complete, consistent, authentic* and *timely*, as shown in Figure 2.1.

♦ *Accurate:* A system or information is said to be accurate if it has not been modified by an unauthorised entity, either inadvertently or intentionally.

♦ *Complete:* A system or information is said to be complete if it has not been destroyed (completely or partially) by an unauthorised entity, either inadvertently or intentionally.

♦ *Consistent:* A system or information is said to be consistent if its modification or manipulation is as specified, and only by authorised entities.

♦ *Authentic:* A system is said to be authentic if its proof of identity can be established.

♦ *Timely:* An information is said to be timely if it can be proved to have not unlawfully delayed (that is, TTL exceeded) by an unauthorised entity either inadvertently or intentionally.

Figure 2.1: Computer network integrity attributes

The timing attribute of integrity is mostly implemented implicitly in secure applications, for example, the application of timestamps and session keys in Kerberos. Kerberos is a computer network authentication protocol, which allows individuals communicating over an insecure network to prove their identity to one another in a secure manner. Kerberos prevents eavesdropping or replay attacks, and ensures the integrity of the data transported across the network. The protocol was developed at the Massachusetts Institute of Technology (MIT) in the late 1980s.

Since computers are unable to provide or preserve all integrity qualities [1], computer networks are said to have integrity when they (or their offered services) are *accurate, complete, consistent* and *authentic*. The *timing* quality of integrity is not explicitly mentioned because, most integrity preserving mechanisms implicitly implement the *timing* quality. For example, Kerberos, Extensible Authentication Protocol (EAP [170, 189]) and One-Time-Password (OTP [148]).

The integrity of computer networks is maintained in two complementary ways: first, by authenticating (*proof of the authenticity*) or validating the identities of potential communicating parties; second, by protecting computer networks, their communications and offered service from *unauthorised modification, tampering* or *destruction*. Hence, to show that computer networks and their offered services are accurate, complete, consistent and authentic, computer networks need to be evaluated on these two aspects, as follows:

◆ Proof of the authenticity of communicating entities (authentication), as well as

◆ Ensuring that mechanisms to prevent *unauthorised destruction, modification* or *alteration* of information, data and systems are utilised.

2.3.2.1 System integrity

System integrity is a requirement that a system performs its intended function as designed, free from deliberate or inadvertent unauthorised manipulation or tampering of the system [39]. With data integrity, system identity validation is required to ensure that the communicating systems are the actual systems and have not been compromised by an adversary.

Systems identity validation (authentication) is one aspect of integrity that is often ignored when discussing information or data integrity. For instance, according to the Computer Science and Telecommunications Board [36], data integrity is defined "as a requirement that information and programs are changed only in a specified and authorised manner". A *program* is an application, such as Word processing, database management system that must perform certain functions according to specified (underlined) instructions. By the integrity definition above, the authentication of interacting entities is neither explicitly mentioned, nor implicitly guaranteed. Conversely, implementation of authentication-based systems requires that the identities of communicating entities be always ascertained before a connection is established. For example, in a site-to-site VPN, systems participating in communication must be authenticated before an established connection is maintained.

2.3.2.2 Data integrity

Data integrity guarantees that an application or information must not be modified or destroyed (completely or partially) by an unauthorised entity, either inadvertently or intentionally, and that any authorised modification or destruction must be as specified. Note that guaranteeing the genuineness of transported information requires authenticating the identities of entities that convey the information, and are involved in the communication.

It is pertinent to mention that integrity is not the same thing as authentication, they are distinct and unique. Information integrity requires combining i) *authentica*tion of communicating systems; and ii) *mechanisms that prevent* unauthorised destruction, modification or alteration of systems and services. Hence, authentication is a necessary requirement toward achieving information integrity.

2.3.3 Availability

The *availability* of computer networks, computer systems and their offered services is a fundamental requirement of computer network security. Systems and services need to be available to legitimate owners and users of the systems at *agreed times*, and at *acceptable levels* as specified in the quality of service agreed in a service level agreement. However, often times, they become unavailable due to faults, attacks or errors in a service.

2.3.3.1 Systems availability

Systems availability is when both the system and the communications network are available to legitimate entities. For example, if the network link (for instance, a fibre optics cable between a gateway router and an access-layer router) fails, although the servers behind the access-layer routers are up, access to these servers is unavailable at the time to legitimate entities. System or network failures, together with network performance bottlenecks (such as, restricted network bandwidths) affect the availability of resources to legitimate users.

2.3.3.2 Information availability

Information availability is when the application or software running on a system is available to legitimate entities. If the software (for example, Microsoft Excel) crashes, although the computer system containing the information is functional, but data stored in it will not be available. With the exception of software failures, other data availability concerns are application peak usage (performance related availability), and software bugs. Application peak usage may occur when the application becomes overwhelmingly busy during times of peak utilisation, and with extra load, either due to an attack or a fault, this may result in a system that is unable to perform within acceptable levels of service delivery (SD) and service level agreements (SLA). *Software bugs* are developmental faults in software design/development that manifests during software operations as errors that make the software unusable at the time, or cause depreciation from its optimum performance. Availability of computer networks requires both the system and the information to be available.

A major threat that impacts the availability of computer networks is *denial of service (DoS)* and *distributed denial of service (DDoS)* attacks. DoS attacks are major threats to the availability of computer networks, clogging up systems and network resources leading to performance bottlenecks, such that computing resources become unavailable, or perform at unacceptable levels.

2.4 Importance of security

The original and primary purpose of computer networks is to provide effective means of communication. That same need is still apparent today. However, what has become critical for most organisations in the 21st century is how to protect computer networks and their offered services (such as data and information) that use public networks as a transport medium for communication. Invariably, this task of protecting computer networks and their communications is both challenging and complex. Managing information security for organisations is challenging, because of the ever-growing dependence of organisations on technology to drive businesses and to create a competitive advantage. Organisations rely significantly on technology (for instance, the Internet) for business operations, secure business transactions and open business administrations.

Certainly, organisations are now more dependent on the use of computer networks for their operations compared to a decade ago, governments depend on the use of computing services for their administration, institutions depend on effective use of computers and their communications for delivering training and administration, while the military requires secure communications to disseminate classified information. These demands placed on computer networks have made their protection critical.

Another challenge in managing information security for organisations comes with global outsourcing (offshore) and the use of in-house third-party personnel to deliver information security (onshore) for the enterprise. In general, business outsourcing (whether offshore or onshore) offers tremendous merits, and in most cases helps the enterprise to lower its operating cost. Unfortunately, security outsourcing introduces entirely new sets of challenges to the enterprise:

◆ First, the scope of security management for the enterprise increases.

◆ Second, security boundaries of the enterprise become fuzzy and undefined when security is outsourced.

◆ Third, various points of inter-connectivity are created to allow third party access to confidential and classified assets, and

♦ Finally, various levels of trusts are established between the enterprise and its third-party organisations. A known concern with this way of doing business is that trust relationships could be exploited or abused; customer and employee privacy may be violated. Nevertheless, managing these new dimensions in the enterprise is in itself complex.

Outsourcing or global outsourcing to drive business operations for the enterprise has its place in the emerging economies but, undeniably, outsourcing comes with a variety of vulnerabilities and threats that put the enterprise at risk. In this respect, conscientious and dependable security requirements are needed to address these new security risks introduced by global outsourcing.

The complexity of managing information security for organisations is evident with the scope of corporate assets required to be protected in organisations. Unfortunately, threats that exploit vulnerabilities in valued assets are evolving. Vulnerabilities are found continuously in most assets, attacks to computer networks are emerging, while attack tools are growing. For example, attack tools are now distributed across the Internet that can be remotely managed by an adversary with Internet access. These factors make managing information security for organisations extremely complex.

To manage information security for an organisation, one approach is to implement technical security controls to prevent threats and mitigate attacks that target valued assets. Unfortunately, the use of technical controls alone is insufficient in efficiently managing information security for organisations [208, 216, 11]. Situations exist where efficient information security management is not feasible with technical controls alone, but by satisfying other security requirements, such as legislative and regulatory compliance. Therefore, to efficiently manage security for organisations, contemporary, conscientious and dependable security requirements are needed, which are not only driven by technical requirements, but also by environmental, regulatory, legislative, compliance, environmental and cultural demands of modern economies and globalisation. Current and emerging factors influencing security management in organisations are identified and discussed. These factors cover technical, legislative, administrative, compliance, regulatory and environmental concerns of security management.

2.4.1 Security management

Security management is the process of managing information security for an organisation in order to achieve secure and dependable services. Achieving secure and dependable security for an organisation largely depends on the organisation's security awareness, protection, monitoring, investigative, assurance and survivability plans afforded to its valued assets. It is important that enterprise security management covers collectively technical, administrative, compliance and legislative security requirements necessary to support the organisation. These factors are essential in providing, maintaining, achieving and sustaining efficient, compliant, secure and dependable networks, communications and services for the organisation.

The dynamics in managing information security motivate exploring the synergy in security management. Today, organisations face considerable challenges in managing security to accomplish its goals of protecting their valued assets, creating business opportunities, and achieving returns on investment. What was once achieved by developing and implementing sound technical controls is no longer guaranteed. Instead, organisations must now consider how they are going to succeed in the face of increasing regulatory, legislative, compliance and technical complexities that challenge most security investments in the ever-changing risk environment.

Protecting computer networks, their communications, or transit data is no longer dependent on deploying sound technical controls alone, but largely dependent on other security requirements, such as compliance, legislation, culture or the environment. It is certain that security is now an essential requirement for doing business in a globally computerised cyberspace. Technical, management and regulatory security compliance are seemingly mandatory security requirements in today's business. BS7799 (ISO 27001-2), Gramm-Leach-Bliley (GLB) Act, Control Objectives for Information and related Technology (CoBIT), Payment Card Industry Data Security Standard (PCI DSS) and IT Infrastructure Library (ITIL) are examples of security compliance standards that drive businesses today, depending on the operating environment of the organisation, - financial, health, telecommunication, or academic. In the financial sector, GLB, ISO 27001-2 and PCI DSS are highly recommended, if not mandatory; while in the telecommunications arena, ITIL, ISO 27001-2 and CoBIT are recommended, and in the health sector, HIPAA is a mandatory framework. To an extent, legislation and regulatory compliance are becoming increasingly essential drivers (information security requirements) for business relations. These requirements when satisfied assist the organisation in achieving the required protection to its valued assets based on best practices. They include operational, technical, legislative, regulatory and compliance security needs.

2.4.2 Factors influencing security in most organisations

Information security management can be both complex and challenging. The complexity stems from the pervasive and multi-functional nature of information security, first, to protect organisations valued assets, to achieve secure and dependable information assurance, and second, to advance business relations for the organisation by creating platforms for trust, business alliance and collaboration. Further, the ever-growing dependence of organisations on technology to drive businesses and to create a competitive advantage makes information security management for organisations extremely challenging. These challenges facing organisations in managing information security are numerous and inherently diverse.

A traditional approach in addressing these challenges includes the use of technical controls to identify vulnerabilities, prevent threats and mitigate attacks targeting their valued assets. While technical controls are useful in protecting valued assets, unfortunately, technical controls alone are insufficient in providing dependable security and information assurance required in a contemporary global enterprise.

Global outsourcing, consumer-centricity, security compliance and legislation as emerging global business drivers have imposed new security requirements that complicate traditional perspective in security management. Hence, current and emerging factors affecting security management in organisations are identified and well-discussed, such as technical, legislative, cultural, compliance and regulatory issues (see Figure 2.2). These factors are discussed as follows:

- security perception

- security risk Acceptance

- return on investment (RoI)

- finance

- security outsourcing

- vulnerabilities in systems

- threats and attacks

- security policies and standards

- security awareness and training

- senior executive support for security initiatives

- privacy

- legislation

- regulatory compliance

- business operating environment (BOE)

- culture

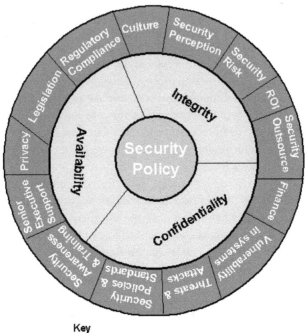

Key
- ○ Security Policy
- ○ Security Requirements
- ● Factors Affecting Information Security Management

Figure 2.2: Factors affecting information security management in organisations

2.4.2.1 Security perception

Organisations perceive security differently. What is acceptable to one organisation may not be to another. For example, academic institutions perceive security requirements differently to the military or financial institutions where security threat levels are thought to be very high. According to C P Pfleeger and S L Pfleeger [38]: "Universities make very good targets for attack. Universities are havens for free exchange of ideas. Thus, their access controls typically are configured to promote sharing and wide access to a population that changes significantly every semester".

One of the reasons why academic institutions operate relatively weak security controls is thought to be because of their business paradigms. The primary aim of an academic institution is to foster research and to provide an enabling environment for research. Sharing of ideas among federated research groups and the dependence of one unit on another does not encourage the adoption of very strict security controls. On the other hand, the military's primary objectives are to protect the nation, and therefore, implement much more rigorous and complex security controls. Similarly, financial institutions are also believed to implement very strict security controls because of the nature of their business environments and fear of liability for consequential financial losses due to security breaches. Thus, organisation perception of security affects their security readiness, processes and implementations; which is largely dependent on the underpinning roles and operations of the organisation. ISO/IEC 27001:2005(E) Information Security Management Systems, (BS 7799-2), begun by determining the value of the information protected and then assesses whether the security procedures, processes, and solutions are appropriate given the risk of financial loss due to a security breach [166]. More valuable assets require stronger protection. Security is strong when it is appropriate.

Regular security briefing and security awareness programmes is highly recommended to ensure organisations' security investments are not inadvertently abused due to security ignorance (lack of security-awareness culture). Security awareness or security awareness culture is the overall organisational attitude toward security, one that everybody in an organisation should practice is essential for organisations, in order to provide or maintain acceptable security protection to its valued assets.

2.4.2.2 Security risk acceptance

Security risk is a combination of the *likelihood* of an asset being compromised and the *impact* the attack would have on the asset together with the *consequential effect* on the organisation if the attack happens. Security risk acceptance level is a measure of acceptable risk. Acceptable risk is the *residual risk* an organisation is willing to undertake in the event of a break-in, violation or attack. In most business organisations, this is usually incorporated into the service level agreement (SLA), a contract that stipulates an acceptable level of service. For example, financial institutions have a percentage of acceptable risk for loans and mortgages, which differs among banks. This risk is insurable and often absorbed by re-insurance underwriters that undertake the liability. This explains why security in some cases, has been defined as the process of reducing risk or the likelihood of harm [37], to organisations' risk acceptance level.

Information security is not a one-size-fits-all proposition. Each organisation has a unique set of risks and must create unique solution strategies to mitigate those risks [205]. Risks come in different aspects when managing information security. It occurs with options an organisation chooses against those not taken. For example, when designing and implementing information security (IS), most organisations' choice of IS products, or scope of implementation is dependent on budget, especially for small to medium sized organisations that have minimal budgets for information security. Cost therefore brings its own risk, in the sense that there is a trade-off between how much money is available for a security project against the assets to be protected, and the scope of the protection afforded to those assets. In most cases, due to constrained budgets for security projects, valued assets may not receive adequate protection, and often, recommended security controls are not used in protecting valued assets.

2.4.2.3 Return on investment (RoI)

Return on investment is a ratio of returns of an investment over the cost of that investment. A significant issue with security or IT investments is that there are no acceptable performance measures or metrics to evaluate the efficiency of a security investment. Unfortunately, not all organisations perceive security as an investment too. Hence, it is difficult for those organisations who do not perceive security as an investment to evaluate its returns. According to Caralli et al. [208], most organisations perceive security as expenditure. This view of security as overhead is an unfortunate outgrowth of the lack of inclusion of measurements and metrics as essential elements of security management. To build a business case for a security investment, several metrics can be utilised. For example, risk analysis has been suggested as RoI metric in the context of incident avoidance, impact analysis, and residual risk [208]. Security RoI to create statistics based on the number of incidents that happened in an organisation when security controls are in place, versus the number of incidents that happened when there were no security controls in place, is a useful metric when evaluating returns on security investments.

Security is an essential driver in modern business. It creates trust, and attracts business relationships from loyal customers, business partners and the government. In this respect, RoI for security investments can be evaluated in terms of opportunity cost. That is, the opportunities organisations loss if they do not have adequate security investments in place to safeguard their valued assets; or opportunities organisations loss due to absence of security certification, accreditation or compliance.

2.4.2.4 Finance

A significant factor with most IT or security investments is funds to carry out projects. Small-sized organisations often have very constrained budget for IT or security investments compared to medium-sized enterprises. With the exception of security perception, returns on investment and finance affect organisational readiness to security. That is, the amount of money the organisation is willing to invest on IT or security ventures. This can be extremely challenging for most small-sized organisations. Unfortunately, security projects are very expensive and capital intensive too. In the absence of standard performance metrics to measure RoI for security projects, it will be extremely challenging for CISOs (chief information and security officers) or CIOs (chief information officers) to persuade board of directors of the benefits and necessity of security investments.

2.4.2.5 Global outsourcing

It is now evident that outsourcing (offshore or onshore) has its place in the modern global economies. Outsourcing offers significant advantages, such as reduced operating cost, improved speed of service delivery, global presence and global reach. However, outsourcing presents complex challenges to security and privacy in organisations. As organisations rush to leverage this emerging trend in outsourcing, they often underestimate the scope and impact of the security challenges posed in a global sourcing environment [214]. According to Gartner research [212], there are significant differences with the issues faced while addressing traditional security issues from those by global outsourcing.

With global outsourcing, there will be legislative, regulatory and compliance considerations, strong cultural differences and perceptions around security, privacy and network protection. These constitute significant and complex organisational issues. For example, laws in two different geographical locations (say, two continents) are bound to differ. For instance, Europe and India work on different sets of legal value systems. To the enterprise with global presence, a major challenge is establishing and maintaining a strong and consistent security program that spans the entire organisation in the different geo-locations, where ethos, legislation and regulatory compliance requirements are bound to differ.

There are morale and psychological issues too with outsourcing. For example, according to Partha Iyenhar of Gartner [212], an important factor of specific relevance to companies in the UK and Europe is the issue of how to handle security and privacy at in-sourced centres (that is, their own subsidiaries) in offshore locations. Most often, companies are faced with the dilemma of having different policies in place for their in-house employees in the local market, and different, more stringent policies for their offshore employees. This can created morale and psychological issues in the offshore location where people feel like second-class employees who are somehow less trusted than those employed in the organisation's home office.

There are various ways organisations have worked around these concerns. For example, non-disclosure agreements (NDA) exist to prevent third parties from disclosing confidential information; security clearance (SC) to check background details of a third-party contractor; and other schemes such as standards certification (for instance ISO 27001-2), and legislative mandates, such as the European directives on data privacy (the safe harbor). Nevertheless, the risks involved with outsourcing require very thoughtful security requirements, which enterprises must address in order to become successful with the venture.

2.4.2.6 Vulnerabilities in systems

A vulnerability in a system is a weakness in that system or in its protection processes, which can be exploited to change, hinder, obstruct or abuse the system's normal operations. A weakness in a system is not necessarily limited to a weakness in its design (design flaw); it could also be due to the absence of, or failure in the protection processes for that asset. For example, a failure on the part of senior executives to implement, encourage or enforce the right levels of security awareness in an organisation can lead to vulnerability, as this lapse or lack in implementing the right security measures can be exploited to harm its assets. Generally speaking, multiple vulnerabilities in and around critical assets put assets at significant security risk, because the likelihood of those vulnerabilities being exploited by threats or attackers becomes higher. With multiple or chains of vulnerabilities being present, it is highly likely that the asset could be inadvertently or deliberately abused. Therefore, it is important security holes (vulnerabilities) within and around critical assets are mitigated (patched) using adequate technical and process-based security controls.

Regular risk assessment, risk management, and business impact review (BIR) are recommended to identify vulnerabilities that may exist in valued assets of the organisation, mitigate perceived attacks to valued assets, and assess business impact in the event of an attack.

2.4.2.7 Threats and attacks

A threat to a computer network exploits vulnerability (or chains of vulnerabilities) in systems to harm them, or predispose them to harm, leading to loss in the confidentiality, integrity or availability of systems resources. Threats to computer networks are on the increase, especially those that use public networks (for example, the Internet) as a transport medium [15]. Understanding vulnerabilities in systems is critical to understanding the threats they represent [40]. Since vulnerabilities in systems and threats that exploit them cannot be completely avoided [10], it is imperative that both must be appropriately controlled. Extended discussion on threats and attacks targeting computer networks is presented in the next chapter.

2.4.2.8 Security policies and standards

The provision of adequate protection controls for organisations' security infrastructure relies on effective implementation of coherent, contemporary and efficient security policies and standards. These are the fundamental building blocks of any security implementation.

Security standards are a distinct set of information security *guidelines* that consist of processes, procedures, methodology and training that assists security personnel in implementing the right set of security controls. Security standards are a catalogue of best security practices comprising technical, management, principle, process and maturity-based guidelines, such as ISO/IEC 15408, ISO/IEC 27001, GAISP, GAPP and ISO/IEC 21827 respectively. An information security standard should be carefully evaluated in relation to an organisation's security requirements. Improper implementation or selection of an inappropriate information standard can have significant implications for the assets which it aims to protect. Security controls enable organisations to manage and protect their computer, information and network services. And security controls consist of mechanisms that provide guidance to connections seeking access to information assets, such as authentication, authorisation, auditing, as well as physical access controls.

A security policy is an organisation's *underlining rules* and *regulation* that aims to address specific security issues for the organisation. It is therefore pertinent that a security policy for an organisation underlines clear rules and instructions on how to administer, manage and maintain secure information management and technological infrastructure of that organisation.

In a nutshell, security policies stipulate *rules* and *regulations* that assist in protecting an organisation's management, information and communication systems; while *security standards* describe *guidelines* for management, technical, process, maturity or operation controls that assist an organisation implement, evaluate, monitor, operate and maintain generally accepted good security practices.

Policies and standards are essential for organisations to implement, maintain or operate acceptable good security practices. Organisations need to adopt security standards appropriate to their business needs. Policies and practices must be constantly and continuously reviewed to ensure that they are implemented according to defined scope and rules; and that they remain up to date and relevant to the organisation. Strictly, practices need to be audited to ensure they comply with the policies, and policies need to be periodically reviewed to ensure they meet business needs and current management directives on security. However, even with excellent security policies and adequate standards in place, it is not guaranteed that an organisation's information resources are secure. The aim of security policies, practices and procedures is to achieve residual risk, that is, to lower the total risk involved with an organisation's assets to the least minimum by having adequate safeguards, countermeasures and security controls in place. Thus, according to NIST [41]: "It is important to note that security policies and practices may be largely dependent upon laws, regulations and organisational decisions around *acceptable risk* and appropriate risk mitigation. No policy or practice, even if implemented exactly as planned, can ensure that an organisation's information is 100% secure". Although policies and standards are essential in maintaining accepted good security practices, the existence of prescribed security processes in organisations does not mean that the goals of the processes are achieved [42]. Therefore, the task of securing organisations information systems cannot rely only on having a security policy or adopting an excellent security standard. Efficient and adequate protection controls must be sought in order to defend against security threats, limit vulnerabilities and mitigate security attacks, while excellent security awareness culture is also essential.

2.4.2.9 Security awareness and training

It is believed that organisations that have adequate security awareness initiatives and training programmes in place more effectively secure their valued assets compared with organisations that do not have security awareness programmes in place. Security awareness programmes assist organisations to communicate acceptable security practices to their employees. Without regular security briefings, security operations reduce to mere "security processes", because it is awareness that drives security for most organisations. Although organisations security practices need to be communicated to all employees, they also must be maintained and continuously reviewed. According to Siponen [42]: "Merely setting up training sessions or presenting information security policies and guidelines will not ensure employees actually follow the information security procedures correctly". What is required from an organisational perspective is a security-awareness culture where everyone is responsible for the security of the organisation by being aware of what are acceptable and unacceptable security practices in the organisation. For example, according to a survey conducted by PricewaterhouseCoopers [210], the challenge to most organisations is to create a security-aware culture. Making staff aware of the risks and their responsibilities helps them act in a sensible and secure manner.

2.4.2.10 Senior executive support for security initiatives

Security initiatives are hardly respected when they do not have senior executive support. For organisations to maintain acceptable levels of security, security initiatives must either be supported or enforced by senior executives. According to the SANS Institute [94]: "The existence of prescribed security processes in organisations does not mean the goals of the processes are achieved". These policies (security initiatives) require senior executive support.

2.4.2.11 Privacy

Privacy affects information security management in most organisations. Often, privacy and security run in parallel. According to Schneier [201], it is like security *versus* privacy: which is more important, and what are we ready to give up? Certain security practices violate privacy, (are anti-privacy); similarly, certain privacy concerns obstruct and restrict effective implementation of security controls. For example, 'lawful IP intercept', and traffic inspection features used on data communications networks, which are built-in in most operating systems can be obtrusive. Major vendors of computer networks have built-in traffic analysis and traffic engineering features. Understandably, these features are useful either in troubleshooting communications faults, or investigating security forensics (penetrated attacks), but their inappropriate use may contravene privacy.

Other examples include the *national ID cards*, warrantless eavesdropping, massive data mining, email sampling/inspection, and *stop and search*. These are practices the government has put in place as security measures either to deter the supposed enemy or terrorists, but in the actual fact, they are obtrusively taking away our social liberties and freedom. Conducting traffic analysis and security auditing without users' authority or consent is unlawful and anti-privacy no matter the circumstance. Security requirements that enable security administrators to inspect users traffic do not necessarily agree with ethical privacy principles. The question is no longer whether security is any more important than privacy, or the case of liberty *versus* control as Schneier discussed [201]. I suspect that security and privacy can work together and are essential organisational requirements.

2.4.2.12 Legislation

Legislation and export restrictions affect information security management. They influence how organisations implement, monitor and manage information security. Export restrictions on cryptographic software are used to regulate how software is distributed. For examples, Cisco's software end user license agreement stipulates that Cisco's IOS software with security feature sets is restricted, and export rules are imposed with respect to the U S export control laws, together with the U S export administration act, and its associated regulations. In this respect, certain countries are not allowed to download this software, and hence, by law, such countries are not allowed to use this software.

With the rising trend in global outsourcing, especially from U.S. and European companies outsourcing IT, Software and BackOffice functions to India, data privacy of, personal information protection, and health records data protection become critical. Unfortunately, legislation of personal data protection in India is completely different from that of the U S or E U. According to [213], India has no data privacy protection legislation at this time. This is why the E U directives on data privacy protection mandate its member states to establish a legal framework to protect the fundamental right to privacy with respect to personal and health records data.

The E U directive on data protection of 1998 (safe harbor) is a comprehensive data protection legislation that orders its member states to establish a legal framework to protect the fundamental rights to privacy with respect to processing personal data that has extraterritorial effect. It prohibits the transfer of personal data or health records data to non-European Union nations that do no meet the European adequacy standard for privacy protection. The U.S. and the European Union share the goal of enhancing privacy protection for their citizens [198]. Clearly, legislation regulates and influences the use and practice of information security for organisations in the global community.

2.4.2.13 Regulatory compliance

Regulatory compliance and certification are security initiatives with significant impact on information security practices. Standards regulate how information security management is being implemented, managed and conducted. For example, ISO 27001-2 is a security standard that recommends best practices for information security management. Organisations seeking accreditation go through a regulatory compliance process. Complaint organisations are perceived to possess essential drivers to earn trust and hence attract business relations with other organisations. Regulatory compliance creates business partnership, instil customer confidence and trust in information assurance, but it comes with a cost: both financial and time resources are expended. Compliance enforces organisations to adhere to certain levels of information security assurance, which is indeed helpful. However, should security compliance, or management compliance become a mandatory requirement? This is going to attract a very lengthy discussion amongst practitioners and researchers in the information security space.

Security compliance, as we highlighted, involves both financial and temporal (time) resource. To the small-sized organisations, this is perceived as another unnecessary burden that distracts business operations as opposed to enhancing information security assurance. To the medium-sized organisations, it is a business gain by being compliant, in order to win trust of other organisations, and consequently fosters business relations. However, security compliance alone can not provide the necessary security and dependability required to reduce security risks organisations face today. Security best practices together with security compliance are the key to reducing security risks.

2.4.2.14 Business operating environment

Operating environment we mean the geographical location where the organisation is operating, and technological challenges that exist in that location. This is one area that is often overlooked when it comes to managing security, because very often, we focus our attention on the developed world, where geographical location and technological challenges have very little influence on how an organisation manages security. Take, for instance, some countries in Africa, Asia or South America, where telecommunications infrastructure are scarce, limited, and expensive. How do organisations in such places manage security? It is extremely difficult for organisations in such environments to efficiently manage security, adhere to regulatory and security compliance, cultivate a healthy security culture or implement the right mix of countermeasures to mitigate attacks. Unreliable communications due to frequent power failures, limited IT infrastructure, and unaffordable IT equipment are inhibiting factors to organisations in such places. Similar circumstances may exist in natural disaster-prone areas where risks from natural disasters affects telecommunications infrastructure.

2.4.2.15 Culture

By culture, we mean the customs, ideas, values of a particular civilisation, society or social group, especially at a particular time [209]. With global outsourcing, the size and scope of an organisation's operations increase, so maintaining a consistently high security across the global enterprise (consisting of many unclear boundaries) becomes challenging. One critical issue that results with global outsourcing or global expansion of an organisation is differences in cultural, social and psychological ideologies among the geographically disperse people working for the organisation. According to Johnson and Goetz [216], outsourcing and off shoring bring new partners into an extended enterprise, with different technologies, cultures, and sensitivities to information management. These conflicting ideologies affect how consistently security is managed and maintained in organisations. Some projects, acquisitions or mergers may fail as a result of the difficulty inherent in managing cultural, social and psychological relationships in organisational change. For example, according to American Express Keith Appleyard [207], Indian companies also struggle with the cultural issue of access control being given on the basis of role rather than rank. Senior managers cannot cope with the idea that lower-ranked members of staff have access to something they don't.

2.5 Summary

In this chapter, key concepts and terminology used to describe *computer security*, *network security* and *computer network security* are discussed. It was shown that although computer security has been extensively researched, computer security terminologies are still used inconsistently.

Traditional computer security issues comprising of confidentiality, integrity, and availability of information and systems were examined. The need for computer network security was highlighted, and factors affecting security implementation in most organisations were discussed. Security perception, risk acceptance, global outsourcing, returns on investment, vulnerabilities in systems, threats and attacks, security policies and standards, security awareness and training, support from senior executives on security, privacy, culture, legislation, and regulatory compliance were identified as notable factors influencing successful security implementation in organisations.

Managing information security for the modern global enterprise was shown to be challenging and complex. There are perceived security and privacy concerns from social networking services, such as *Facebook*, *MySpace*, *YouTube*, and also from meta-universe (Metaverses), such as *Second Life*. Similarly, with security and privacy implications of emerging technologies, such as risks posed by wireless (mobile) computing, Voice over IP (VoIP), and Web 2.0, yet to be accounted. Technical controls alone are believed to be insufficient in addressing the evolving risks output of emerging technologies. Hence, social, legal, privacy and trust requirements were investigated in appropriately managing the new dynamics in information security for the global enterprise.

The new security requirements for the global enterprise are now beyond traditional security requirements. Thus, conscientious, contemporary and comprehensive security requirements are now needed to adequately manage security for the enterprise. The new security requirements are driven by regulatory security compliance, technology, legislation, privacy, culture, environment and operations needs of emerging practices, such as global outsourcing, social networking services, IT in the cloud, and mobile computing. It is pertinent to note that these factors influence the dependability of information security management in organisations.

Chapter 3

Understanding threats and attacks
to computer networks

A critical review of security threats and attacks, and their impacts on computer networks is provided. A new security attack classification in relation to attack timelines is introduced and well discussed. Approaches to security attack detection, prevention and mitigation are discussed, with special emphasis on intrusion detection systems (IDSes). Existing IDS designs are reviewed, while a new classification for intrusion detection systems based on sensor detection construct is provided.

3.1 Introduction

Computer systems are vulnerable to various attacks that can subject or predispose assets to various types of harm. The effects of these attacks vary considerably; some affect the confidentiality, integrity or availability of data, while others affect the confidentiality, integrity or availability of system [1].

According to Brinkley and Schell [34], a security threat is one that participates in an exploitation, either by gaining unauthorised disclosure or by modifying information, leading to information-oriented computer misuse. They identified six types of threats to information, such as *human error, user abuse of authority, direct probing, probing with malicious software, direct penetration,* and *subversion of security mechanism.* Further, they provided a distinction between *threats to information* and *threats to computers.* Countering information-oriented computer misuse requires preventing the unlawful access of both *legitimate users,* and *non-users.* Countering resource-oriented computer misuse only requires keeping non-users from unlawful access to confidential resources. That is, computer misuse aims to prevent computer and information abuse from non-legitimate users of the system. Threats to information are fundamentally different from threats to computers. While threats to computers are difficult to prevent, threats to information are much more difficult to prevent [34].

Evaluating the different types of security threats discussed by Brinkley and Schell, one would soon observe that these types of threats are caused by deliberate human actions on valued assets. As computer security emerges, in 2001, NIST [1] incorporated the idea of *non-deliberate computer misuse* such as errors and omissions, and threats caused by natural disaster, such as fire and flood. These threats cause damages to information and computer systems. Hence, NIST's classification of security threats include: *errors and omissions, fraud, disgruntled employees, fires, water damage, hackers*, and *viruses*. Fire and flood are natural disasters that occur in some places damaging and destroying valued assets. Errors and omissions are caused by non-deliberate human actions, while fraud, worms and viruses are caused by deliberate malicious intents. It is pertinent to note that there is a distinction between the action that causes harm, and the entity whose action caused the harm. This separation leads to *threats* and *threat agents*.

A threat agent is an entity with the capability to introduce threats to assets [43], whose adverse actions are performed on assets. These adverse actions by threat agents can cause *faults, errors*, and *failures in* systems [49]. A *system failure* is an event that occurs when the delivered service deviates from the agreed service level based on the quality of service agreed upon on the SLA. A system may fail either because it does not comply with the specification or because the specification does not adequately describe its function. *Error* is that part of the system state that may cause a subsequent failure. *Fault* is defined as the adjudged or hypothesised cause of an error [49].

Threats to computer networks are classified in terms of *natural disaster* related faults and *human* actions oriented threats [49] that cause harm to assets or predispose assets to harm. Harm to computer networks, occurs in the form of *destruction, disclosure, modification, interruption of data, system and/or denial of service* that result due to natural causes or human-oriented actions. Human-oriented threats exploit vulnerabilities in systems, either deliberately or inadvertently; while natural disaster oriented threats happens without human related actions.

3.2   Threats and their impacts on computer networks

3.2.1   Natural disaster threats

Natural disaster are physical disasters that occur without human actions, such as: fire, flood, earthquake, hurricane and tidal waves. These disasters cause harm to computing infrastructure, such as damage, destruction and interference, which cause computing infrastructure to function abnormally, or stop functioning. Natural disaster do not exploit vulnerabilities that may exist in computer networks, rather physical disaster occur in areas vulnerable to certain natural circumstances. For example, tropical fire often happens in Africa, and hurricanes in South America. The distinction is that natural disasters are not caused by human-related actions.

3.2.2 Human-oriented threats

These are threats relating to human actions that cause faults in systems. Human-oriented actions include deliberate, non-deliberate, inadvertent, malicious, and non-malicious actions. According to Avizienis et al. [20], the two categories of human-related threats are: 1) unintentional and 2) intentional, leading to: developmental faults, physical faults and interaction faults, as shown in Figure 3.2.

3.2.2.1 Developmental faults

Development faults include fault types that occur during development, such as software bugs, hardware errata, design faults (wrong design of equipment, error in dimensioning) and firmware caveats. These types of faults remain undetected during normal program, program testing or hardware development, but may manifest themselves during system operation, and often times in inexplicable circumstances.

3.2.2.2 Physical faults

Physical faults include fault types that affect hardware infrastructure, such as damage to hardware toolkits, its sub-part, firmware, or content. These include system failures caused by excessive temperatures, abnormal environmental conditions (flooding, fire, earthquakes, hurricane, tidal wave and human physical abuse) that affect equipment performance or operation.

3.2.2.3 Interaction faults

Interaction faults include faults that occur due to external interaction with the system. There are many use cases of external internal causing faults in a system. For example, mistakes by systems operators, maintenance personnel, cleaners and others with access to the system that lead to incorrect operation, system shutdown, or accidental physical damage, such as accidental disconnection of equipment, or cable cut [20].

3.2.3 Errors and omissions

Errors and omissions affect the integrity of computer networks. Errors and omissions predispose systems to harm, or create vulnerabilities in systems; and can be caused by all types of users (novice and expert users). For example, a data entry error made by a novice user, or a programming error made by an expert user can cause a system to malfunction. Similarly, an omission (either from a novice user or systems expert) to carry out system backup can led to data losses. Unfortunately, if the system crashes and there is no backup available to be used to restore the system to its last successful state, then there is a problem. Errors and omissions in systems occur frequently. The recent animated cursor (ANI [178]) vulnerability in some versions of the Microsoft Windows operating system is caused by a programming error in design. Errors can occur during all phases of the systems life cycle [1]. It is claimed that 65% of losses to organisations are as a result of errors and omissions, according to a survey of computer-related economic losses [44].

Programming, design and *development errors* often called 'bugs' or 'caveats' constitute other major concerns. For example, according to Arbaugh et al. [45], complex information and communication systems give rise to design, implementation, and management errors. These errors can lead to a vulnerability (flaw) in an information technology product that could allow violations of a security policy.

Installation and *maintenance errors* are another source of security problems. For example, an audit by the Presidents Council for Integrity and Efficiency (PICE) in 1988 found that every one of the ten mainframe computer sites studied, had installation and maintenance errors that introduced significant security vulnerabilities [1].

3.2.4 Deliberate software threats

Deliberate software threats pose serious problems to computer networks, and are on the increase, as shown in Figure 3.1. Examples of deliberate software threats include network worms, viruses and trojans. Other types of threats of growing importance include malicious codes, malware, adware and spyware.

Figure 3.1 shows the losses in US dollars caused by different types of threats obtained from CSI/FBI 2006 crime survey [72]. As shown, viruses topped the list; however, other new types of threats are beginning to emerge, such as cyber-threats (terrorism and cyber-warfare). These types of threats accounted for a significant amount of dollar losses in 2006 compared with previous years, and have been highly publicised after the US 9/11 incident [206].

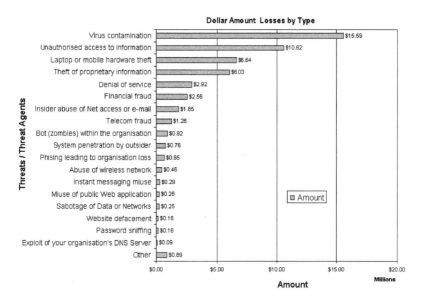

Figure 3.1: Dollar amount losses due to security threats [72]

3.2.5 Cyber threats

Cyber threats are a new form of computer network threats that are used in electronic warfare, terrorism, and espionage. The recent electronic attacks on Georgia, where important government websites and portals where constantly 'flooded' by spurious requests in a second, which led to many of these sites being unavailable to legitimate users, highlights the prevalence of cyber threats. Similar attacks were witnessed in 2007 by the Estonian government. Some attacks took the form of denial or distributed denial of service attacks, as hundreds of thousands of "zombie" computers launched various forms of service requests a second on Estonian websites, which led to many of these sites being temporarily unavailable to service legitimate user requests.

3.2.6 Insider Threats

Insider threats are threats imposed by internal users of a system. Internal users of the system are those users with legitimate access to the system. Insider threats include privilege escalation by an internal user in order to conduct an unauthorised action. It is shown that insider attacks are the most prevalent attacks witnessed in the enterprise leading to critical data losses. For example, insiders can copy confidential and sensitive files. They can escalate password and privilege of their legitimate accounts of the system. They can also plant trojan or scripts to automatic delete certain files or corrupt logs in order to avoid being detected. Unfortunately, insider attacks are hard to detect, because network protection is usually against external access to the system. Internal users with good knowledge of the network also know which assets to tamper without being swiftly detected.

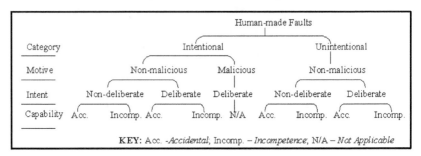

Figure 3.2: Classification of human-made faults [20]

A classification of human-action faults shown in Figure 3.2 is adapted from Avizienis et al. [20]. This figure is used to determine the *category, motive, intent* and *capability* of human-action threats. For example:

◆ Network errors and omissions: *unintentional, non-malicious, non-deliberate, accidental human actions faults.*

◆ Deliberate software threats: *intentional, malicious, deliberate human-action faults.*

◆ Cyber threats: *intentional, malicious, deliberate human-action faults.*

◆ Insider threats: *intentional, malicious, deliberate human-action faults.*

◆ Natural disasters: *unintentional, non-malicious, non-deliberate, accidental natural-action faults.*

3.3 Security threats and attack timeline

To examine how threats exploit vulnerabilities in assets, a requirement is to investigate a taxonomy of threats. Threats have been classified based on vulnerabilities that exist in systems [34]. Unfortunately, a classification of threats based on identifying potential vulnerabilities an attacker exploits to harm an asset is not sufficient in identifying possible countermeasures required to protect valued assets. Hence, a classification of threats based on attack timeline, which is essential in efficiently and timely identifying countermeasures that are adequate in protecting valued assets is proposed.

The purpose of classifying threats based on attack propagation timeline is as follows:

♦ to examine when in a threat's propagation dynamics the threat will cause most significant harm (or damage) to assets; and

♦ to identify countermeasures that are possible at each specific stage of the attack, in order to efficiently and timely mitigate the attack. In this respect, a classification of attacks based on an attack timeline is investigated.

The attack classification is a three-stage attack classification based on an attack timeline, namely: the *probing, penetration* and *perpetuation* (the **3P**) stages, shown in Figure 3.3.

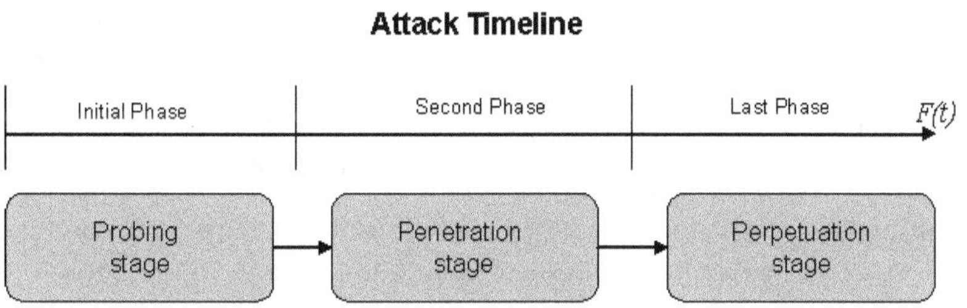

Attack Timeline

Figure 3.3: Security threat propagation and attack timeline

3.3.1 Probing stage

The probing stage is the earliest stage in an attack timeline. It is also known as the *reconnaissance stage.* This phase is primarily for information gathering. The probing stage is when vulnerable networks and systems are discovered through processes such as probing, scanning and sampling. For example, an attacker may use portscan (ICMP, TCP or UDP) techniques to discover and characterise networks and systems that are online, and to identify services, processes or applications running on these systems, or other systems. Social engineering deception techniques also can be used to gather information about a person or a system as part of the probing stage. The information gathering stage is known to be a precursor to attack.

3.3.2 Penetration stage

The penetration stage is the second stage in an attack timeline. This occurs when an attacker (or a threat agent) tries to circumvent security controls to create opportunities to cause harm to the system. Two subcategories are recognised:

◆ **Unauthorised access**: this occurs when an attacker intentionally (deliberately and maliciously) tries to bypass access control mechanisms to harm or predispose a system to harm. For example, brute force attacks and dictionary attacks.

◆ **Denial of service:** this occurs when an attacker that does not require authorised access invades a system to deliberately and maliciously harm a system. Examples include, network intrusions, network worms, denial of service attacks (DoS) and distributed denial of service attacks (DDoS).

3.3.3 Perpetuation stage

The perpetuation stage is the last stage in an attack timeline. It occurs when an attacker has successfully penetrated networks or/and systems unlawfully for malicious intent. Four subcategories are recognised:

◆ **Disclosure:** when the intent is unlawfully disclose information or system, consequently leading to a breach of confidentiality.

◆ **Manipulation:** when the intent is to alter information or system configuration or operation, leading to an abuse of information or system integrity.

◆ **Destruction:** when the intent is to manipulate or destroy (partly or in whole) assets (information/system), leading to abuse of integrity and availability.

◆ **Cleaning-up**: when the attacker removes evidence of the attack in order to prevent being detected using forensic evidence, so as to avoid criminal prosecution.

At each stage of the attack timeline different countermeasures are required. For example, at the *probing stage*, host and network-based intrusion detection systems are required to detect port scans. It is shown that this stage is very important for a successful attack, since the probing stage is a precursor to attacks. It is shown that the success of an attack has a high dependence on the thoroughness of its reconnaissance [54].

At the *penetration stage*, strong access control mechanisms are required together with denial of service mitigation tools. For example, authentication, authorisation and accounting mechanisms, firewall systems, and DoS mitigation systems are required. At the *perpetuation stage*, efficient forensic systems are required together with efficient network monitoring systems.

It is evident that at each stage of the attack timeline different countermeasures are required. Hence, a classification that investigates security threats in terms of *attack timeline* pertinently recommends countermeasures that are efficient and timely in mitigating attacks at every stage of their propagation, and therefore, is more adept in protecting systems. There is no doubt that such a classification is more effective at evaluating emerging security threats and attacks than existing taxonomies that investigate vulnerabilities in systems without considering threats propagation dynamics.

3.4 Approaches to security threat detection, prevention and mitigation

This section discusses approaches and techniques utilised to detect, prevent security threats to, and mitigate attacks on computer networks. Special attention is given to intrusion detection systems (IDSes), and notable contributions in IDS engineering are presented.

To detect security threats, such as *intrusion, exploit, or computer misuse*, an approach is to use sensors (also loosely known as detectors) to detect threats. This is referred to as intrusion detection. Intrusion detection is the process of intelligently monitoring the events occurring in a computer system or network, analysing them for signs of violations of the security policy [55]. But the process of intrusion detection is performed by an intrusion detection system. An intrusion detection system is likened to a burglar alarm in a computer site [56]. The aim is to defend computer networks by using a combination of an alarm that sounds whenever security has been compromised, and a security administrator (site security office - (SSO)) that responds to the alarm and takes appropriate mitigating actions.

According to Helmer et al. [57], IDSes are *reactive systems* that attempt to detect, analyse and respond to malicious activities targeted at computing and networking resources.

Another approach to protecting systems from harm caused by security threats is the use of *preventive systems* to prevent threats targeting systems and networks. This approach comprises the use of access and admission control frameworks that stipulate admission conditions (rules and policies), which entities seeking network connection into corporate infrastructure must satisfy prior to gaining network acceptance, as shown in Figure 3.4. Major vendors in both the network infrastructure and operating systems arenas have recognised the need for such approaches in protecting corporate infrastructures. Examples include Network Admission Control (NAC) [58] by Cisco Systems Inc., and Network Access Protection (NAP) [59] by Microsoft. These initiatives aim to prevent the introduction of foreign security threats into managed corporate infrastructure. A detailed discussion on preventive systems is presented in section 4.3.1.

Another approach to threat detection is the use of *retrospective systems* to detect threats solely for the purposes of litigation, post mortem analysis, re-engineering, evaluation of products, and security forensics. A discussion of this class of systems is presented in section 4.3.3.

We recognise that not all classes of attacks can be prevented. For example, studies have shown that denial of service attacks are difficult to prevent, and can only be mitigated [50, 51]. In this respect, it is recommend that all the approaches discussed namely, preventive, reactive and retrospective ought to be seamlessly deployed together for better protection of valued assets. Approaches to security threat detection, prevention and attack mitigation are viewed from the perspective of the classification provided in Figure 3.4.

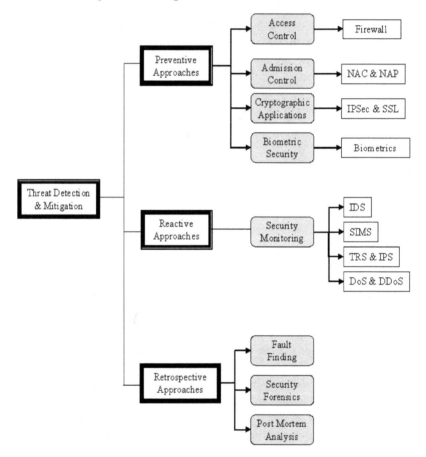

Figure 3.4: A high-level classification of approaches to security threat detection and attack mitigation

3.4.1 Preventive approaches

These are approaches distinctively used in preventing threats or attacks from penetrating into monitored or corporate LANs. Preventive security models include access control mechanisms, admission control frameworks and cryptographic applications. Access control mechanisms such as firewalls are specialised detectors that classify traffic (into malicious and non-malicious), and are able to prevent malicious traffic targeting secure infrastructures. Admission control mechanisms such as the NAC and NAP focus on prerequisite security admission policies for computer networks seeking network connection to an enterprise. Cryptographic applications such as Internet Protocol Security (IPSec) and Secure Socket Layer (SSL) are security protocols that allow access only to authentic (trusted) parties. A detailed discussion of preventive approaches is presented in section 4.3.1.

3.4.2 Reactive approaches

These are approaches for mitigating attacks that preventive approaches could not prevent. Since not all types of attacks can be prevented, reactive approaches are used as complementary systems to protecting valued assets. For example, denial of service or distributed denial of service can only be mitigated, but could not prevented. Hence, approaches that focus on mitigating attacks as opposed to preventing attacks become very relevant and appealing. These comprise of security monitoring approaches deployed to proactively monitor the network, such as intrusion detection systems (IDS), security information management systems (SIMS), threat response systems (TRS), intrusion prevention systems (IPS), and DoS mitigation systems, as shown in Figure 3.4. A detailed discussion of reactive approaches is presented in section 4.3.2.

3.4.3 Retrospective approaches

These are approaches used solely for evaluating security breaches aimed at postmortem examinations, security forensics and legal purposes. Retrospective approaches comprise security mechanisms used for fault finding, security forensics and post mortem analysis that assist in evaluating systems in the event of a security breach in order to gather crime scene evidence to enable the asset owner to pursue criminal litigation against the attacker, and also for the purpose of system re-evaluation towards survivability. A detailed discussion of retrospective defence approaches is presented in section 4.3.3.

3.5 Intrusion detection systems

In the past 20 years, intrusion detection systems (IDSes) have evolved and are now very sophisticated. IDSes are not only used to detect and control the level of attacks launched on computer networks, but also, used in cyberspace situational awareness and impact analysis. A survey of approaches in intrusion detection systems shows that emerging intrusion detection systems now combine multiple sensors in gathering attacks evidence. An important proposition that makes emerging IDSes very capable of gathering a wide variety of attack evidence, which were not possible with previous ID systems, consequently making emerging IDSes able to detect attacks that would have ordinarily gone undetected with current systems.

3.5.1 Survey and classification of intrusion detection systems

In 1987, a seminal work from Denning [85] made an inroad into the field of intrusion detection systems. The paper presents a classic model of intrusion detection, and a general framework for intrusion detection systems, called IDES (intrusion detection expert systems). A classification presented in the paper was anomaly-based detection (threshold-based detection), which is based on activity profiles. An activity profile is a baseline profile of a particular action. IDES function by comparing a template profile to a real-time activity profile. A real-time activity profile is generated every time the network is monitored; however, to check for anomalies, the real-time activity profile is compared against the template profile.

In 2000, Axelsson [56] presented a survey and taxonomy of intrusion detection systems. The paper provides a classification of intrusion detection systems principally based on *detection techniques* and *system characteristics*. The three main detection techniques demonstrated in the classification were, *anomaly, signature-based* and *signature-inspired*. However, *anomaly-based* systems were further classified into systems that are supervised (programmed) and unsupervised (self-learning). Similarly, *signature-based* systems were further sub-classified as supervised, while *signature-inspired* systems were further sub-classified as unsupervised.

System characteristics include *time of detection, granularity, audit source, type of response, data processing, data collection, security* and *interoperability*.

Axelsson's taxonomy is rich and well presented. It classified IDSes in terms of detection technique and made further separation based on the constructs of the techniques. For example, it provided a separation between *anomaly-based, signature-based* and *signature-inspired* systems.

In 2006, Gates [86] used two sets of criteria, namely *detection technique*, and *type of network data* to classify intrusion detection systems. Although Gates's work focused primarily on detecting distributed port scans, the approaches investigated in her paper are those that are able to detect other types of threats and attacks in addition to port scans.

Another type of classification seen in the literature is based on *type of response* provided by an IDS or IPS. Primarily, there are two types of responses identified, namely, *passive* and *active* responses. Some IDSes can offer both a passive response or an active response against an attack, depending on their assessment of the attack evidence. A class of intrusion detection systems that passively respond to threats and attacks, or used solely for attack detection, are conventionally known as IDS. The other class that actively respond to perceived attacks, are referred to as *intrusion prevention systems (IPS)* or *threat response systems (TRS)* according to Benjamin and Ramachandran [77]. IPS or TRS are built to automate their responses to perceived attacks. A combination of responses is possible, such as drop, deny or reset a connection deemed malicious.

It is recognised that other classifications exist in the field of intrusion detection systems, for example, Botha et al. [78], classified IDSes in terms of host-based, network-based, application-based and target-based monitors. This relates to where an IDS is placed in the network to monitor traffic. Similarly, a class of IDSes is referred to as hybrid systems. These are IDSes that combine both *threshold* and *signature-based detection techniques* in their analysis [78].

Investigating the field of intrusion detection systems, we observed that emerging IDS initiatives are using *multiple heterogeneous sensors* in their detection of threats and attacks. For example, Siaterlis and Maglaris [82] employed multiple sensors in detecting and mitigating denial of service attacks. Hall and McMullen [109] described various solutions that combined multiple sensors to detect attacks, system faults, improved attack tracking, identification and detection. Haines et al. [186] discussed a correlation system that deployed numerous sensors to provide better attack detection. Tim Bass [177] demonstrated the need for next generation intrusion detection systems to use multiple sensors in their analysis. It is believed that next-generation cyberspace intrusion detection systems will require the fusion of data from myriad heterogeneous distributed network sensors to effectively create cyberspace situational awareness. Chen et al. [179] described an approach for intrusion detection systems in ad hoc networks that combined data from multiple sensors to provide accurate detection of cyber attacks. Siraj and Vaughn [180] described how they used evidence from multiple sensors for alert correlation in a distributed environment.

IDS correlators is a class of IDSes that use multiple sensors to detect intrusions and attacks. They work on the premise that evidence from multiple sensors used to detect attacks provides better understanding of the attacks than a single sensor perspective. According to Haines et al. [186], "Previous results indicate that no single IDS can detect all cyber attacks. IDS research continues, but researchers have also turned their attention to higher-level correlation systems to gather and combine evidence from many different intrusion detection systems and to make use of this broader evidence base for better attack detection."

Hence, to provide a comprehensive survey of IDS approaches a new classification is proposed - *the sensor detection construct*. The sensor detection construct, is a classification that evaluates IDSes under numerous criteria, but based on three primary metrics, namely: *detection technique, type of data* available to the sensors, and potential for *multisensor fusion* capability, discussed below.

3.6   Sensor detection construct

Despite advances in IDS engineering, IDS classification is still an open research issue. With the rapid development in intrusion detection systems, it is difficult to have a complete classification or taxonomy of ID systems. Existing classifications lag in time with advances in ID engineering, and therefore, insufficient in classifying recent advances in the field. Sensor detection construct is a classification that is used to survey current, and the most recent open source intrusion detection system. Hence, the classification aims to complement existing classifications, such as those by Gates [86] and Axelsson [56]. The metrics used in evaluating current and emerging contributions in the field is simple and straightforward, and are as follows:

- ◆ detection techniques

- ◆ type of network data

- ◆ position

- ◆ type of response

- ◆ multisensor fusion capability

When using sensor detection construct to classify an IDS, we investigate the *detection techniques* the sensors apply to detect threats and attacks, *the type of network data* available to the sensors when analysing attack evidence, whether the sensors are able to detect attacks on *hosts or networks*, whether the IDS combines more than two sensors (*multiple sensors*) in its detection engine, and finally, the *type of responses* to sends to perceived attacks, as shown in Table 3.1. Other attributes not shown in Table 3.1, are whether an IDS provides realtime, near realtime or/and non-realtime response to attacks; and a potential attribute that will be worth checking is if an IDS is aware or able to report enterprise-wide situations (cyber situational awareness) of threats and attacks.

3.6.1 Detection technique

Detection technique refers to the underlying principle that the IDS uses to detect security threats and attacks. Three subcategories of detection technique are identified, *threshold*, *algorithmic* and *visualisation*.

3.6.1.1 Threshold-based systems

Threshold-based systems (*anomaly-based* [85, 56, 86]) watch for abnormalities in the traffic being monitored. The construction of detectors in this class of systems starts by forming an opinion on what constitutes normal for the monitored network, and then deciding on what percentage of the activity to flag as abnormal, and how to make this particular decision[56]. Examples of threshold-based IDSes include, IDES [85], EMERALD [87].

3.6.1.2 Algorithmic-based systems

Algorithmic-based systems (signature-based or misuse detection systems [56, 55, 85]) function by using decision rules and apply detection methods such as sequential hypothesis testing, probability inference, time series analysis, neural networks and genetic algorithms. Examples of algorithmic-based IDSes, include: Bro [88], GASSATA [89], IDIOT [174], SNORT [127], and NSM [173], as shown in Table 3.1.

3.6.1.3 Visualisation-based systems

Visualisation-based systems focus on presenting the data to the user in some visual representations that assist security administrators to detect and mitigate threats or attacks. Examples of visualisation-based IDSes include: GrIDS [83], NVisionIP [92], PortVis [93], Onwubiko and Lenaghan [17].

3.6.2 Type of network data

IDSes require *packet-level information, flow-level information*, or both as shown in Table 3.1. *Packet-level information* provides connection details, such as IP address, packet payload, and traffic header information. According to Gates [54] this level of detail allows signatures of known attacks to be used on the data to determine whether the packet payload contains an attack. *Flow-level information* (for example, Juniper's *cflowd* and Cisco's *netflow* protocols) provide summarised connection information. *Netflow* is a 5-tuple unidirectional sequence of packets; each packet shares the 5-tuple values. Several versions of netflow exist, namely, v_1, v_5, v_6, v_7, v_8 and the more recent v_9; but v_5 is the most used of them all. A netflow packet is shown as:

$$netflow\ packet = \langle ip\_src, ip\_dst, tcp\_src, tcp\_dst, proto \rangle$$

Where ip_src = source IP address, IP_dst = destination IP address, tcp_src = source TCP port, tcp_dst = destination TCP port, and proto = IP protocol.

3.6.3 Position

Position applies to where an intrusion detection system is placed in the network to monitor traffic. Hence, IDSes have been classified based on position. For example, there are host-based, network-based, application-based and target-based intrusion detection systems [78]. IDS placement is a significant consideration when deploying intrusion detection systems. This is because the amount and quality of data (traffic) observed by the ID system have some relationships to where and ID system is placed in the network. This in turns determines the degree of protection the ID system provides to the organisation. If an intrusion detection system is placed in a network that is not of major concern to an organisation, it is likely that the ID system may not be able to observe anomalous traffic, and unable to provide adequate protection to the critical information assets it's meant to protect. IDS placement should be at the following points in the network:

◆ behind a pair of firewalls towards the external-facing interface.

◆ at peering points (especially public peering points).

◆ at points of interconnection to third parties, such as vendors, customers, ISP.

◆ at extranet interconnection.

◆ at points of interconnection among various departments, such as finance, HR, R&D and Engineering.

3.6.4 Multisensor fusion

Given that sensors are designed to gather and detect specific threats, according to Staniford et al. [181], and Axelsson [56], specific sensors or specific intrusion detection systems are better at detecting a class of threat than others, (for example, Staniford et al. claimed in [181] that EMERALD is not capable of detecting slow stealthy scans). According to Hall and McMullen [109], "there is simply no one perfect sensor"; that is, no single sensor or type of sensor has the capability to detect, locate or identify all cyber attacks. In this respect, it is recognised that a security monitoring approach where multiple sensors are deployed to monitor, gather and collate security attack evidence across the entire network is desirable.

The premise is that the deployment of multiple, specialised and cooperating sensors to detect, gather and collate pieces of attack evidence produces better results in detecting a variety of threats perceived on enterprise networks than those that rely on the capability of a single sensor to do the same job, which is the case with most intrusion detection systems. This philosophy underpinned the classification of threat detection systems based on multisensor fusion, as shown in Table 3.1. Security information management systems monitor the network with multiple sensors to efficiently detect and mitigate attacks perceived on a population of computer networks. A *multisensor fusion* is an initiative in security monitoring, where multiple sensors (*comprising packet-level* and/or *flow-level*) are deployed to collate security threat or attack evidence on the entire network. Examples of multisensor fusion in security monitoring include Siaterlis and Maglaris [82], Haines et al. [186], Chen and Venkatarmanan [179], and Onwubiko and Lenaghan [17].

The scope of a single sensor in detecting a variety of threats or attacks is limited. Approaches that deploy multiple sensors to monitor and detect threats are a step forward in detecting varying threats/attacks perceived on the entire network compared to approaches that rely only on a single sensor. For example, Haines et al. [186] used multiple correlators that combine pieces of evidence from various sensors to detect specific attacks and to identify attack targets. They argued that multisensor correlation focuses on taking diverse information from at least two sensors and combining it to form an integrated picture of an attacker's activity. This is important to an analyst because it improves and substantiates the accuracy of a hypothesis regarding an attack.

3.6.5 Type of response

Here, an investigation is carried out to determine the type of response provided by IDSes. Two types of responses are identified, namely, passive and active responses. A class of intrusion detection systems that passively respond to threats and attacks, or used solely for attack detection, are conventionally known as IDS. The other class that actively respond to perceived attacks are referred to as intrusion prevention system (IPS) or threat response system (TRS) (see Benjamin and Ramachandran [77]).

Intrusion prevention systems are built to automate their responses to perceived attacks; however, some IPSes can be configured to alert security administrators who are monitoring the systems. A combination of responses is provided by intrusion prevention systems, such as drop, denial or reset traffic connection deemed stealthy or/and malicious. In this study though, intrusion prevention systems are referred to as intrusion detection systems. A different set of classification other than 'type of response' classification is provided herein, as in sensor detection construct.

IDS	Year	Detection technique	Network data type	Position	Type of response	Sensor fusion
IDES [85]	1987	Threshold	Packet level	Network	Passive	x
MIDAS [79]	1988	Threshold	Flow level	Network	Passive	x
NSM [173]	1990	Threshold	Packet level	Network	Passive	x
IDIOT [174]	1994	Algorithmic	Packet level	Network	Passive	x
GrIDS [83]	1996	Algorithmic, Visualisation	Packet level	Host, Network	Passive	x
Bro [88]	1998	Algorithmic	Packet level	Network	Passive	x
SNORT [127]	1998	Threshold	Packet level	Network	Passive, Active	x
GASSATA [89]	1998	Algorithmic	Packet level	Network	Passive	x
Staniford et al. [181]	2002	Algorithmic	Packet level	Network	Passive	x
Siaterlis and Maglaris* [82]	2002	Algorithmic, Threshold	Flow level	Network	Passive	√
Haines et al.* [186]	2003	Algorithmic, Threshold	Packet level, Flow level	Host, Network	Passive, Active	√
Gates et al. [80]	2003	Algorithmic	Flow level	Host, Network	Passive	x
PortVis [93]	2004	Visualisation	Flow level	Host, Network	Passive	x
NVisionIP [92]	2004	Visualisation	Flow level	Host, Network	Passive	x
VisFlowConnect [84]	2004	Visualisation	Flow level	Host, Network	Passive	x
OSSIM* [63]	2005	Threshold, Algorithmic, Visualisation	Packet level, Flow level	Host, Network	Passive	√
SQUIL* [81]	2005	Algorithmic, Visualisation	Packet Level	Host, Network	Passive	√
Onwubiko and Lenaghan* [17]	2005	Threshold, Algorithmic, Visualisation	Packet level, Flow level	Host, Network	Passive	√
OSSEC [64]	2008	Algorithmic, Visualisation	Packet level	Host	Active	x

Table 3.1: Classification of IDSes based on Sensor Detection Construct

Table 3.1: Classification of IDSes based on Sensor Detection Construct
Key: x - *means a single sensor*; √ - *means two or more sensors*

Table 3.1 shows the sensor detection construct classification. It is used to classify key contributions in IDS designs in the literature. The order in which the IDS contributions appear in the table is based on the year the IDS was developed or when its code was made available to the public. The contributions marked with (*) means that such contributions can also be referred to as security monitoring and event correlation initiatives.

3.7 Summary

Threats and attacks to computer networks are discussed, and different approaches to controlling threats and mitigating attacks are presented and explained. Five major categories of threats are evaluated, such as *errors and omissions, deliberate software threats, natural disasters, cyber threats* and *insider threats*. Cyber threats, such as, terrorism and cyber warfare are on the increase since the US 9/11 incident. However, *deliberate software threats*, comprising of network worms, viruses and trojans still topped the rankings, in terms of harm caused by threats leading to significant financial losses [72]. Human-oriented threats were further classified in terms of *category, motive, intent* and *capability*. For example, deliberate software threats and cyber threats were identified as caused by *intentional, malicious, deliberate human-related faults*, while, errors and omissions were identified as caused by *unintentional, non-malicious, non-deliberate, accidental human-related faults*.

The various IDS initiatives used for detection, prevention and mitigation of attacks are identified and discussed. They were classified into three general detection approaches, namely: threshold-based, algorithmic and visualisation, as shown in Table 3.1. The types of traffic data available to these IDSes were identified as 'flow-level' and 'packet-level' data, while, the type of response provided by the IDSes are a combination of passive and active responses.

Senor detection construct is the new classification used to classify IDS engineering based on five interrelated metrics, namely, detection technique utilised by the approaches, type of data available to the IDS, position of IDS in the network, the enrichment of multisensor capability *in the analysis* of threat evidence and type of response provided by the IDSes. The richness of the *sensor detection construct* classification is evident when well-known classifications, such as Denning [85], and Gates [86] can be loosely mapped directly into the *classification*, as shown in Table 3.1.

Chapter 4

Defence approaches for protecting computer networks

This chapter discusses different approaches employed by organisations to protect their computer systems and computer networks. Current and emerging approaches are compared, and a taxonomy of security defence approaches is presented.

4.1 Introduction

Security defence systems are used to protect computer networks against security attacks in three fundamental ways: they are used to prevent known attacks to computer networks (preventive); they are used to respond to attacks that have penetrated networks (reactive); and also, to investigate break-ins (retrospective) after attacks had happened. Before discussing emerging security defence approaches, current approaches to security defence are examined, and compared to emerging approaches. A classification of security defence approaches is provided; and the relevance of defence models to three application domains, such as security monitoring, distributed systems and electronic commerce is demonstrated.

4.2 From localised to distributive defence approaches

A traditional network security approach is to use localised systems, such as user authentication, encryption and firewalls to protect computer networks as the first line of defence [5]. But localised approaches offer stand-alone security countermeasures to end-user systems or to specific sections of the network. They do not have total visibility of the entire network, hence they are limited in perspective.

Localised defence systems operate in isolation, and at specific points in the network. Each possessing only fragments of evidence about the overall state of the network. Coupled with the lack of integrated mechanisms to coordinate inputs from localised defence systems, it is believed that such security approaches are inadequate to address the security requirements imposed by emerging attacks, such as a distributed attack. For example, localised defence systems are inconsistent in protecting computer networks [96]; while traditional network security approach of using localised defence systems is insufficient in preventing emerging attacks [6]. Emerging attacks are distributed in nature, and often coordinated, so mitigating them with stand-alone localised systems is often challenging. An example of an emerging security attack is illustrated in Figure 4.1.

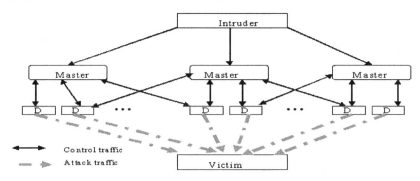

Figure 4.1: An instance of a distributed attack

Figure 4.1 is an example of a classic distributed attack system [97]. A distributed attack system consists of *intruders, masters, daemons and victims*. The *intruder* controls a small number of "*masters*", which in turn control a large number of *daemons*. These daemons (denoted with a "D") can be used to launch packet flooding or other attack types against *victim* (a target system). Daemons are software agents installed on most sites, typically through the exploitation of well-known vulnerabilities that lead to root privilege on the compromised system. In fact, some of the daemon programs do not require root privilege to launch an attack. One significant characteristic of such attacks is that they are distributed in nature and therefore originate from different egress points (the daemons), although controlled from a single source (the intruder). To mitigate emerging security attacks, such as the attack illustrated in Figure 4.1, a paradigm shift in security defence is necessary.

4.2.1 Traditional localised security approach

With the traditional security approach, each countermeasure is localised on individual clients, with each countermeasure having a single perspective on the network traffic, and providing uncoordinated countermeasure actions based on its

77

limited view of the network, as shown in Figure 4.2. It is believed that such countermeasure approaches do not cater for transient mobile user populations on the network. Therefore, what is required is a different type of security approach that caters for mobility on the network, focusing on defending both the edge and core of the network.

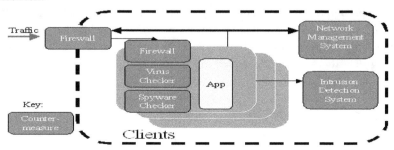

Figure 4.2: An illustration of a localised security concept

Figure 4.2 is an illustration of a localised security concept. The sensor, analysis and response mechanisms are all built in a single client (say, an end user laptop). Although the client can detect and respond to attacks, its response is limited to threats seen and perceived by the client. This type of security approach is limited in perspective (scope) and therefore insufficient in protecting an enterprise network.

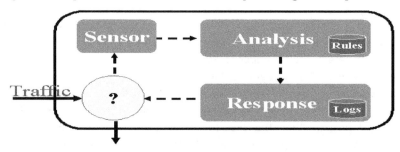

Figure 4.3: Functional decomposition of a localised countermeasure, for example, a firewall

Figure 4.3 is an example of a functional decomposition of a localised countermeasure, such as a firewall. It shows how the system detects, analyses and responds to attacks. The mechanism is to inspect traffic at the ingress and egress for suspicious activities, and when suspicious activity is detected, responses are provided. Again, its perception is localised and limited.

Stand-alone systems detect, record, and may take action to mitigate attacks. In contrast, a distributed security mechanism operates across a population of hosts on the network. Distributed approaches offer three significant advantages over localised approaches, namely their abilities to:

- ◆ collate evidence about attacks across a population of hosts rather than an individual host.

- ◆ analyse evidence about attacks across a population of hosts rather than an individual host.

- ◆ coordinate the deployment or reconfiguration of multiple countermeasures across a network.

In these respects, distributed security approaches possess the capability to identify emerging attacks earlier and provide more efficient and effective responses than localised security approaches. Hence, to provide appropriate countermeasures to emerging security attacks, the need for distributive defence approaches in protecting computer networks is investigated. Distributive defence approaches are shown to successfully handle emerging threats through a distributed framework of heterogeneous systems that cooperate to achieve effective defence [95]. Similarly, it has previously been shown that distributive defence systems that possess the capability to detect attacks perceived on a population of hosts on the network are sufficient to mitigate attack sessions perceived on the entire network [14].

4.2.2 Distributed security mechanisms

The shifting paradigm from standalone countermeasures to more distributed mechanisms is visible in the growing deployment of corporate and open-source security initiatives. First, the deployment of security information and event management (SIEM) systems to monitor enterprise networks [14]. SIEM systems integrate, correlate and normalize security events from multiple sources to provide a unified analysis of the state of an entire network.

Second, an active network approach in security management has recently been utilised to provide distributed security defence to computer networks [6]. The active network approach is a distributive initiative for defending computer networks by pushing responses (countermeasures) as near as possible to the source of attacks, where they can produce efficient and appropriate mitigation effects [98].

Third, major vendors in both the network infrastructure and operating systems arenas have recognised the need for frameworks for distributed security infrastructures; for example, Network Admission Control [58] by Cisco Systems Inc., and Network Access Protection [59] by Microsoft. Details of these initiatives are discussed in section 4.3.1.2.

Finally, the open source community currently have OSSIM (Open Source Security Information Management) [63], SQUIL (the Analyst Console for Network Security Monitoring) [81], and AWCC[171] (the Applied Watch Command Center) as examples of open source distributed security frameworks.

It is pertinent to note that security frameworks that distribute sensors throughout the network and are able to integrate their individual perspectives are a step forward. They promise to detect a variety of attacks targeting the enterprise compared to standalone approaches. However, gathering evidence of attack is only half the solution. Both powerful analysis techniques and well-coordinated responses are needed. Analysis techniques are needed that can model the relationships between events to sift the data more effectively. Patterns of response are needed that coordinate individual countermeasures to yield a coherent defensive realignment of a network.

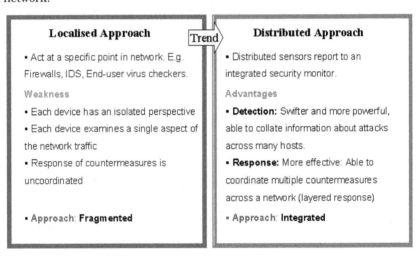

Figure 4.4: Trend in security defence: from localised to distributed

Figure 4.4 shows the trend in security defence from a localised to a distributed security approach, and outlines advantages of the distributed approach over the localised approach.

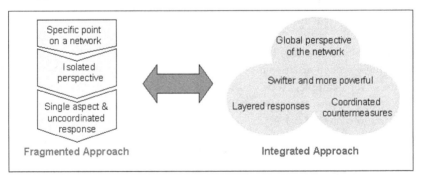

Figure 4.5: Localised versus distributed security approach

Figure 4.5 is a diagrammatic illustration of the comparison between localised and distributed security approaches. Localised countermeasures are fragmented, each layer performs specific, but uncoordinated actions, while, the distributed defence model integrates overlapping layers of security components together to protect the network.

4.3   Security defence models

In deciding how best to protect computer networks and their communications from security attacks, a new classification scheme is drawn based on specific functions performed by separate defence models as shown in Figure 4.6.

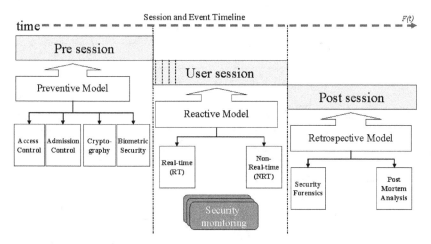

Figure 4.6: Classification of security models with an indication of their focus

Specific functions of defence models are summarised as follows:

◆ to prevent threats and attacks to computer networks (preventive models).

◆ to defend computer networks from successful network intrusions (reactive models).

◆ to investigate security break-ins, policy violations or compromise (retrospective models).

Figure 4.6 shows the proposed security classification that divides the task of protecting computer networks and their communications into three specific areas based on the tasks they perform, as follows:

◆ Preventive security models *prevent* attacks from violating the network security policy, compromising security controls or assets.

- ◆ Reactive security models *defend* computer networks from network intrusions, threats and attacks that have penetrated systems.

- ◆ Retrospective security models provide *trace-back* capability for attacks and investigate policy violations and break-ins to corporate assets.

4.3.1 Preventive security models

Preventive security models are used to prevent known security threats and attacks targeting computer networks. They focus primarily on denying or blocking known security attacks. Preventive security methods include *access control methods, admission control approaches, cryptography* and *biometric security* as shown in Figure 4.7.

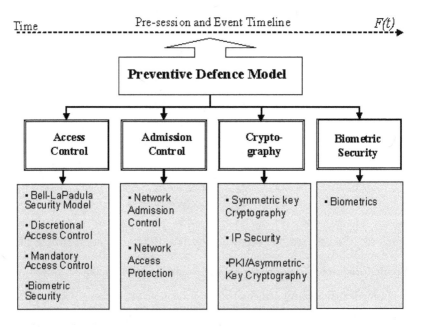

Figure 4.7: Preventive defence classification

4.3.1.1 Access control methods

Access control methods are used to protect corporate assets by controlling who gains access to networks, what services are available to them, and the privileges associated with users based on a pre-defined policy. Access control policies are based on access control models, for example, Biba [99], Bell-LaPadula model [31], Lattice model, role-based and discretionary access controls [101]. For *network services*, access controls are based on pre-defined rule-based instructions that allow, drop, block or/and log certain traffic. For example, gateway devices, such as routers, switches or firewalls, use filters (access control lists) to permit, deny or log certain traffic based on predefined policy components, such as traffic source, destination, type of protocol or a combination of these (see RFC 1858 [183]). For *information services*, access controls are based on flow analysis, a mechanism that ensures information flows in systems range from secure to less secure, according to stipulated levels of trust.

4.3.1.2 Admission control methods

Admission control mechanisms are used to protect corporate assets by controlling what gains admission into corporate networks, by ascertaining that services and systems accessing a corporate network are legitimate, compliant, and adhere to the corporate security policy. This implies checking that a system requesting access to corporate networks has the latest patches, anti-viral updates, recommended user-based IDS and a personal firewall. When a system requesting access is lacking in any of these regulatory admission control credentials, the admission request is forwarded to a remediation service from where the latest updates have to be downloaded and installed before privileged access can be granted. Admission control mechanisms are corporate initiatives to protect enterprise networks. Examples of such initiatives include Microsoft's NAP [59], and Cisco's NAC [58].

NAP is a policy enforcement platform built into recent iterations of the Microsoft Windows operating system. It allows security policies to be set, such as requirements on the operating system patches and anti-virus updates, which restrict clients from accessing network services until the client demonstrates compliance. This approach helps to prevent and limit the level of new threats introduced into corporate networks.

NAC is a security initiative to address threats targeting corporate networks. The NAC framework is an authentication-based network admission approach. NAC validates software credentials running on a client (PC, PDA and other devices) that requests access to a LAN. NAC's software validation process includes; checking operating system (OS) fingerprint, OS patch level, service packs and anti-virus versions installed on the device requesting network access, as defined in the security policy. Software validation helps minimise the level of threat introduced into a network by newly connected hosts.

4.3.1.3 Cryptography

Cryptography is used to protect information resources and assets from threats such as misuse, traffic analysis, and replay attacks by preserving the confidentiality and integrity of communications. For example, cryptographic applications such as Internet protocol security (see RFC 2411 [204]) are used to encrypt packets being transported among trusted parties. Cryptography provides secure communications among trusted parties, such that foreign or eavesdropping adversaries cannot identify the transported payload. It also assists in transporting shared secret keys securely among trusted parties.

4.3.1.4 Biometric security

Biometric security is a verification-based preventive security approach. It aims to identify entities by authenticating them. This may involve series of physical identification process, such as iris and retinal scans, speech, facial feature comparison and facial thermograms, and hand geometry or behavioural characteristics of the entity [188]. Generally, biometric security is preferred over pin-chip, password or token-based identification methods because it is perceived to be more secure and dependable.

4.3.2 Reactive security models

Reactive security models focus on mitigating attacks, which the preventive security controls could not prevent. Preventive security controls such as firewalls, user authentication and cryptography are regarded as first-line protection mechanisms [5], while reactive security models are used for second-line defence of computer networks. Figure 4.8 shows a reactive defence classification model. It comprises of security components that assist in controlling threats and mitigating attacks.

Reactive security mechanisms are deployed in security monitoring to provide real-time, near real-time and non-real-time defences against attacks targeted at computer networks, as shown in Figure 4.8. These include intrusion detection systems, security information management systems, threat response systems, and DoS mitigation systems used to monitor corporate assets for security breaches, policy violation, compromise or attack.

4.3.2.1 Security information management systems (SIMS)

SIMS are defence systems used to monitoring computer networks to identify and detect security threats and attacks. Their main function is to correlate, normalise and assess security events from varying network sources to provide a unified actionable logic for protecting an enterprise network. Recently, the functionality of SIMS has expanded to incorporate event management, which is why recent implementations of SIMS now go by the word SIEM, meaning security information and event management. Whether SIMS or SIEM, both gather, correlate and analyse events from myriads heterogeneous defence systems to identify and detect situations in networks (cyberspace situation awareness). *Correlation* is a technique applied to show the relationship of security events coming from different sources in the network. This enables the system to compare and analyse sequences of security events, thereby allowing for improved detection capabilities. *Normalisation* is a technique applied to format the correlated security events in a particular pattern, which helps in prioritising events in a given context.

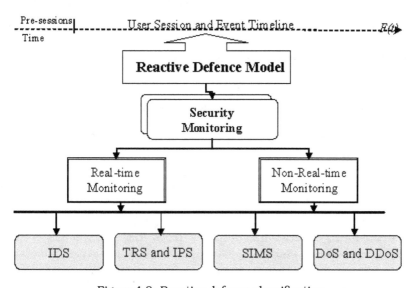

Figure 4.8: Reactive defence classification

The relevance of SIEM is seen in areas such as enterprise network monitoring, alert correlation, attack identification and tracking, and vulnerability assessment. For example, in the security provider arena, the SIEM market is very competitive with commercial offerings such as, Arcsight's Enterprise Security Management (ESM) [60], Cisco's Monitoring, Analysis and Response System (MARS) [61] and Checkpoint's Unified Threat Management (UTM) [62]. From the open source community, recent developments include, the Open Source Security Information Management [63], the Analyst Console for Network Security Monitoring [81] and the Applied Watch for Command Center [171].

It is very challenging to monitor and manage enterprise networks for organisations without efficient security information and event management systems in place. However, the astuteness in SIEM solutions is provided by the analysis of security events and the audit trails obtained from various network sources. These sources output security events in different formats. More so, security events provide only symptomatic evidence, such as, high CPU utilisation history, access-list violations, and failed resource. Therefore, a requirement for SIEM solutions is to incorporate powerful analysis, capable of examining and combining diverse pieces of evidence in order to detect attacks, and consequently provide effective counter-measures in return.

As shown previously, current SIEM implementations are only utilised for correlating security evidence about attacks, none provides automated response capabilities [16]. Similarly, a major concern (drawback) with proprietary (commercial) SIEMs is that their analysis techniques are classified as "*trade secrets*", and therefore not available for public scrutiny or evaluation, even for research purposes. Hence, it is difficult to evaluate their effectiveness. Which is why it is not surprising that Bruce Schneier raised the question whether "SIMS is a solution or part of the problem [65]?"

4.3.2.2 Threat response systems and intrusion prevention systems

TRS or IPS are inline intrusion detection systems that provide active responses to perceived attacks. Responses provided by TRS and IPS are automated, active and able to provide instant mitigation of perceived attacks. It is important to remember that when an IPS is not configured to provide instant response, in an in line mode, it defaults to a normal IDS; since current IDSes still struggle with appropriately classifying threats, most IPS work in simulation mode. IPS simulation mode is when an IPS functions as a normal IDS, and report their observations as alerts to security administrators, who then must investigate each alert to determine whether it is malicious or not, and hence recommend appropriate countermeasures where necessary, and if applicable. An example of a well-known open source intrusion detection system that can function also as an IPS is SNORT [127].

4.3.2.3 DoS and DDoS mitigation

DoS and DDoS mitigation approaches include mechanisms that help security administrators to mitigate denial of service attacks, or distributed denial of service attacks respectively. DoS attacks are a special class of attacks that aim to inhibit the availability of networks and computing resources to legitimate users. Note that DoS agents do not require network log-in access in order to adversely affect a network. This makes DoS attacks difficult to prevent. According to Gartner Research [66], 50% of companies without effective mitigation strategies will suffer financial or service loss as a result of "botnet" attack by 2007. A botnet attack is a special type of attack that uses "bots" or "zombies" to launch distributed DoS attacks on computer networks. DoS mitigation approaches have been suggested in both the academic literature and commercial arena. For example, Siaterlis and Maglaris [82] suggest a multisensor data fusion approach towards DoS detection, while Mölsä [74] uses a cross layer of defence mechanisms to mitigate DoS. Commercial offerings also exist, such as Arbor Peakflow DoS mitigation [75] by Arbor Networks, and Cisco Guard [76] by Cisco Systems Inc.

4.3.3 Retrospective security models

Retrospective security models focus on investigating break-ins after attacks have happened and comprise *security forensics, network fault finding, and post-mortem analysis,* shown in Figure 4.9.

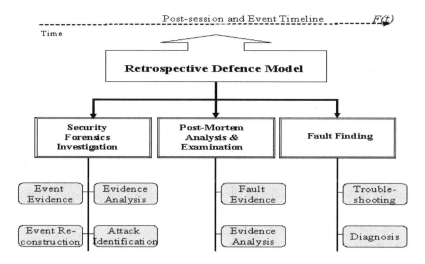

Figure 4.9: Retrospective defence classification

4.3.3.1 Computer and network security forensics

Computer forensics, also known as digital forensics, is a relatively new area of research that investigates security break-ins after attacks have happened. It centres on gathering forensic evidence (often as part of a criminal investigation) from computers, computer networks, and in general from electronic media [103]. It comprises both the legal proceedings for liability and technical aspects of investigative searches, which encompasses digital crime scene investigation, authorisation, crime reconstruction and crime prosecution [105].

Network forensics regarding network attacks that had happened involves *event evidence* gathering, event *evidence analysis, event reconstruction* and *attack identification* and detection, as shown in Figure 4.9.

Event evidence gathering involves collection of security logs, alerts and events, which must be stored persistently for later use. Evidence analysis involves collating gathered event evidence (that is logs, alerts, and alarms) from different sources, such as IDS, firewalls, anti-viral servers etc in order to deduce what attacks the events constitute. Event reconstruction is a process whereby the events are reconstructed in order to ascertain that the attack was possible through such events;

and finally, attack identification is the endpoint of a forensic investigation in order to identify and detect attacks that had occurred by analysing already gathered logs, alerts, alarms and events.

4.3.3.2 Post-mortem analysis

Post-mortem analysis is traditionally associated with fault management and process longevity, where a trace-back examination is conducted to investigate a possible cause of a fault, error or failure in systems that helps to avoid recurrent faults, errors or failures in systems. Post-mortem analysis comprises *fault evidence gathering* and *evidence analysis*. Fault evidence gathering is the process whereby the output of actions, tasks or steps taken to complete a particular project is gathered and logged. This is to assist the individual to evaluate how the project was completed, its success rate, and if the project was successfully completed or not. Evidence analysis is the process of analysing pieces of evidence gathered while a project is being executed (that is, outputs from fault evidence gathering phase) to recommend better ways of realising the same project, and to avoid recurrent faults, errors or failures in project if the project was unsuccessful.

4.3.3.3 Fault finding

Fault finding is a process whereby faults that exist in computer networks are identified and resolved. This encompasses *fault troubleshooting* and *fault diagnosis*. Fault troubleshooting aims to identify a possible cause of a computer network issue, that is faults, errors and failures. This process attempts to pin-point the actual cause of the fault, error, omission or failure. Fault diagnosis is the process by which the identified fault is finally resolved. Both fault troubleshooting and diagnosis involve series of testing to isolate and resolve the fault. It is important to say that in some environments, these two processes involved in fault finding, are combined into one, often referred to as fault diagnosis.

Further, since computer or network failures can be as a result of threats (malicious), faults (accidental and inadvertent) or a combination of both, a recommended requirement for retrospective models is to conduct both a post-mortem examination, and a forensic investigation in the aftermath of a security breach.

4.4 Application domains of security defence approaches

This section demonstrates the usefulness of security defence approaches to organisations, and highlights how security defence approaches have been successfully applied in specific application domains, such as security monitoring, distributed defence systems and electronic commerce. It is imperative to note that preventive security approaches on their own are insufficient in protecting network security attacks. Similarly, neither a reactive system, nor a retrospective system is sufficient on its own in protecting networks. Therefore, what is recommended is an integrated (layered) defence framework that is composed of preventive, reactive and retrospective defence mechanisms with the capability to adequately protect computer networks.

4.4.1 Security monitoring

Security monitoring is essential in detecting security attacks, and is characteristically *real-time* and produces *significant amount of event logs*. In security monitoring, corporate assets are monitored for suspicious network activities, such as, network behaviour, policy violation or computer misuse. Network activities, such as threats, faults or attacks are *abrupt* in nature. But abrupt network activities offer only symptomatic evidence which may not necessarily happen as a result of security attacks, but happen as a result of other issues that occur in the network, such as:

♦ genuine network behaviour with slight deviations in known patterns (normal and genuine).

♦ faults in the network (inadvertent and accidental).

♦ incorrectly classified traffic (normal and genuine).

For example, *genuine network change* resulting in deviation from established activity patterns or traffic thresholds can trigger an intrusion detection system to report an alert (a false positive). This is because of changes in the network or traffic parameters or thresholds. Although the activity in question is genuine, the deviation from predefined profiles will be large enough to cause an alert to be reported. A *fault* in the network, such as a card failure leading to a link down, will be reported as a network change. Although, the card failure could be *accidental* or *inadvertent*, an alert will be triggered. Finally, an incorrectly classified traffic (even though non-malicious), for example, huge traffic or a result of a backup activity, will certainly trigger an IDS, since the traffic has exceeded a preset traffic utilisation threshold. A similar situation occurs when there is a high peer-to-peer contact from a host to many hosts. Thus, *network changes* can be as a result of many issues. The difficulty here is in appropriately evaluating network activities in order to pertinently detect an attack. The gathering of network activity logs, for example, event logs or audit trails, provides only suggestive evidence, such as high CPU utilisation, access-list violations, failed resource requests and attempted intrusions. Therefore, appropriate analysis is required to collectively correlate, fuse and combine multiple pieces of evidence in order to conclusively detect security attacks perceived on a population of hosts in the network. In this respect, defence models are useful, imperative and unavoidable in detecting and mitigating security attacks.

4.4.2 Distributed defence services

According to Mirkovic et al. [51], it is challenging to successfully defend against emerging attacks using a single defence system. They argue that a single defence system is not sufficient in mitigating emerging attacks, such as distributed denial of service attacks. Hence, what is required is a distributed defence infrastructure with the capability to detect, defend against and deter attack penetrations. Distributed defence applications gather attack evidence across the network to infer attack levels or the state of the network being monitored. They employ powerful and intelligent analysis. Concrete attacks can be detected and consequently appropriate countermeasures applied to mitigate perceived attacks.

Distributed defence applications are used in security monitoring to detect and respond to security attacks. For example, DefCOM (the Defensive Cooperative Overlay Mesh) is a distributed framework for DDoS defence that consists of heterogeneous defence nodes organised in a peer-to-peer network [95]. Distributed defence applications are utilised in the analysis of battlefields situations [109] and in electronic commerce to protect participating parties in agent-based distributed systems. Aircraft configuration management is another distributed application [110] where security defence mechanisms are deployed for both security and safety checks.

4.4.3 Electronic commerce

The world wide web and electronic mail have revolutionised the way businesses are conducted, becoming the prime vehicle of contemporary e-commerce, which has been vastly broadened and redefined [15]. Both have brought numerous benefits, such as ease of communication, geographical coverage, information dissemination, marketing and business administration. However, they have also introduced an entirely new set of vulnerabilities and attack vectors to mission critical information systems, especially content security related attacks, such as, viruses, worms, trojans, electronic fraud, phishing, pharming, and electronic warfare.

Countering these threats to critical information systems requires an integrated layer of appropriate countermeasures. Security defence approaches are used in electronic commerce to provide secure transactions. Defence mechanisms deployed to electronic commerce include a set of preventive security approaches, reactive security approaches and retrospective security approaches.

4.5 Summary

Existing security approaches to computer networks use *localised systems* that operate in isolation, but *localised systems* are limited in the evidence of attacks they gather in the network. They are often insufficient in mitigating emerging security attacks. Thus, distributed defence approaches have been suggested to complement localised defence systems, or replace them.

An in-depth discussion of distributive defence approaches is provided, and both schematic and semantic representations of distributive defence models are discussed, as shown in Figures 4.7, 4.8, and 4.9.

A new classification that divides the roles of defence systems into three *(preventive, reactive* and *retrospective)* defence approaches was discussed. Preventive defence methods include *access control, admission control, cryptographic protocols* and *biometric security.* They aim to prevent known security attacks that target corporate networks. Reactive defence models are deployed in security monitoring to provide real-time, near real-time, and non-real-time monitoring capabilities. Reactive defence systems mitigate attacks that have penetrated networks, for example, denial of service attacks, networks worms or trojans. Finally, retrospective defence methods include, *security forensics, post-mortem examination* and *fault finding systems,* that investigate security break-ins after attacks have occurred, or evaluate network failures in order to minimise their re-occurrence.

The application of defence models to *security monitoring, distributed defence services* and *electronic commerce* is discussed. Security defence models are applied to security monitoring for identifying and detecting specific threats and attacks launched on the network, especially, attacks targeting critical information systems or infrastructure are presented. With distributed defence services, security systems are deployed to mitigate attacks, while in electronic commerce, security mechanisms are deployed to counter e-commerce threats, such as content security threats, identity theft, electronic fraud and phishing.

Since the primary goal of a security defence system is to enable the effect of an attack on a victim to be alleviated by identifying appropriate, sustainable and timely countermeasures to attacks. A layered integrated security framework is therefore required to adequately protect computer networks from *threats,* control *vulnerabilities* and mitigate *attacks,* as discussed in section 4.3, by combining *preventive defence models* that counter known threats, misuse and attacks to computer networks; *reactive defence models* that defend computer networks from exploits and attacks that have entered the network and finally, *retrospective defence models* that assist in investigating and examining security break-ins.

Chapter 5

Integrated security assistance framework

This chapter provides an introduction to the integrated security assistance framework (ISAF), developed to assist in accurately identifying and detecting widespread attacks in computer networks. A brief description of each component of the framework is presented, while in the following chapters, each component of the framework is discussed in detail.

5.1   Introduction

An integrated security assistance framework is a new paradigm in security defence based on *sensors, analysis, and response* that is used to detect existing and emerging security attacks. A high-level description of the framework followed by a detailed discussion of the framework's design principle, and component requirements (general and specific) is presented in this chapter. The next chapter (Chapter 6) focuses specifically on the response component of the framework, while in Chapter 7, the signalling mechanism of the framework is discussed.

As seen in Chapter 4, traditional defence mechanisms struggle to cope with the demands of emerging security attacks. Traditional defence methods are insufficient in mitigating distributed and evolving security attacks perceived in most enterprise networks today. Successfully mitigating emerging attacks requires a paradigm shift. Instead of deploying localised defence mechanisms that operate in isolation, an integrated framework of defence mechanisms is required that not only possesses the potential to detect attacks perceived across a population of hosts in the network, but also possesses the capability to include human expertise in its analysis. An integrated security assistance framework is a defence initiative that includes human expertise (security administrators) in defending computer networks from security attacks.

Technologies to protect computer networks are emerging, so are vulnerabilities in computer networks, and and threats that exploit these vulnerabilities to harm the assets. Vulnerabilities in computer networks are shown to be on the increase. With day-zero vulnerabilities, that is, freshly identified vulnerabilities also on the increase [111], it is difficult if not impossible to fully automate responses to attacks that exploit these kinds of vulnerabilities. In fact, automating responses to these freshly identified vulnerabilities could lead to the network launching a denial of service of attack on own systems. For example, fully automated systems can lead to what are effectively denial of service attacks to its systems by blocking traffic to or from legitimate systems due to false positives.

An innovative way to respond to security attacks that exploit unknown or freshly identified vulnerabilities in computer networks is to involve human expertise in their responses. This way, security administrators can evaluate complex attack scenarios in conjunction with automated analysis techniques, while attacks with known signatures can be simultaneously responded to by built-in adaptive response mechanisms.

5.2 An integrated security assistance framework: sensors, analysis, and response

An integrated security assistance framework is a distributed defence framework that unifies security mechanisms to provide enterprise-wide security defence to computer networks. The framework offers capabilities for distributed threat detection, integrated analysis and coordinated response via security spaces. It also offers extension mechanisms to involve human countermeasures in protecting networks. The ISAF framework is underpinned by the sensors, analysis, and response security paradigm.

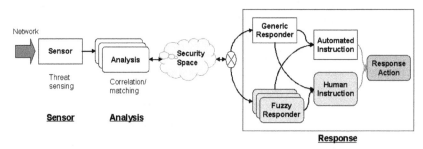

Figure 5.1: A high-level representation of an integrated security assistance framework

An integrated security assistance framework defines three types of component, as shown in Figure 5.1: *sensor components* that contribute evidence about security-

94

related events; *analysis components* that implement autonomous software agents capable of synthesising evidence; and *response components* that implement countermeasures. Response components can be configured to incorporate *human expertise* in decision-making in protecting networks. An abstract *security space* provides a medium through which components communicate. The logical components of the framework are realised on physical network nodes. A physical network node may realise one or more logical components and may interact with one or more security spaces.

The underlying concept in this framework is the capability for sensors to connect, contribute and communicate security information to the analysers (analysis component), where pieces of attack evidence are combined and analysed. In the analysis component, appropriate countermeasures are recommended, while in the response component, recommended countermeasures are executed. Responses made could be the reconfiguration of security policies to mitigate perceived attacks, or a combination of sequences of countermeasure actions.

Thus, the ISAF framework, as shown in Figure 5.1, allows:

◆ multiple sensors to be used to gather and report security events perceived on a population of the network to an analysis component.

◆ the use of powerful analysis techniques to correlate, analyse and combine pieces of evidence reported by sensors.

◆ the analysis component to provide a visual representation of perceived attacks.

◆ security administrators offer human expertise in providing a set of response to mitigate perceived attacks.

As a result, the ISAF framework provides capabilities for real-time (RT) distributed sensing of attacks, near real-time (NRT) integrated analysis and coordinated responses to perceived attacks on the network. However, it incorporates human decision-making in the analysis of attacks, and relies on security spaces for signalling and coordinating security-related information among its components, that is, its sensors, analysers and responders.

It is pertinent to note that defence systems that provide capabilities for automated countermeasures, and involve human expertise in providing countermeasure actions are a step forward. They pertinently and significantly offer extensive and appropriate responses to attacks. Therefore, they are better models than systems that provide only a set of uncoordinated responses [16].

The integrated security assistance framework for protecting computer networks was first proposed in 2005 by Onwubiko et al. [14]. Since then the framework has

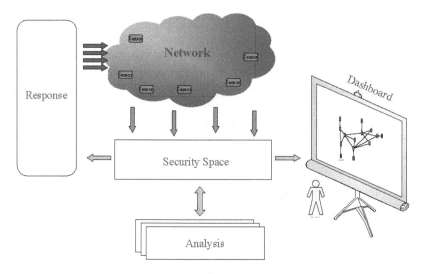

Figure 5.2: A schematic diagram of the ISAF framework, when realised.

been used in analysis-applications using graph representation for security monitoring [17], with a genetic algorithm to solve the NP-complete optimisation problem
of graph matching [18], graph-based representation of security information management systems [10], to evaluate security risks [12], and suggested for countering
terrorism and organised crime. A schematic diagram of the ISAF framework is
shown in Figure 5.2 to illustrate its use in security monitoring.

5.3 Distributive security approach

A distributed security approach divides the task of securing a network into separate functions for sensing, analysing and responding to attacks [112], the task of
securing a network implies:

- ◆ sensing threats: sensors are distributed across the network to gather and
  communicate attack evidence perceived.

- ◆ analysing pieces of attack evidence: efficient techniques are utilised to analyse, synthesise and evaluate attack evidence communicated by the sensors.

- ◆ responding to attacks: adequate countermeasures are deployed in mitigating
  perceived attacks based on collective human and automated decisions from
  the analysis.

- ◆ these security inputs are coordinated through a signalling mechanism (security space) that enables sensors, analysers, and responders to connect, con-

tribute and communicate security related information.

5.3.1 Security assistance paradigm

The security assistance paradigm is a network defence initiative that incorporates human expertise in the analysis of security events, threats and attacks. Thus, security assistance in an integrated security framework allows human assistance in the analysis of attacks and in decision making. The premise for an integrated assistance approach is threefold:

♦ first, the analysis of information from the whole network is more pertinent than any individual countermeasure perspective.

♦ second, a response that coordinates multiple countermeasures is potentially more effective than that which can be achieved by the sum of the responses of a set of standalone countermeasures.

♦ third, frameworks that involve human expertise in the analyse of perceived attacks are more flexible and subtle in decision making than systems whose responses are fully automated. For example, fully automated systems can be easily lead to denial of service to its own network by false positives.

Furthermore, the need for an assistance security framework is appealing because in network security, both security countermeasures and security threats are evolving. New vulnerabilities to computer networks are found continuously. Similarly, emerging threats and attacks are becoming intelligent [113], hence, fully automating responses to these class of attacks can be very challenging. Therefore, what is required is a framework that incorporates the expertise of security administrators in its analysis. It is shown that such frameworks are appropriately more extensible, flexible, and a step forward in providing better understanding of emerging attacks than those that tend to automate all responses, which can significantly complicate their behaviour [16].

According to Schneier [65], security systems (tools) are only as effective as the people that use them. To automate every response a security system offers can be challenging. For example, it has been shown that security information management systems struggle to live up to their promise, because they are missing the essential ingredient that so many other computer security products lack, that is *human* assistance. Firewalls often fail because they are configured and maintained improperly. IDSes are often inefficient because there is no one to respond to their alerts, or to separate the real attacks from the false alarms. SIMS will have the same problem, unless there is a human expert monitoring them [65]. This reaffirms the unrivalled advantages of integrating human expertise with powerful adaptive analysis in providing appropriate responses (countermeasure actions) to mitigate attacks on computer networks.

5.4   Areas where the framework has been applied

The integrated security assistance framework can be deployed in security monitoring as shown in Figure 5.3, in distributed data fusion, as shown in Figure 5.4; and suggested for countering terrorism and organised crime discussed in section 11.4.1.

5.4.1   Application of the integrated security assistance framework in a multisensor LAN

The application of the integrated security assistance framework to multisensor data fusion is aimed that using the framework:

◆ to gather independent evidence of security attacks by sensors.

◆ to combine and analyse pieces of security evidence gathered by sensors deployed in the network.

A high-level representation of the ISAF framework in a multisensor LAN to identify and detect widespread attacks perceived in the network is shown in Figure 5.3.

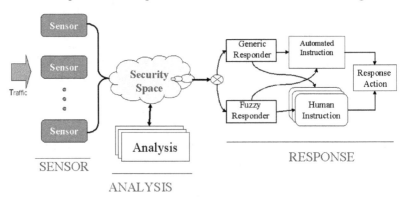

Figure 5.3: Application of integrated security assistance framework in a multisensor LAN

The figure shows how sensors are distributed to gather security evidence in the network. Pieces of evidence gathered are communicated to the analysis component, where they are analysed and synthesised to deduce exact attacks perceived on the network, with appropriate countermeasure actions (responses) recommended to the responders. Each of the components, such as sensor, analysis, security space, and response of the framework are discussed in section 5.2.

5.4.2 Application of the integrated security assistance framework in a distributed data fusion LAN

The application of the ISAF framework to a distributed data fusion system is described in Figure 5.4. The aim is to distribute the analysis, such that each sensor has the capability to collate piece of attack evidence it perceives independently, while a higher level interpretation is obtained via the integrated fusion and analysis module. Hence the task is divided as:

◆ each sensor senses security attack evidence, analyses and reports its belief for the attack.

◆ beliefs from sensors are combined at the integrated fusion and analysis module.

◆ decision is made based on the aggregated intelligence regarding the attack.

◆ responses are recommended for each attack identified,

◆ finally, the responses are executed to mitigate the perceived attacks.

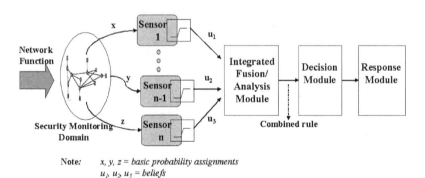

Note: x, y, z = basic probability assignments
        u_1, u_2, u_3 = beliefs

Figure 5.4: Application of security assistance framework in a distributed data fusion

Pieces of evidence gathered by the sensors are collated in an integrated fusion and analysis module, for analysis and in identifying the perceived attacks. Inferences made are communicated to the decision module where recommendations are provided as to which response or chain of response will adequately mitigate the perceived attacks.

5.5 Framework requirements

The requirements of distributed systems involve identifying both the functional and non-functional properties [110]. So in discussing the requirements of the *security assistance framework*, a separation is made between general design properties and the more concrete requirements of the framework. The functional properties are the specific requirements of each component of the framework, while the general requirements are the global properties of the framework. Thus, the requirements of the framework under consideration are divided into two, namely, general and specific.

5.5.1 General requirements of the framework

The general requirements of the framework address general concerns, such as how scalable is the system? Is the system interoperable with existing systems? How open, fault-tolerant, secure and flexible are the mechanisms? Thus, general requirements of the framework are identified as follows:

◆ the approach should be simple, scalable, responsive, flexible, robust and future proof to identify potential points of failures, and sources of potential threats to the system.

◆ the goal is to assist security administrators in their decisions rather than fully automating every response of the system (and consequently, significantly complicating its behaviour).

◆ the impact of the approach on existing network services or infrastructure should be minimised.

◆ the approach should be secure, allowing the dependable and confidential exchange of information about security attacks.

◆ the approach should be flexible and sufficiently open ended to accommodate a wide range of analysis techniques.

◆ the approach should be deployed on a single system or on many systems, this allows for resource sharing among distributed components, which is often a necessary and sufficient property of distributed systems.

5.5.2 Specific requirements of the framework

Specific requirements (functional requirements) of the framework focus on addressing specific needs of each component of the framework. That is, the *sensor requirements, analysis requirements, signalling requirements* and *response requirements*. Thus, the specific requirements of the framework are to:

- support the distributing of sensors throughout the core and edge of the network (core, edge and user hosts) to gather evidence of security threats/attacks perceived in the network, hence providing secure monitoring capabilities.

- allow security components, sensors, analysers and responders to dynamically connect, contribute and communicate security information through security spaces.

- support integrated analysis of pieces of evidence about attacks gathered by sensors. That is, evidence such as attack signatures for known attacks, and also, symptomatic evidence, especially for threats with unknown attributes, symptomatic evidence includes resource exhaustion, high peer-to-peer contact ratio, system unavailability.

- allow analysers to correlate, normalise and combine attack evidence.

- support the provision of appropriate and expressive representations of security attacks in the analysis.

- support the automated discovery of the analysis components of the infrastructure by the sensors allowing them to forward security related information.

- support the involvement of human assistance in decision making and in selecting appropriate responses.

- support the deployment and coordination of multiple responses.

- provide appropriate and coordinated responses (counter measures) to mitigate perceived attacks by combining automated and human assisted responses.

5.6 Design principles

The design rationale guiding the development of the distributive security assistance framework is presented and summarised as follows:

- to provide an innovative framework for detecting threats that exploit freshly identified vulnerabilities (day-zero attacks). These attacks may not have no known preventive measures (controls) available at the time, since their fingerprints are very much unknown.

- to avoid being led to denial of service to its own network due to false positives from distributed attacks.

- to avoid deceptive intrusion or other forms of network deception.

The provision of appropriate responses to emerging security threats, especially, threats that exploit or even extend freshly discovered vulnerabilities in systems highlights the importance of the security assistance defence framework. Often there are no stipulated controls to prevent threats, or mitigate attacks that exploit or extend freshly identified vulnerabilities in systems. One of the reason for this is because the attack's fingerprints are unknown, hence, adequate security controls have not been provided to mitigate the attacks. Therefore, mitigating threats that exploit freshly identified vulnerabilities may require a combination of countermeasures or the reconfiguration of multiple defence mechanisms. A major concern in mitigating such threats are that they do not match or suggest known attack attributes. Instead their attributes are vague, symptomatic and uncertain. Thus, the provision of automated or even semi-automated responses for these types of fuzzy and symptomatic attack evidence may consequently complicate the behaviour of security defence systems. In this respect, human assistance is incorporated in the decision-making process. This makes defence systems pertinently more flexible and extensible in providing adequate responses to mitigate such attacks. Thus, the goal is to assist security administrators in decision making while still providing lightweight automated responses to attacks with known signatures.

The design paradigm behind the integrated security assistance systems of incorporating human expertise in decision making, and in recommending appropriate responses to attacks, together with their relevance to 21st century network, is shared by other network security researchers. For example, Lee et al. [114], argue that to operate effectively, a defence mechanism may require extensive human intervention and several other security mechanisms. These dependencies affect the cost-effectiveness of attack detection and response. Similarly, Schneier [65] argues that security defence systems require human expertise to provide better security.

5.7   Framework components

A review of the components of the framework is provided, while briefly discussing the high-level operation of the framework. An in-depth discussion of each component is provided in the next two chapters. Chapter 6 discusses the response component of the framework, while Chapter 7 deals with the signalling requirements of the framework.

The framework comprises four separate domains, namely:

◆ attack detection in the framework (sensor).

◆ attack analysis in the framework (analysis).

◆ attack response in the framework (response).

◆ signalling and integration in the framework (security space).

5.7.1 Attack detection in the framework (sensor component)

Attack detection in the framework is implemented through the distribution and integration of existing open source security sensors, such as, SNORT, NTOP, PADS, ARPWATCH, SPADE and TCPTRACK to form a sensing engine that passively monitors the network. The sensor component collates security events, either by gathering concrete attack evidence based on exact matching of attack signatures, or through more symptomatic ways, such as identifying deviations in traffic thresholds (baseline for traffic utilisation) or abnormal network behaviour. In either case, pieces of evidence gathered from distributive sources in the network are communicated to the analysis component, where these pieces of evidence are combined to determine if an attack is perceived, and to accurately identify and detect that attack.

5.7.2 Attack analysis in the framework (analysis component)

Pieces of evidence about attacks perceived in the network through the sensors need to be analysed to detect specific attacks that are ongoing, not just on a single host but on the entire network. Therefore, it is appealing to synthesise pieces of attack evidence perceived on the whole network (integrated analysis) rather than provide individual analysis of attacks perceived on separate parts of the network, or on an individual host, as shown in Figure 5.5.

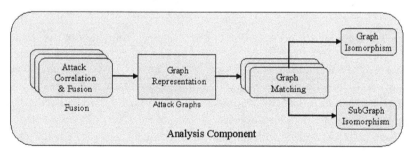

Figure 5.5: High-level representation of the analysis component of the framework

It is pertinent to note that security mechanisms that analyse attacks perceived on the entire network are better at providing an accurate representation of the overall attacks perceived in the network compared to those that analyse only a subset of network.

The analysis techniques employed comprise:

- the use of the Dempster-Shafer theory of evidence to combine multiple pieces of attack evidence gathered by sensors, in order to accurately detect the attacks.

- the use of graph-based representations to visualize resultant attacks.

- the use of graph matching techniques to compare *template graphs* to *data graphs* obtained from monitoring the network.

The analysis techniques are discussed in detail in Chapter 8.

5.7.3 Attack response in the framework (response component)

The framework recommends the use of automated responses that are passive, although active responses to counter attacks are possible, but recommended and administered only by security administrators.

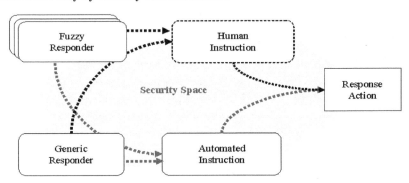

Figure 5.6: High-level representation of the response component of the framework

The response mechanism of the framework comprises five components, as shown in Figure 5.6, namely: *generic responders* that apply "hard" responses to attacks. A hard response is a security response applied to an attack whose signature is recognised. *Fuzzy responders* apply a "soft" response. A soft response is a security response applied to threats with unknown threat attributes or for freshly identified threats that have no existing counter measures in place at the given time. *Automated instructions* are instructions recommended by generic responders. *Human instructions* are response actions recommended by fuzzy responders, but applied to fuzzy-type threats through security administrators. *Response action* is a resultant counter measure instruction that must be executed to mitigate an attack.

A soft response to a security threat is employed when the analysis evidence is not so concrete, rather suggestive. A hard response is implemented when the analysis suggests known security threats that match existing *threat template* or *threat profile*.

A threat template is a template of known security vulnerability definition (threat signature); while a threat profile is a baseline profile of known security breaches.

Responses to attacks can be precise at times (for known attack signatures), for example, *if port=445 and type=TCP, and priority=high, and reliability=high, then log.* Reliability = high means the peer-to-peer contact ratio must be very high, which suggests the Sasser worm that uses the Microsoft Windows directory service of TCP port 445. However, some responses can be very fuzzy, in which case, a single counter measure may not be adequate, and therefore, complex instructions may be required. For example, *if* daily utilisation exceeds a certain threshold, and *if* packets per second (pps) is higher than the baseline threshold (pre-set threshold), *then* traffic behaviour suggests intrusive activities. This is not precise because traffic patterns are seen to change even with normal behavioural utilisation and may not suggest a real attack. Such fuzzy-type threat behaviour is vague and suggestive, and it therefore requires careful analysis to deduce exactly that a threat is perceived. In this instance, the expertise of security administrators is utilised in appropriately recommending responses to such attacks. Detailed explanation of the response mechanism is discussed in Chapter 6.

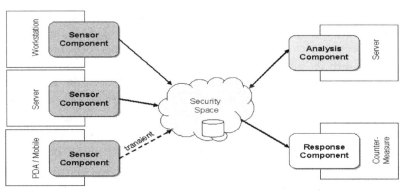

Figure 5.7: Security space - the signalling mechanism of the framework

5.7.4 Integration and signalling in the framework

Evidence of an attack perceived in the network is shared amongst the components of the framework through a middleware referred to as a *security space*, as shown in Figure 5.7.

A security space is an abstract space, where messages are queued (push/pull). The space guarantees that security messages are queued, stored and fetched by the security components and that requesting components (sensors, analysers, and responders) can connect, contribute and communicate security related information. A high-level representation of the signalling mechanisms of the framework is as shown in Figure 5.7; however, detailed discussion of the signalling mechanism is provided in Chapter 7.

5.8 Summary

An integrated security assistance framework that helps provide efficient and timely counter measures to emerging security threats or attacks perceived on a population of hosts in the network is discussed. The ISAF framework is composed of three components: *sensors, analysis,* and *response.* Sensors gather evidence of attacks seen on the entire network and communicate their evidence to the analysis component. In the analysis component, pieces of evidence are combined and analysed to identify the exact attacks perceived on the network. Finally, responses are recommended to mitigate perceived attacks. Responses can be automated or human assisted. However, a fundamental design construct of the framework relies on its ability to include security administrators in the decision making and furthering of security responses to attacks. Hence, the ISAF framework is designed not only as a distributed network defence system, but also as a security assistance framework that incorporates the expertise of security administrators in mitigating attacks.

Both the functional and non-functional requirements of the framework are discussed. The non-functional requirements being the general requirements of the framework, such as scalability, openness, interoperability, robustness and resource sharing. The functional requirements of the framework are the unique requirements of its various components such as the requirement for sensors, analysis, signalling and response, respectively. The mechanics of each component in the framework have been examined, while specific techniques employed in the analysis component are explained in subsequent chapters. The overall objective of this chapter was to introduce the framework and to explain its high-level operational and intellectual underpinning.

It is imperative to mention that the central theme of this research is not aimed at developing another type of IDS, rather a framework that clearly describes an approach in network security defence that accurately identifies and detects widespread attacks perceived in most enterprise networks in the 21st century. This approach in security defence recommends the distribution of multiple sensors across the network to gather pieces of security evidence about threats or attacks perceived in the entire network, which are combined with a powerful expressive representation, and evidential techniques to detect widespread attacks perceived on federated and distributed LANs.

Chapter 6

The response component of the framework

This chapter provides detailed discussion on the response component of the framework. The chapter also provides explicit discussion pertaining to the application of the response mechanism in the framework as a whole. In the next chapter, the signalling mechanism of the framework is provided including its mathematical formalisms.

6.1 Introduction

The need for a coordinated response in the framework is investigated. The requirements of the recommended response mechanism are evaluated. These include both general and specific requirements. General requirements are the *functional* aspects of the mechanism, while specific requirements are the *non-functional* aspects of the mechanism. Limitations of current response mechanisms are explained and improvements the new response mechanism provides over existing response mechanisms are well discussed.

The significant reliance of proactive monitoring of computer networks on security information and event management systems, requires that appropriate and comprehensive countermeasures to attacks perceived in the entire network are offered [16]. But responding to widespread attacks is currently challenging. Hence, to address this issue, a new security response mechanism that combines automated (static and dynamic) security response with human assistance in providing responses to mitigate attacks is introduced and discussed.

6.2 Limitations of existing response mechanisms

Response mechanisms to attacks perceived on computer networks exist, but they are implemented from a localised perspective. For example, the use of firewalls to drop, reset and log malicious sessions; or the use of intrusion prevention systems to execute filters to detect vulnerability exploits. Unfortunately, these mechanisms although independent, provide individual responses that are fragmented. Their responses are isolated and uncoordinated, and therefore insufficient in mitigating widespread attacks.

Responses from localised mechanisms are efficient from the individual end-user perspective but they provide isolated responses. Each device offers security responses based on its own limited view of the network. In terms of providing a unified comprehensive response to attacks, current response mechanisms are insufficient because they aim to protect individual systems or the small part of the network in which they are able to capture traffic. In return, the responses provided may not be sufficient in mitigating attacks perceived in the entire network. An instance of widespread and distributed attack is shown in Figure 4.1.

According to Marcus [112], existing response mechanisms such as, remediation services, patching and firewall systems struggle in mitigating recent attacks on corporate networks because they lack the capability to implement flexible and adaptive responses such as dynamically adjusting preventive security controls, self reconfiguring detection systems, self adjusting internal system parameters, or providing multiple chains of responses.

Similarly, existing responses are shown to be unable to swiftly mitigate emerging attacks that appear to be distributed and coordinated [9, 6]. And there are concerns that *monotonic responses*, such as drop, alert, and reset provided by existing response mechanisms, are insufficient to mitigate emerging threats or attacks that exploit multiple chains of vulnerabilities in a succession of network systems [96].

6.3   The proposed response mechanism

A response mechanism that possesses the capabilities to coordinate the deployment or reconfiguration of multiple responses across the network is investigated and discussed. A defence system that provides capabilities for automated countermeasures and still includes human expertise in determining response actions pertinently and significantly offers extensive, appropriate, and richer responses than models that provide only a set of uncoordinated individual countermeasure actions.

The new response mechanism comprises five components, as shown in Figure 6.1, namely, generic responders, fuzzy responders, automated instruction, human instruction, and response action.

The task of responding to attacks in an integrated defence framework is divided into separate functions as follows:

◆ passive response: response aimed to inform security administrators about the state of the network, and the different situations that may exist in the network. Passive response does not apply any mitigation whatsoever, it is more of an observational response sent to security administrators. Passive response can be sent by both generic and fuzzy responders.

◆ active response: response via automated and human-assisted response aim to swiftly mitigate an attack. Active response includes response from generic and fuzzy responders.

◆ automated response: response automatically deployed by the responders to mitigate attacks on a population of the network. Automated response includes response from fuzzy responders, generic responders, and automated instructions.

◆ human assisted response: response applied by security administrators. Security related information is communicated by alert messages to administrators who apply adequate countermeasures to the perceived attacks.

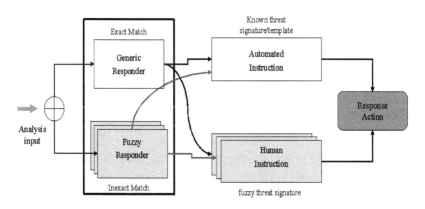

Figure 6.1: The proposed response mechanism

A passive response is a response that does not alter the state of the network, and hence, does not mitigate an attack. It aims to be silent, and rather report the state of the network to security administrators, who may take ownership in mitigating possible attacks. An active response is a response (or collection of responses) executed to provide instant mitigation to an attack. It can be provided automatically, or via a security administrator. An automated response is a response provided through automation, such as scripts and background programs, for example, cron jobs that are executed automatically without human intervention. Human assisted response is a response the system provides through security administrators who evaluate resulting responses to determine its effectiveness and consequences when applied in the network.

As shown in Figure 6.1, both fuzzy and generic responders offer human assisted and automated responses through human instruction and automated instruction respectively. Similarly, both fuzzy and generic responders provide passive and active responses. The distinction between fuzzy and generic responders is that generic responders evaluate perceived threats whose signatures are already known and available, while fuzzy responders evaluate freshly identified threats whose signatures are unknown and unavailable. These instructions (automated and human-assisted) provide responses that are efficient, comprehensive, and possessing the capability to provide appropriate and extensive security controls to mitigate a wide variety of attacks.

The logical components of the framework are realised on physical network nodes. A physical network node, such as a system or a network appliance, may realise one or more logical components and may interact with one or more responders.

The role of responders in an integrated security framework is to execute responses recommended by the analysis component where security threats are analysed [16]. The premise for a coordinated response mechanism in the framework is threefold:

◆ first, the analysis of information from the whole network is more pertinent than any individual countermeasures perspective.

◆ second, a response mechanism that coordinates multiple countermeasures is potentially more effective than that which can be achieved by the sum of the responses of a set of point countermeasures.

◆ third, a response mechanism that combines both automated and human countermeasures provides extensive and richer mitigation controls to attacks than that which can be achieved by the uncoordinated individual counter-measures.

6.4 Design principle

Three design principles guide the response approach:

◆ the approach should be simple, scalable, responsive, extensible, flexible, robust and future proof.

◆ the goal is to assist security administrators in their decisions whilst still providing lightweight automated response to attacks.

◆ the impact of the mechanism on existing network services or infrastructure should be minimised.

6.5 Response requirements

The requirements for a response mechanism in the framework are that it:

◆ supports passive, active, automated and human-assisted responses that allow the framework to mitigate attacks and prevent (control) threats perceived in the network.

◆ allows the combination of chain of responses.

◆ allows automatic and adaptive reconfiguration, remediation, re-distribution and re-deployment of responses.

◆ be flexible and sufficiently open ended to accommodate a wide range of responses.

6.6 Security requirements

Security requirements of the response mechanism are necessary to protect the responders from attackers who may want to compromise the responders in order to manipulate responses rendered by the framework. To ensure that responses made by responders are accurate, legitimate and authentic, authentication, a set of security requirements are stipulated. Thus the security requirements of the response component include:

◆ to ensure reliable and secure responses are executed.

◆ to support strong authentication, authorisation and accounting mechanisms in the framework, such as RADIUS, TACACS+, RSA securID, or a combination of mechanisms.

◆ to allow only authenticated responders to execute responses in the framework.

◆ to allow secure interaction between automated and manual response provided by security administrators.

6.7 Components of the response mechanism

6.7.1 Generic responder

Generic responders are underpinned on rule-based logic. Generic responders are utilised, and are more efficient, in mitigating threats with known signatures, or fingerprints. For example, if the analyser reports an attack as a UDP-type worm exploiting computer resources on UDP port 3304. The analyser must also express its belief (probability mass) to indicate its confidence that the perceived attack is taking place. This piece of security evidence is sent to the generic responder that then executes a filter to drop, deny and log UDP port 3304 from a specific source as a response action to the perceived attack.

When an attack is perceived on multiple hosts in the same subnet, the resultant countermeasure is executed on the gateway device that is closest to the target systems. For instance, when a worm is sensed on a subnet infecting computer networks, the response applied is on a gateway router or switch, particularly, on the interface carrying traffic to the infected systems. In this way, the effectiveness of the applied response (chain of response) in mitigating the attack is realised. Similarly, when attacks perceived on an entire network are not localised to a single subnet but rather to different subnets, then isolating a specific subnet to apply the resultant response is difficult since it is perceived on many different subnets. Applying responses to every subnet may lead to a denial of service to a population of the network. In these circumstances, *generic responders* alert security administrators for human decision-making and countermeasure recommendations. This design construct is a significant proposition with the response mechanism described, as the aim is to develop an *assistance system* (a system that assists security administrators in mitigating attacks) rather than automating all the functions of the system, which could significantly complicate its behaviour.

6.7.2 Fuzzy responder

Fuzzy responders are implemented using the *D-S rule of combination* as an inference mechanism in recommending response (or set of response) to mitigate attacks. The complexity involved in recommending a set of response to attacks whose pieces of evidence are often symptomatic, fuzzy and vague is enormous and challenging. It requires not only analysing complex attack scenarios in selecting a set of responses to adequately mitigate the attack, but also in decision making as to the consequence(s) a chosen response may have on the overall protection of the network. For example, newly identified attacks whose countermeasures are now widely available, what set of response is required? and what consequences are there with the chosen set of responses? This type of questions or decision making is often the case with a fuzzy responder; hence, human assistance (security administrator) is required in the decision-making process in selecting a set of responses, and in evaluating their consequences in protecting the network.

Response to attacks can be executed either through automated instructions or human assisted instructions, as shown in Figure 6.1. Responses from fuzzy responders include:

◆ adjusting preventive security mechanisms, such as, updating anti-virus checkers, or lowering security guards.

- redirecting traffic to a remediation service for the latest patch updates.

- dynamically adjusting detector settings, for example, instructing a firewall to drop or log a specific session or an IDS to log and mitigate an attack session.

- traffic re-route, similar to traffic redirection.

- response re-distribution. This involves redistributing various responders to provide a set of coordinated responses to perceived attacks.

- applying a combination of responses, for example, logging a specific session and redirecting it for remediation.

6.7.3 Automated instruction

Automated instructions encompass static and dynamic responses applied to attacks of known signatures. Automated instructions provide automated responses to security attacks. These include self-reconfiguration of security measures, such as detectors or analysers; or execution of a mix of responses. For example, sending signals to the firewall to block certain traffic, or the use of security guards to prevent a specific vulnerability incident. These instructions are automated because their attack sessions are of known signatures (for *misuse-type*) or of predefined attack profiles (for *anomaly-based*).

Static automated instructions are *hard* responses, such as:

- dropping traffic to certain ports because of perceived vulnerability.

- re-directing traffic to remediation services, if the system requesting connection is not compliant to a security policy.

- alerting and logging certain activities due to perceived threat activity.

- resetting traffic if it is perceived to be malicious; however, *reset* is not recommended because the attacker may use the NACK information sent by the response mechanism to infer that it was dropped by a defence system.

- denying traffic that is perceived to be malicious if there is a rule enforcing it to be dropped.

6.7.4 Human instruction

Human instructions are applied when attack analysis suggests very complex attack scenarios that may require multiple responses at different network segments to mitigate the attack. Often, such attacks may not be previously known, hence, its attack signature, fingerprint or threat profile may not be known or made widely available. For example, *freshly identified threats* whose signatures are unknown and appropriate counter measures are not fully developed. However, if the attacks perceived match known templates, then automated instructions are applied. Human instructions are administered by security administrators who evaluate the analysis output and associated risks. Hence, they are able to recommend effective responses. The overall *response mechanism* described in this section is designed as an *assistance response system* where responses are *partly automated* and *partly human assisted*. Fully automating the system which may significantly complicate its behaviour is not recommended.

6.7.5 Response action

Response action is the resultant response that is directed to attacks to control or stop their propagation. It is the overall response obtained from a collective responses offered by the framework. The effectiveness or efficiency of a set of countermeasures applied against an attack depends on the recommended response action, as shown in Figure 6.1.

6.8 Summary

The response mechanism of the framework is novel, straightforward and of great potential in addressing both current and emerging cyber attacks. The response mechanism is designed using the same design paradigm as the ISAF framework. Therefore, as a response assistance system, the responses provided by the mechanism are partly automated and partly human assisted.

The need for a response mechanism for the ISAF framework has been discussed, while existing response mechanisms are shown to be limited in scope. Hence, existing response systems are insufficient in providing the required level of responses needed to mitigate emerging security attacks that appear to be distributed, evolutionary and aggressive.

Responses provided by the new response mechanism of the ISAF framework are reliable, efficient and dependable in mitigating current and emerging security threats and attacks targeting enterprise networks. This is because it offers a variety of responses to attacks, such as passive, active, automated and human assisted. Automated responses are offered to attacks whose behaviour or characteristics are known, and its attack signatures are identified; for example, Code Red, Sasser worms or the Slammer worm. Human assistance is recommended for newly identified attacks, whose signature is unknown and appropriate countermeasures to mitigate the attack may not have been fully developed or widely distributed; for example, "day zero" attacks.

The response mechanism of the ISAF framework comprises five components: generic responders, fuzzy responders, automated instruction, human instructions and resultant response action. Generic responders provide automated response to mitigate attacks, *fuzzy responders* recommend human assistance in mitigating attacks. *Automated instructions* are automatically executed to provide active response in countering attacks, while *human instructions* are provided by security administrators in mitigating attacks. Finally, the resultant *response action* is executed either automatically by automated instructions or manually by security administrators.

Both the general and specific requirements of the proposed response mechanism are discussed. These include support for both automated and human assisted counter measures, how to combine responses to achieve effective results in mitigating attacks, how multiple responses can be combined, such as reconfiguration, re-distribution and re-deployment.

A fundamental property of the proposed response mechanism is that it incorporates human assistance in its decision making and response controls.

Chapter 7

Security spaces - the signalling mechanism of the framework

This chapter provides detailed discussion on the signalling component of the ISAF framework. The chapter also provides explicit discussion pertaining to the application of security space - the signalling mechanism in the framework, and other security domains, such as federated, distributed and multisensor LANs.

7.1 Introduction

A characteristic feature of a system, or a complex system, is its ability to allow coordinated interaction among its components. Although a system is seen as a single unit, it is actually made up of several other components that interact in some meaningful and orderly fashion. It is permissible to say that, in most systems, this capability is provided by a middleware that enables various components of the system to share and interact together. This analogy is true with security space, the signalling component of the framework. As a middleware it defines, aligns and coordinates the various components of the ISAF framework, enabling these components to function together as a single unit. One of the challenges, as we shall see later, is how to define and implement such a signalling mechanism in order for it to allow transient mobility of end user devices to report their observations to its management systems without static (hard coded) configuration of the address of its management systems. For instance, sensors are allowed to join and leave the system dynamically without a statically configured address of its management system. This encourages the sensors to automatically discover its management to which it sends its alerts.

7.2 The proposed signalling mechanism

The coordination of security related information and intra-process synchronisation among the components in the integrated security assistance framework is through a signalling mechanism. This signalling mechanism allows sensors, analysers and responders to share intelligence about threats and attacks perceived in the network. The signalling mechanism is known as a security space. A security space is an abstract space (middleware) through which components of the framework, namely *sensors, analysers, and responders* interact, share security related information and intelligence about attacks perceived in the network, as shown in Figure 7.1.

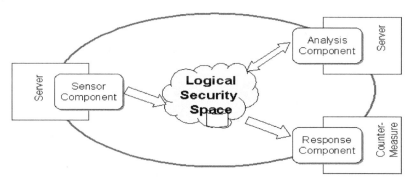

Figure 7.1: The proposed security space in the framework

The space guarantees that security messages are queued, stored and fetched by the security components. It defines a message format for the event gathered by sensors that conforms to the intrusion detection message exchange format (IDMEF [203]).

A security space is defined over a set of network nodes, each of which can contribute or access evidence about security related events. It is distinct from any underlying network addressing scheme or physical topology. It is pertinent to note that security spaces can be open or closed depending on whether an arbitrary node can join them or whether authentication and authorisation are required. The logical mechanism can be realised on physical network nodes, such as systems or network appliance. A physical network node may realise one or more logical security spaces.

7.3 Motivation

The concept of a security space is based on that of a *tuple space* first developed in the early 1980s in relation to the parallel programming language called Linda [115].

A tuple space provides a virtual shared memory (VSM) for the exchange of messages in the form of tuples. A tuple is a list of elements of potentially different types; for example, *(19:45, Alert, 17, port 135 probed)*, is a four-item tuple containing a timestamp (*time of alert*), a string (*event type*), an integer (*protocol number*) and a string (*port probed*). Tuple spaces have very simple semantics, comprising three primitive operations as follows:

- ◆ **put:** a tuple into a space.

- ◆ **take:** tuple out of a space.

- ◆ **read:** a copy of a tuple from a space. Note: the tuple still remains in the space.

Figure 7.2 shows the security space's position in the framework. It shows how the various components contribute (*put*) security information to the space, use (*take*) information from the space, and communicate (*read*) security information from the space.

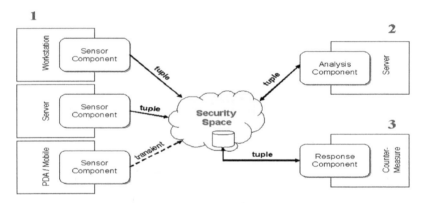

Figure 7.2: Illustration of a security space application

Tuple spaces are characterised by three properties:

- ◆ they support the asynchronous exchange of messages between processes. This means message exchange among sources occurs concurrently. For example, one source (say, a firewall) can write message to the space at the same time that another source, (say, an IDS) is writing to the space, and at the same time another source (say, an analyser) is reading message from the space.

- ◆ they are a form of associative memory, that is, the contents are accessed by matching the values and types of elements rather than by an address.

- ◆ they store messages persistently, that is, message written to the space remain until explicitly removed.

The semantics for interacting with a security space are minimal. Four primitives are defined. Most physical nodes will host sensor components, which will write messages to the space, but in addition, analysis components can *read* messages, *remove* or take messages and *subscribe* to be notified when changes to a space occur, as shown in Figure 7.2. All messages written to the space are *time stamped* on arrival and identify the sender's address.

Tuple space and shared memory programming have attracted recent research investigation in areas of distributed applications, such as blackboard, shared network and client-server messaging systems. JavaSpaces [116] from Sun Microsystems, *Tspaces* from IBM, and LIME (Linda In a Mobile Environment) [117] highlight the emerging relevance of security spaces in distributed applications.

JavaSpaces *("the space")* is a unified mechanism for dynamic communication, coordination, and sharing of objects between Java technology-based network resources like clients and servers. *The space* provides developers with the ability to create and store objects with persistence, which allows for process integrity.

LIME is a communication middleware supporting logical mobility of hosts, agents or both based on tuple space. It provides a lightweight interface for rapid and dependable development of mobile applications. TeenyLIME and TinyLIME are a set of middleware for wireless sensor networks (WSN) that enables multiple mobile monitoring stations to access the sensors and share their collective evidence through wireless links [195]. TinyLIME is an extension of LIME that makes sensor data available through a tuple space interface, providing a medium for shared memory between applications and sensors.

The IDMEF (RFC 4765) is a recent initiative to standardise information sharing in intrusion detection and response systems. It is a model data implemented in XML. IDMEF is essentially useful for allowing intrusion detection source (or 'sensor') to report alert messages deemed suspicious to the manager (or 'console') [192].

7.4 Limitations in current mechanisms for exchanging security-related information

Traditional signalling mechanisms for networks exist. For example, the *Syslog protocol* (IETF RFC 3164 [119]), and the *simple network management protocol* (IETF RFC 3416 [118]).

7.4.1 The Syslog protocol

The Syslog protocol allows a device to send event notification messages across IP networks to event message collectors also known as Syslog servers [119]. Hence, offering a potential mechanism for clients to send information about security related events. However, Syslog requires the manual configuration of the IP address of a Syslog server (which may differ for each network the user attaches to) and provides no acknowledge to the user if the message was delivered or not. Moreover the original Syslog protocol is widely used but is neither secure nor dependable. Although reliable alternatives have been proposed [200], they are not yet widely deployed. The design assumptions implicit in the Syslog protocol dictate its use by permanently connected devices that send messages to pre-configured event message collectors. It is vital to mention that Syslog was not originally designed to address the signalling needs of a large numbers of transiently connected end user devices, such as laptops, desktops, and personal digital assistants (PDAs), as shown in Figure 7.3.

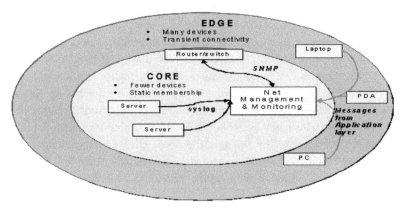

Figure 7.3: Expanding the signalling of threats to incorporate signalling from the network edge

7.4.2 Simple network management protocol

Simple network management protocol (SNMP) is a management protocol that allows the exchange of management information between networking elements, this includes security related information. SNMP [versions 1 and 2 (SNMPv2 includes SNMPv2 party-based, SNMPv2u, and SNMPv2c [153])] lacked authentication capabilities, which resulted in several vulnerabilities, such as:

◆ masquerading attack.

◆ modification of information.

◆ message sequence and timing modifications.

◆ disclosure.

Although SNMP version 3 includes both authentication and encryption mechanisms to provide security; like Syslog, SNMP still requires the configuration of the IP address of the management server to which traps will be sent due to limitations in dynamic discovery capabilities of end devices, as shown in Figure 7.3. Unlike Syslog though, SNMP provides a mechanism for a central management server to contact the client to alter its configuration. Although TCP variants of SNMP exist, SNMP is traditionally a UDP-based protocol and consequently is unreliable. It has no delivery acknowledgment and lacks knowledge of state information (is non-stateful).

In summary, both Syslog and SNMP evolved for monitoring the performance of network cores. These consist of network devices or servers that are permanently connected and statically configured with a target IP address for Syslog messages or SNMP traps. Although core devices are the focus for attacks that target the networking infrastructure, they represent a relatively small proportion of the actual hosts that populate networks. A reliable and dynamic signalling mechanism is therefore needed that caters for the masses (the edge, core and transient mobility of end user computing devices PDAs).

To address the message exchange problem in the framework, a security space as a lightweight message exchange mechanism is investigated. A security space is an abstract space (middleware) through which security components (sensors, analysers and responders) connect, contribute and communicate security related information. Security space is based on tuple space that allows multisource agents to communicate security related information securely. It allows communication not only from a sensor to a manager, but also from sensors to other sources. It also defines message exchange format for the sensors, the analysers and the responders that conform to the IDMEF.

7.5 Design principle and requirements

The role of signalling in a distributed security framework is to allow distributed sensors to dynamically direct information about events to an analysis unit where it can be collated and responses determined. In discussing the needs of the signalling mechanism, the emphasis is on its design principles and requirements. The requirements comprise functional and non-functional requirements, that is, general and specific requirements of the mechanism.

7.5.1 Design principle

Four design principles guide the proposed mechanism:

- the approach should be simple, scalable, responsive, flexible, robust and future proof.

- the goal is to allow sensors to dynamically join and leave the infrastructure without fixed preset configuration.

- the mechanism should support multiple heterogeneous sources (e.g. sensors, firewalls, IDSes, AV etc) to interact and share security intelligence.

- the impact of the mechanism on existing network services or infrastructure should be minimized.

7.5.2 Signalling requirements

The requirements for a signalling mechanism in a security framework are that it:

- supports the distributing of sensors throughout both the core and the edge of the network, even to end user devices.

- allows sensors to dynamically join and leave the network.

- supports the automated discovery of the analysis components of the framework by the sensors allowing them to forward security related information.

- be highly scalable to include large numbers of sensors in transiently connected edge devices.

- be secure, allowing the dependable and confidential exchange of messages.

- be flexible and sufficiently open ended to accommodate a wide range of devices and potential message types.

7.5.3 Security requirements

A security space allows messages to be queued (push/pull), and can be open or closed depending on if an arbitrary node can join the space, or whether authentication and authorisation are required. Security is a major concern with security space because an arbitrary node is allowed to join or leave dynamically and freely if the space is open. If the space is closed, then the identity of a node seeking to join the space must be authenticated and authorised before it is allowed to join the space. It is highly recommended that security space's implementation stipulates desirable authentication, authorisation and accounting mechanisms to ensure the security of the space.

It is pertinent that reliable and secure message exchange happens in the ISAF framework. In this respect, the following mandatory security requirements are essential, to:

- ◆ support strong authentication, authorisation and accounting mechanisms, such as RADIUS, TACACS+ or both.

- ◆ allow only authenticated nodes to join the space,

- ◆ allow authenticated nodes to share intelligence based on the necessary rights gained when authorised.

Non-mandatory security requirements are desirable and highly recommended, and these include:

- ◆ support for network admission control in the space. Network admission control is a security policy that stipulates the necessary security compliance requirements in the space. For example, it specifies software patches, firewall, intrusion detection system, or operating system service levels expected for every node requesting access to the space. Each node is expected to comply with the specified security requirements before they can gain privileged access to the network.

- ◆ allowing nodes that have shown security compliance into the network, and to participate in a communication, only if they have satisfied admission control requirements.

- ◆ supporting strong cryptographic and data integrity algorithms for encrypting and hashing data/evidence sent across to the analysis component. For example, advanced encryption standard (AES) and SHA-1 are recommended encryption and hash algorithms respectively for the *space*, which the sources (sensors, analysers, and responders) agree upon while encrypting, decrypting and hashing evidence shared among them.

7.6 Security spaces in network security

The application of security spaces to two specific domains is examined, namely, multisensor environment, and federated sensor environment.

7.6.1 Multisensor environment

In a multisensor environment multiple sensors are distributed across the network to monitor the entire network. Security spaces analysis in a multiple sensor environment investigates how security information from different sensors from the same corporate network (single autonomous system) can be analysed.

This includes how to identify which sensors reported an information, which source has subscribed for that information, and which source would be interested

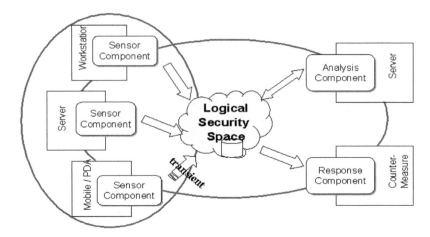

Figure 7.4: An illustration of a security space in a multiple sensor scenario

in that information. It is important to note that these sources (for example, sensors, analysers and responders) are from the same corporate network within a single autonomous system.

As illustrated in Figure 7.4, multiple sensors are distributed to gather and report threats and attacks perceived on a population of computer networks. As shown, there are different types of sensors deployed; there are server sensors, workstation sensors, and mobile or PDA sensors, each gathering specific security evidence of a class of attack. Evidence of attacks gathered by sensors needs to be conveyed securely through the space to the analysis component, where it can be collated and analysed. The challenge is to show and explain how *unique sensor information* can be communicated without ambiguity or error in the message.

7.6.2 Federated sensor environment

In a federated sensor environment, as shown in Figure 7.5, the semantic relationship of the loosely associated security information sent across the different small autonomous systems/groups (often called federations) within the same corporate network is examined.

Federated networks comprise several member networks that share some level of trust, although member networks still retain their own administrative and management controls. With each network (federation) constructed and run separately, managing their relationships can be problematic. Therefore, the challenge is to demonstrate how security spaces can be deployed in such an environment as the underlying signalling mechanism of the framework.

The description of a logical *security space* within a federated network, encapsu-

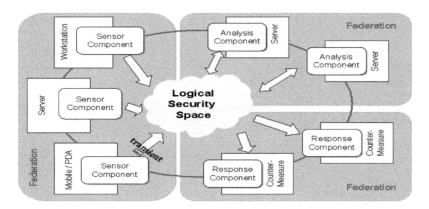

Figure 7.5: An illustration of security spaces in a federated sensor scenario

lated in the sensor, analysis, and response defence paradigm, is as shown in Figure
7.5. The federated network has three separate autonomous federations, each having its own control. The components of the framework are deployed separately on
different federations. There is a sensor federation, an analysis federation and a
response federation.

7.7 Security spaces formalism

The discussion on security spaces started by describing with examples what a tuple
is. Recall from section 7.3 that a tuple is a list of elements of potentially different
types. For instance, $(19 : 45,' Alert', 17, port135\ probed)$, is a four-tuple event. Hence,
the number of elements of the event is four. Before formalising the definition of a
tuple, the following assumptions made in regards to security events are made.

◆ a security event is either an alert or an alarm message. An alarm (audible) is
an escalated alert message. An alert is a prioritised security event logged or
sent via email to security administrators. However, these two types of messages can mean the same thing in certain environments.

◆ the number of attributes in a security event is finite, and depends on the
attributes a particular log vendor considers important. Hence the number
of attributes described in a security event varies from vendor to vendor. To
describe a standardised computer event attributes, the common event expression (CEE [199]) was organised by MITRE, and is currently investigating how
to streamline computer event description. However, in this discussion, the
number of attributes in a security event is limited to five: timestamp, source IP
address, protocol number, destination IP address, and 'signature type'. Note

that both source port (sp) and destination port (dp) are ignored (as shown in Equation 7.1).

◆ signature type is the attack signature deduced by the sensors, such as portscan, network worms or policy violation.

Definition 7.1: *A security event* (E) is an alert message that contains a list of elements of potentially different types. Thus:

$$E = (t, e_t, s_{ip}, d_{ip}, proto, s_t, s_p, d_p) \qquad (7.1)$$

Where:

$t =$	*timestamp*
$e_t =$	*event_type*
$s_{ip} =$	*source_ip_address*
$d_{ip} =$	*destination_ip_address*
$proto =$	*protocol*
$s_t =$	*signature_type*
$s_p =$	*source_port*
$d_p =$	*destination_port*

For example, *E = (19:50, Alert, 192.168.0.10, 192.168.0.3, TCP, Spade:Closed dest port used, 34725, 850)*. In this discussion, the number of event attributes in the list is limited to five: *timestamp, source IP address, destination IP address, protocol number* and *signature type*. This is to conform with the implementation reported in Chapter 8.

Definition 7.2: *A tuple* is a list of event attributes sent by a sensor for a particular activity, thus given τ as a tuple, then,

$$\tau = (t, s_{ip}, d_{ip}, i, a) \qquad (7.2)$$

Where: t is the timestamp, s_{ip} is the source IP address, d_{ip} is the destination IP address, i is the protocol number and a is the signature type.

The *space of a tuple* is defined as the number of attributes in an event. That is, the number of attributes of an event. For example, τ_8 is an eight-tuple space, if $E = (t, e_t, s_{ip}, d_{ip}, proto, s_t, s_p, d_p)$. Whereas, $E = (t, e_t, s_{ip}, d_{ip})$ is a four-tuple space τ_4. To define an event or a tuple in a multisensor environment, a *sensor id* is required. A sensor id represented as ξ is what ties (maps) an event to its originating sensor.

Definition 7.3: *A security event in a multisensor environment* (E_ξ) is described as an event that contains a list of elements of potentially different types, including the contributing sensor's id. Thus,

$$E_\xi = (t, \xi, e_t, s_{ip}, d_{ip}, proto, s_t, s_p, d_p) \qquad (7.3)$$

where E_ξ denotes an event from *sensor* ξ. For example, an event from a sensor, where *sensor id* is denoted as 1, is given as: E_1 = *(19:50, 1, Alert, 192.168.0.10, 192.168.0.3, TCP, Spade:Closed dest port used, 34725, 850)*. Now, supposing it is a named sensor, say, the *sensor id* is *p0f* (meaning, passive operating system fingerprint); then the event is described as: E_{p0f} = (19:50, p0f, Alert, 192.168.0.10, 192.168.0.3, TCP, Spade:Closed_dest_port_used, 34725, 850).

Definition 7.4: *A tuple (τ_ξ) in a multisensor environment* is defined as a list of sensor event attributes. Thus,

$$\tau_\xi = (t, \xi, s_{ip}, d_{ip}, i, a) \tag{7.4}$$

Where: *t = timestamp, ξ = sensor id, s_{ip} = source IP address, d_{ip} = destination IP address, i = protocol number and a = signature type.*

In a multiple sensor environment, we generalise a tuple (τ_ξ) as of the various sensors. Thus,

$$
\begin{aligned}
\tau_{p0f} &= (t, \xi_{p0f}, s_{ip}, d_{ip}, i, a) \\
\tau_{snort} &= (t, \xi_{snort}, s_{ip}, d_{ip}, i, a) \\
\tau_{pads} &= (t, \xi_{pads}, s_{ip}, d_{ip}, i, a) \\
\tau_{ntop} &= (t, \xi_{ntop}, s_{ip}, d_{ip}, i, a) \\
\tau_{arpwatch} &= (t, \xi_{arpwatch}, s_{ip}, d_{ip}, i, a)
\end{aligned}
\tag{7.5}
$$

The *sensor id* information in a tuple is what is used to differentiate the sources of security information provided by the sensors. This is vital when analysing and incorporating sensor beliefs about attacks. The *sensor id* is a single discriminator used to distinguish the same events but from different sensors in a multisensor environment.

7.8 Analysis of security spaces

The analysis of security spaces is conducted in two domains: first, when the sensors are distributed in a single domain, that is, the same autonomous system (AS); second, when sensors are federated in different domains (different autonomous systems).

7.8.1 Single domain (distributed LAN)

When all the sensors are in a single domain, this scenario decomposes into a multisensor scenario. The analysis of the multisensor scenario had already been discussed in section 7.7. Whereas managing multisensor information in different domains is synonymous with managing multisensor information in a multiple domains environment.

7.8.2 Multiple domains (federated LAN)

Domain information is important to associate sensor evidence to a specific domain. With domain information, events can be managed consistently in a multiple AS domain. To manage security information in a federated domain, domain information is required. To include domain information in a security event, denote Δ as the domain information. Thus, a security event from a sensor in a multi-domain environment is defined in definition 7.6.

Definition 7.6: *A security event in a multi-domain environment* $(E_{s\Delta})$ *is defined as an event that contains a list of elements of potentially different types, including both the* originating sensor *and* domain identities. *Thus,*

$$E_{s\Delta} = (t, \xi, \Delta, e_t, s_{ip}, d_{ip}, proto, s_t, s_p, d_p) \tag{7.6}$$

For example, a description of an event from a sensor (pOf) in a UK domain is shown as: $E_{(p0f)(UK)}$ =(19:50, pOf, UK, Alert, 192.168.0.10, 192.168.0.3, TCP, Spade:Closed dest port used, 34725, 850). Note that domain identity can be *typed* or *named*. The example shown above is for a *named* domain identity.

Definition 7.7: *A tuple in a federated domain environment* $(\tau_{s\Delta})$ *is defined as containing a list of domain event attributes. Thus,*

$$\tau_{s\Delta} = (t, \xi, \Delta, s_{ip}, d_{ip}, i, a) \tag{7.7}$$

Where: t = timestamp, ξ =sensor id, Δ = domain identity (typed or named), s_{ip} = source IP address, d_{ip} = destination IP address, i = protocol number, a = signature type.

Thus, in a multiple domain environment, equation 7.8 is an example of tuples from five sensors in one domain (UK domain).

$$\left.\begin{array}{ll}
\tau_{(p0f)(UK)} & = (t, P0f, \Delta_{UK}, s_{ip}, d_{ip}, i, a) \\
\tau_{(snort)(UK)} & = (t, SNORT, \Delta_{UK}, s_{ip}, d_{ip}, i, a) \\
\tau_{(pads)(UK)} & = (t, PADS, \Delta_{UK}, s_{ip}, d_{ip}, i, a) \\
\tau_{(ntop)(UK)} & = (t, NTOP, \Delta_{UK}, s_{ip}, d_{ip}, i, a) \\
\tau_{(arpwatch)(UK)} & = (t, ARPWATCH, \Delta_{UK}, s_{ip}, d_{ip}, i, a)
\end{array}\right\} \tag{7.8}$$

Generalising this formulation, we have equation 7.9:

$$\tau_{(sensor)(domain)} = (t, \xi_{sensor}, \Delta_{domain}, s_{ip}, d_{ip}, i, a) \tag{7.9}$$

Therefore, both the *sensor id* and the *domain id* are needed in a tuple to differentiate one security event from another.

7.8.2.1 Sub-domain tuple

A sub-domain tuple is a tuple in a federated domain, as shown in Equation 7.10, comprising *sensor id, domain identity* and *sub-domain identity* information. For example, if domain UK is comprised of sub-domains, say, London, Wales and Scotland, a named sub-domain tuple can be generalised as:

$$\tau_{(sensor)(domain)(subdomain)} \;=\; (t, \xi_{sensor}, \Delta_{DOMAIN}, \sigma_{subdomain}, s_{ip}, d_{ip}, i, a) \qquad (7.10)$$

Where: t = timestamp, ξ_{sensor} = sensor ID, Δ_{domain} = domain identity, $\sigma_{subdomain}$ = subdomain identity, s_{ip} = source IP address, d_{ip} = destination IP address, i = protocol number, a = signature type.

7.9 Summary

Signalling is an essential component of most distributed systems, and signalling requirements differ from system to system. With the integrated security assistance framework, a dynamic, extensible, scalable and future proof signalling mechanism, such as security spaces is required. Security spaces allow sensors, analysers, and responders to dynamically join and leave the infrastructure without fixed preset configurations. Further, the distribution of sensors throughout the core, the edge and end-user systems must be supported, which allow different types of attacks and threat attributes to be gathered in the network. Finally, automated discovery of the analysis components in the framework was offered to allow sensors to forward their pieces of evidence seamlessly to the analysis components without preset configurations on the sensors.

The schematic, semantic and formal descriptions of security spaces, and its application in the framework were discussed. Formal description including the analysis of security spaces in distributed sensor, multisensor, and multi-autonomous systems environments was discussed in section 7.7.

Security space is a secure message exchange mechanism for multisource communication that allows for heterogeneous multi-agent communication. It is distinct from any underlying network addressing scheme, such as IP addresses or physical topology. Hence security spaces can be open or closed depending on whether an arbitrary node can join them or whether authentication or authorisation is required.

The need for a signalling mechanism for the framework was explained. The requirements for the integration of the sensor, analysis, and response components of the framework was outlined for different monitoring environments, such as, single domain, multisensor and federated LANs.

The usefulness of the proposed signalling mechanism in multisource data fusion is promising. The mechanism can be used for sensor to sensor communication, and also for multi-agent communication or in a heterogeneous multisource fusion. It allows both authentication and authorisation of the sources in the fusion system in order to ensure that compromised sources are not allowed in the communication, and that any source seeking to join the space are authenticated and authorised. To adapt an alert or alarm message to the proposed message exchange format is relatively simple. This is as discussed in section 7.7; the format depends on the definitions provided, primarily for an event or a tuple. The degree of complexity of the format depends on the number of event attributes required. The alert or alarm message is then described to conform to the event or tuple definition depending on the environment. There should be one-to-one correspondence between an alert message and an event.

Security of the space is a mandatory requirement of the message exchange mechanism. This ensures that the space is secure, allowing the dependable and confidential exchange of messages, data or pieces of evidence gathered and communicated by the sources. Above all, the signalling mechanism conforms to existing IDMEF format.

Chapter 8

Security visualisation

Security visualisation and the Dempster-Shafer theory of evidence are the two fundamental techniques used in this research to analyse attack evidence perceived in computer networks. This chapter provides detailed discussion about visualisation and pattern matching techniques used to analyse security events perceived in the network by various heterogeneous sensors distributed across the entire network. The next chapter provides detailed discussion pertaining to the Dempster-Shafer theory of evidence technique also utilised in the analysis to correlate, combine and synthesise attack evidence gathered by sensors.

8.1 Introduction

Integrated analysis in the framework is achieved by using techniques that are effective and able to detect and identify attacks in real time. Deciding on a particular analysis technique to use in detecting security attacks was challenging. This is due to the nature of emerging attacks targeting corporate networks. Emerging attacks to computer networks are distributed, and often coordinated. Coordinated attacks are harder to detect than traditional attacks, as discussed in section 1.2. Hence, the objective is to employ techniques that assist security administrators to detect, evaluate, analyse and respond to attacks. In this respect, techniques favoured in the analysis are those that:

◆ provide expressive graphical representation of security attacks perceived on networks.

◆ combine separate pieces of attack evidence based on belief function and epistemic reasoning to compute errors, inconsistencies and contradictions in evidence.

◆ investigate both known and unknown attack characteristics through heuristic and pattern matching analysis.

♦ provide real-time (RT) sensing, and near real-time (NRT) overall attack detection.

8.2 Visualisation and pattern matching techniques

Graphs are a rich and flexible data structure for the representation of objects, object attributes and their relationships. A graph is composed of a set of *vertices* and a set of *edges*. A graph vertex is also referred to as a *graph node*. A graph edge is a link between a pair of incident vertices. An edge is referred to as an *arc*, when the link indicates a direction, as defined in section 8.3.1. Usually, a graph vertex represents data or a region, while a graph edge represents a relationship between a pair of incident vertices. Depending on the level of abstraction used to represent the data, a graph provides either a *syntactic* or a *semantic* description of the data [122]. Graph representations are widely used for analysing structural information, and are utilised in diverse disciplines, such as visual analytics, social networks, pattern matching and shape extraction [129].

Graph-based representations are useful in network events visualisation and analysis. They describe attack activities that reveal temporal, spatial, logical or topological relationships of attack interactions. Graph-based representations assist security administrators to visualise threat interactions, attack activity patterns, and to characterise subtle or hidden attributes of attacks. These attributes may often appear to be unrelated at first, but when investigated, their relationships reveal that they are somehow connected. Thus, relations in graph can be useful in detecting stealthy and coordinated attacks.

In network security, graphs have been used in intrusion detection systems, network monitoring and security visualisation to detect network anomalies and attacks [83]. Graph-based representations have been used in network security to analyse network activity for detection and defence [125], and also in SIMS to analyse security events [10]. Visualising port-level activities alone can be a useful indicator to revealing anomalous behaviour. For example, PortVis [93] is a security visualisation application that takes TCP activity of each port in a given time frame to uncover interesting security events through visual pattern analysis. NVisionIP [92] is a network flow security visualisation tool for portscan. VisFlowConnect [84] is a netflow visualisation of link relationships designed to identify anomalous traffic patterns, and can visually indicate the detection of events such as virus outbreaks.

Fundamental to the analysis of graphs is *graph matching*. Graph matching is a technique employed to compute the degree of similarity (dissimilarity) between two graph descriptions. Mathematically, graphs are implemented by two data structures the *adjacency list* and *adjacency matrix*, discussed in section 8.5.1. To check if two graph representations are similar, a graph matching algorithm is used. The algorithm computes a function that checks if the vertices are equal between the two graphs, and if the function preserves the arc invariant property. Graph matching is therefore an approach to checking similarities between graph data structures that helps provide concrete evidence of their exactness. The application of graph matching has been utilised extensively in diverse disciplines to analyse real-world applications and problems. For example, graph matching algorithms have been applied to successfully manipulate and analyse problems in computer vision, machine learning, pattern recognition [175] and, recently, in surveillance systems, shape extraction, and monitoring of computer networks [176].

In this investigation, graph matching algorithms are used to check similarities between a *template graph* and a *data graph*. Where the template graph is a subgraph of the data graph, the algorithms checks for a subgraph matching. A *template graph* is a graph obtained from known attack activities, and a *data graph* is a graph constructed from the testbed data sets obtained by monitoring the network. These techniques enable security administrators to investigate both known and unknown attack attributes, and therefore are a step forward in detecting emerging attacks compared to techniques that are specifically focusing on a class of attack. It is pertinent to note that techniques, such as graph and graph representation that provide expressive visualisation of attacks perceived in the network assist security administrators to:

◆ visualise attack activities and their interactions.

◆ gain better understanding of explicit relationships between attacks.

8.3 Graph representation and use of relation information

To analyse network attacks, an approach is to represent security events in a graph-based representation often referred to as an activity graph. Activity graphs reveal attack activity patterns. The use of relational information in graph representations of attack activities assist to reveal temporal, logical, spatial or topological relationships of security attacks. A visual description of attacks can be useful in offering insights into how attacks can be adequately mitigated. Thus, graph-based representations offer the following strengths:

◆ provide expressive and explicit descriptions of security events or attacks.

◆ reveal attack activity interactions and their relationships.

◆ describe appropriate temporal, spatial, logical or topological relationships among security events/attacks that characterise their attributes.

◆ reveal attack characteristics.

In this research, network attack activities are represented with a graph. Where the *graph vertices* represent the *attacker host* and the *attacked host* (target host), *graph arcs* represent logical relationships such as *attack type* (for example, portscan) as shown in Figure 8.1 or temporal relationships using the *attack timestamp*, as shown in Figure 8.2.

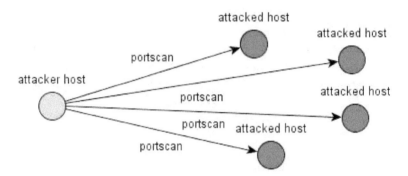

Figure 8.1: Graph description of attack activities based on logical relations

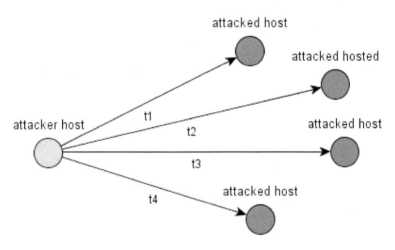

Figure 8.2: Graph description of attack activities based on temporal relations

8.3.1 Graph theory

Definition 8.1: A graph H comprises a set of *vertices* V and a set of *edges* $E \subseteq V$ x V.

$$H = (V, E) \tag{8.1}$$

If two vertices, say $u, v \in V$ are connected and $e \in E$ in H, such that (u, v) implies (v, u) for all u and v in V. Then H is an *undirected graph*, usually referred to as a graph.

Definition 8.2: A *directed graph* or *digraph* G is an ordered pair

$$G = (V, E) \tag{8.2}$$

Where V is a set, whose elements are called vertices or *nodes*. E is a set of ordered pair of vertices, called *directed edges*, *arcs* or *arrows* [138].

Definition 8.3: A *directed attributed graph* is a digraph with labels assigned to the set of vertices and arcs.

$$G = (V, E, \alpha, \beta, V_w, E_w) \tag{8.3}$$

G is a six-tuple, such that:

◆ V is a finite set of vertices.

◆ $E \subseteq V$ x V is a finite set of arcs (ordered pairs of vertices).

◆ V_w is a finite set of vertex labels (numbers).

◆ E_w is a finite set of arc labels (numbers).

◆ $\alpha : V \rightarrow V_w$ is a labelling function for finite set of vertices.

◆ $\beta : E \rightarrow E_w$ is a labelling function for finite set of arc relations.

8.3.2 Pattern activity graph

A *pattern activity graph* is a type of directed attributed graph, as in equation 8.3. A pattern activity graph $PAG = (V, E, \alpha, \beta, V_p, E_p)$ is a six-tuple, such that:

◆ V is a finite set of vertices, representing a security attack attribute.

◆ $E \subseteq VxV$ is a finite set of (logical/spatial) arc relationships between adjacent security attack attributes.

◆ $\alpha : V \rightarrow V_p$ is a labelling function generating vertex attributes.

- $\beta : E \rightarrow E_p$ is a labelling function generating logical, topological, temporal or spatial arc attributes.

- V_p is a finite set of vertex labels (numbers) representing vertex attributes.

- E_p is a finite set of logical, topological, temporal or spatial arc labels (numbers) between logically or temporally consecutive vertices.

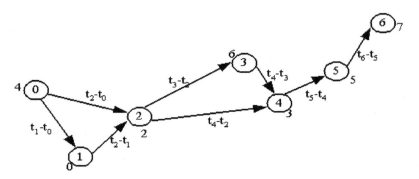

Figure 8.3: An example of a description of a pattern activity graph

Figure 8.3 represents infected computer systems that are temporally related. Graph vertices represent *the attacker* and *attacked nodes*. Graph arcs represent duration of attack ($\Delta\tau$). The numbers in the circles depict iterative graph index $(0, 1, 2, \cdots)$, while the number outside the circles indicate the attribute of attacked or attacker node and their relationship is duration of attack given as $\Delta\tau = (t_n - t_{n-1})$.

As an illustration, applying the pattern attack graph (PAG) definition to Figure 8.3, gives:

- $V = \{0, 1, 2, 3, 4, 5, 6\}$

- $E = \{(0, 1), (0, 2), (1, 2), (2, 3), (2, 4), (3, 4), (4, 5), (5, 6)\}$

- $\alpha : 0 \rightarrow 4, \quad 1 \rightarrow 0, \quad 2 \rightarrow 2, \quad 3 \rightarrow 6, \quad 4 \rightarrow 3, \quad 5 \rightarrow 5, \quad 6 \rightarrow 7$

- $\beta : (0, 1) \rightarrow (t_1 - t_0), (0, 2) \rightarrow (t_2 - t_0), (1, 2) \rightarrow (t_2 - t_1) \cdots (5, 6) \rightarrow (t_6 - t_5)$

- $V_p = \{4, 0, 2, 6, 3, 5, 7\}$

- $E_p = \{(t_1 - t_0), (t_2 - t_0), (t_2 - t_1), (t_3 - t_2), (t_4 - t_2), \cdots (t_6 - t_5)\}$

8.3.3 Graph matching

A graph matching problem is concerned with determining the similarity (dissimilarity) between graph representations. Standard concepts in graph matching include *graph isomorphism*, *subgraph isomorphism*, *maximum common subgraph*, and more recently, the *graph edit distance*.

8.3.3.1 Graph isomorphism

Two graphs G and H are said to be *isomorphic* if they have identical structure, as shown in Figure 8.4.

Formally, an isomorphism between two graphs G and H is a *bijective mapping* between the vertices of G and H that preserves the arc invariant property, that is, that preserves the structure of the arcs.

Since graph representations of objects are often invariant under a number of transformations, for example, spatial transformations such as translation, rotation and scaling [130]. Graph isomorphism is a useful technique to ascertain when one object is a transformed version of another, as shown in Figure 8.4.

Figure 8.4: An example of graph matching of two graphs G and H, matching vertex and preserving arc invariant property.

Definition 8.4: *Graph isomorphism:* A graph G is *isomorphic* to a graph H, if there exists a bijective mapping ϕ from the vertices of G to the vertices of H that preserves all labels and structures of the arcs, as shown in Figure 8.4. That is:

$$\phi : G \to H, \text{ is isomorphic} \tag{8.4}$$

If ϕ is a bijective function, such that:

- $e = (v_1, v_2) \in E(G)$, iff $e' = (\phi(v_1), \phi(v_2)) \in E(H)$, such that $\beta(e) = \beta(\phi^{-1}(e'))$

- $\forall\, e' = (\phi(v_1), \phi(v_2)) \in E(H) \ \exists\, e = (\phi^{-1}(\phi(v_1)), \phi^{-1}(\phi(v_2))) \in E(G)$, and $\beta(e) = \beta(\phi^{-1}(e'))$

8.3.3.2 Subgraph isomorphism

A graph G_s is a subgraph of G if G contains G_s. That is, every vertex $V(G_s)$ in G_s is contained in $V(G)$, and every edge $E(G_s)$ is contained in $E(G)$ as defined by equation 8.5.

Definition 8.5: *A subgraph* $G_s(V_s, E_s, \alpha_s, \beta_s)$ *of* G, *is a four-tuple*

$$G_s \subseteq G \tag{8.5}$$

such that:

◆ $V_s \subseteq V$

◆ $E_s \subseteq E \subseteq V_s \times V_s$

◆ $\alpha_s(v) = \alpha(v) \; \forall \; v \in V_s$

◆ $\beta_s(e) = \beta(e) \; \forall \; e \in E_s$

Definition 8.6: *Subgraph isomorphism:* A mapping ϕ from a graph G_s to a graph G is a *subgraph isomorphism*, if $G_s \subseteq G$, provided ϕ is bijective. That is,

$$\phi : G_s \to G \tag{8.6}$$

such that:

◆ $e = (v_1, v_2) \in (G_s)$, iff $\quad e' = (\phi(v_1), \phi(v_2)) \in E(G)$

◆ $\forall \; e' = (\phi(v_1), \phi(v_2)) \in E(G), \; \exists \; e = (\phi^{-1}(\phi(v_1)), \phi^{-1}(\phi(v_2))) \in E(G_s)$

A subgraph isomorphism exists between two graphs if one graph contains a subgraph that is isomorphic to the other. Subgraph isomorphism is useful if one wants to discover if a given object is part of another object or a collection of several objects [130].

8.3.3.3 Maximum common subgraph (MCS)

The *maximum common subgraph* of two graphs G and H is the *largest subgraph* contained by both G and H. Maximum common subgraph is useful in measuring the similarities between two graph objects. The larger the MCS of two graphs, the greater the degree of similarity between the two objects they represent.

Definition 8.7: Suppose $G_1 = (V_1, E_1, \alpha_1, \beta_1)$ and $G_2 = (V_2, E_2, \alpha_2, \beta_2)$ are graphs. A *common subgraph*, $cs(G_1, G_2)$ is a graph, such that there exist *subgraph isomorphisms* from G to G_1, and G to G_2.

$$G = mcs(G_1, G_2) \tag{8.7}$$

The graph G is called a *maximum common subgraph* $mcs(G_1, G_2)$, if there exists no other *common subgraph* of G_1 and G_2 that is greater than G. That is,

8.3.4 Inexact graph matching

In most real world applications, there may not always exist perfect (exact) matches between graph descriptions. Therefore, a function is required that computes an approximate measure of similarities in graph representations. This leads to a class of graph matching problems often referred to as *inexact graph matching problems*. Inexact graph matching is the process of finding the best possible approximation or matching between two graphs when exact matching is not feasible. Two inexact graph matching concepts discussed in this book are: *error-correcting graph matching* and *Graph Edit Distance*.

8.3.4.1 The error-correcting graph matching (ECGM)

An error-correcting graph matching computes a mapping between the vertices of two graphs so that they approximately coincide, realising that the two graphs may not be exact [129]. Error correcting graph matching is a generalisation of string matching, or string edit distance computation [202]. This involves different metrics to measure the two graphs, for example, cost function is one possible option, deletion, insertion or substitution of vertices and edges.

8.3.4.2 The graph edit distance

A graph edit distance (GED) is a convenient and logical graph distance metric that arises naturally in the context of error-correcting graph matching [130]. Graph edit operations are introduced with GED. Typical graph edit operations include *deletion, insertion* and *substitution* of vertices and edges. These operations are used to transform graph representations. Given a set of edit operations, *a graph edit distance* is defined as the minimum number of operations that transform a graph into another. Thus, similarity in graph representations is measured by the minimum number of operations required to transform one graph to another.

8.4 Graph constructing engine

This section describes the approach used in this investigation to construct the activity graphs employed in this research. In the testbed, various sensors, such as NTOP, SPADE, SNORT, ARPWATCH and POF are distributed across the network to gather security attack evidence. Evidence gathered by these sensors is stored for further analysis. The graph constructing engine is a piece of code that takes collated (normalised) sensor evidence obtained about attacks perceived on the entire monitored network and converts it into graphs. First, the overall goals of the activity graph are explained together with how it accomplishes these goals.

8.4.1 Design goals

The purpose of the graph constructing engine is to build graphs from network attack activities, and to analyse them to see if they represent an exact match to a genuine network attack in a given time period. Specific goals accomplished by constructing activity graphs are as follows:

- ◆ to detect port sweeps, port scans, host scans and stealthy scans.

- ◆ to detect network access and policy violations.

- ◆ to detect network worms and Web attacks.

- ◆ to detect other network anomalies (threats), classified or unclassified in the network.

- ◆ to provide security administrators with a comprehensive and expressive way to visualise network activities (security events), which assists them to detect network attacks, and consequently provide adequate mitigation controls to perceived attacks.

8.4.2 Constructing activity graphs

A graph vertex $(v \in V)$ corresponds to a *security event attribute* and a graph arc $(e \in E)$ represents a *relationship* between two incident vertices. The possible vertex attributes (V_p) are *attack attribute type* (for example, attacker host and attacked host). The arc attributes (E_p) indicate the relationship between two adjacent attack types, such as, type of attack or vulnerability exploit. Examples include, portscan, worm, and policy violation. However, where the graph is modelled in terms of temporal relationships, the temporal arc attributes (E_p) indicate the time of occurrence of the attack, that is, event timestamp, as shown in Figure 8.1.

Although security events are time-stamped extensive temporal evaluations are possible. For example, consider two events, say A and B. A is *"coincidental"* to B, if the two events occurred at the same time. In this case, the objective might be to search for events that occurred at the same time. A occurs *"before"* B, if A's timestamp is earlier than B's timestamp. Here, the objective may be to investigate a break-in after a certain time $t > \tau$. Similarly, other temporal qualities exist, such as *"after"*, *"during"*, *"starts"*, *"ends"*.

8.4.3 Overview

The graph constructing engine is one of the most fundamental aspects of the analysis. Its task is to pull events of network activity from a security events database as shown in Figure 8.5.

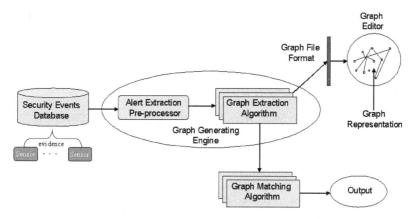

Figure 8.5: Overview of the graph constructing engine

From the security events database gathered by sensors, pertinent information as requested by security administrators are preprocessed and then used to construct activity graphs. The constructed graphs are used by a security administrator to visualise network activity patterns and to identify network attacks, by comparing *template graphs* of known threats to the constructed *activity graph* using graph matching algorithms. Visual inspection of attack graphs in itself is very useful in identifying security attacks, due the attacks characteristic activity patterns.

A high-level description of the graph constructing engine is shown in Figure 8.5. It comprises six components: the *security events database* stores attack evidence as reported by the sensors. An *event extraction pre-processor* extracts security events based on pre-defined conditions. A *graph algorithm* converts predefined security events into activity graphs, the *activity graph* is formatted into a graph file format for visualisation by the *graph file format interface*. Activity graphs are visualised using an *editor* (graph description editor) and finally, a *graph matching algorithm* checks for similarities (dissimilarities) in graph descriptions.

8.4.4   Event extraction pre-processor

Here, an event extraction pre-processor is parsed on the database containing security events to extract events at a given time. For example, an administrator might be interested in knowing the interactions on the network in a given day of the month, say 3 March 2007, as shown in Table 8.1.

The event database has a tendency to grow significantly depending on the size of the network being monitored. The size of the dataset being analysed at a given time may have a significant performance issue on the graph algorithm discussed in section 8.5.1.

Table 8.1: Sample dataset of security events

/* log format: ip_src/ip_dst/signature/timestamp */
172.16.1.1/192.168.0.10/POLICY VNC server response/2007-03-16 04:17:00
172.16.1.1/192.168.0.10/(spp_stream4) possible EVASIVE RST detection/2007-03-16 04:26:05
172.16.1.1/192.168.0.10/(spp_stream4) possible EVASIVE RST detection/2007-03-16 04:26:52
172.16.1.1/192.168.0.10/(spp_stream4) possible EVASIVE RST detection/2007-03-16 04:43:41
172.16.1.1/192.168.0.10/(spp_stream4) possible EVASIVE RST detection/2007-03-21 16:15:14
75.3.17.97/192.168.0.10/ICMP Echo Reply/2007-03-22 12:57:57
75.3.17.97/192.168.0.10/ICMP Echo Reply/2007-03-22 12:57:58
75.3.17.97/192.168.0.10/ICMP Echo Reply/2007-03-22 12:57:59
$\vdots$

Given specified times t_1 and t_2, a security events database is parsed for security events of interest. Security events are described in terms of event attributes of interest, such as event source address (*ip_src*), target host (*ip_dst*), type of threat (*signature*), time of exploit (*timestamp*), protocol type (*proto*). To build an activity graph, the relevant evidence is extracted, such as, *ip_src, ip_dst, signature, timestamp*.

Where:

◆ ip_src = source IP address,

◆ ip_dst = destination IP address,

◆ proto = protocol type.

The algorithm for the extraction is described in *Algorithm* 8.1. Note that the specified time frame t_1 to t_2 reduces to t when $t_1 = t_2$.

Algorithm 8.1 Event extraction pre-processor

Algorithm secEventLog(t_1, t_2):
Input: Begin time t_1, end time t_2.
Output: Security events log "timed_events.log" between $t_1 \leq t_2$
$ip\_src \leftarrow attacker\ address$
$ip\_dst \leftarrow attacked\ address$
$sig\_name \leftarrow threat\ type$ /* (attack signature) */
$time \leftarrow timestamp\ \ of\ security\ event$
$proto \leftarrow protocol\ type$ /* (example, TCP, UDP, ICMP, IP) */
while $t_1 \leq t \leq t_2$ do
    $siglist[\,] \leftarrow (ip\_src, ip\_dst, sig\_name, time, prot)$
end while

Algorithm 8.1 shows an event extraction pre-processor for analysing security events. It uses security event attributes such as, *attacker address, type of protocol, timestamp and type of threat.* A similar idea of using security event attributes such as, host address, timestamp and protocol id, to build activity graphs was also used by Cheung et al. [83] in the design of GrIDS - a graph-based intrusion detection system.

8.4.5 Graph algorithm

The processed events extracted by the "event extraction pre-processor" are fed into a graph algorithm to build an activity graph. The graph algorithm constructs a *pattern activity graph* of the processed events as discussed in section 8.3.2. The constructed activity graph assists security administrators to visualise attack activities in the network, and reveals attack relationships that characterise their patterns. The graph algorithm has gone through four revisions to date. The first and final versions are discussed.

Algorithm 8.2 Graph algorithm (first design)

Algorithm digraph:
Input: Events - "timed_events.log"
Output: Graph in GraphML and Adjacency list
/* events are read from timed_events.log */
data ← events
G ← new graph initialised for data
While not (*data is empty*) **do**
    line ← read in data line by line
    name[ ] *← split line* by a meta data (/)
    attacker ← name[0]
    for *i ← 1 to name.length* **do**
        /* builds activity graph from security events */
        G.addEdge(attacker, name[*i*])
    end for
/* write adjacency list of graph to file and to GraphML file format */
print(G)
end while

Algorithm 8.2 is the first version of the graph algorithm. The methods used in the algorithms were adapted from Sedgewick's implementation [142]. It relies on a graph adjacency list constructed using a linked list data structure for graph arcs, and symbol table data type for vertices and arcs.

The graph representation and graph matching algorithms described in this book are implemented using the Java Programming Language, however other programming or scripting languages can also be used, such as C++, TCL or Perl respectively. In Java programming, a *symbol table* is a data type that associates values to keys. For example, a symbol table, say, *ST ⟨key, value⟩*, assigns a *graph vertex* as the *key*, while *a linked list* (containing adjacent vertices) is the *value pair*. A *key* is the primary reference data. A symbol table is a collection of key-value pairs.

The first implementation of the graph algorithm (that is Algorithm 8.2) had a couple of minor omissions that were resolved in the final design, such as:

◆ parallel arcs.

◆ labels on arcs.

It is important to note that the first implementation is suitable for analysing most security incidents, and have shown to provide very reliable results too.

8.4.5.1 Parallel arcs and arc labels

A *parallel arc* in a graph representation is when the same arc is repeated between the same pair of vertices, as shown in Figure 8.6. An arc label is a label or number used to identify a graph arc.

The idea of parallel arcs and arc labels is essential to the security problem being solved. For example, to understand how many times an attacker exploited the same vulnerability on the same target, parallel arcs are of importance. Again, if the analysed graph is modelled as the interaction between an "attacker host" and an "attacked host", then parallel arcs reveal temporal relationships. For example, without parallel arcs, the graph would not be able to capture such knowledge as the *number of attempts* and the *actual times* when an adversary repeated the same exploit on the same target. This information would be lost without incorporating parallel arcs and arc labels in the design, as shown in Figures 8.6 and 8.7.

Figure 8.6: Activity graph with parallel arcs

Figure 8.7: Activity graph ignores parallel arcs

Figures 8.6 and 8.7 show two graph representations, one with parallel arcs, as shown in Figure 8.6, and the other without parallel arcs, as shown in Figure 8.7. It would be impossible to know how many times an attacker (192.168.0.10) carried a reconnaissance attempt (*ICMP Ping*) on the target host (192.168.1.20) without parallel edges. If the times these attempts were made are important, this knowledge is unavailable except through manual analysis of the security log without parallel edges. Incorporating such knowledge into the design is useful in the detection process of the investigation.

Another advantage of parallel edges is seen in structural analysis of graph representations, discussed in section 8.5.2.

Algorithm 8.3 Graph algorithm (final design)

Algorithm digraph:

Input: Events - "timed_events.log"
Output: Graph in GraphML and adjacency list
/* Events are read from timed_events.log */
$data \leftarrow events$
$G \leftarrow new\ graph$ initialised for data
While not$(data\ is\ empty)$ **do**
  $line \leftarrow read$ in data line by line
  $name[\ ] \leftarrow split$ line by a meta data (/)
  $attacker \leftarrow name[0]$
  for $i \leftarrow 1\ to\ name.length$ **do**
    /* weight or label assigned to graph edge */
    $weight \leftarrow name[name.lenght + 1]$
    /* build activity graph of security event interaction, including weight */
    $G.addEdge(attacker, name[i], weight)$
  end for
    /* write adjacency list of graph to file and to GraphML file format */
$print(G)$
end while

Algorithm 8.3 shows the final design of the graph extraction algorithm. The algorithm is a revised version of the first design, as shown in Algorithm 8.2, which addressed the limitations observed in the first design, such as:

◆ labels on graph arcs.

◆ incorporating parallel arcs.

◆ self-loop.

A loop (or a self-loop) is an arc that connects a graph vertex to itself. Its importance in analysing security activities is to reveal information flows or attack interactions.

The use of a label on a graph arc was introduced in the final version of the algorithm (Algorithm 8.3). The labels used were of different qualities such as temporal, logical, topological or spatial.

Temporal and logical qualities were demonstrated as shown in Figure 10.7 and Figure 10.8. Spatial and topological qualities can be realised using the pattern activity graph discussed in section 8.3.2.

8.4.6 Graph language

A graph editor is a platform used to visualise graphs, such as activity graphs, attack graphs, or data graphs. A graph editor relies on a graph file format, as an interface or language to read and display graphs. Interoperability among different graph file formats has always been an issue with visualising graphs. An effort to formulate an interoperable graph file format began in 2000, when the GraphML [133] project was initiated at the data exchange formats (DEF) Workshop, a subsection of the graph drawing conference [134], to accomplish this quest.

In 2001, at the next DEF workshop, the GraphML working specification, primer and file format were demonstrated. *GraphML* is a comprehensive, easy to use XML-based graph file format that supports most graph extensions, and can be translated to other file format such as, *GXL [184], GML [193], XGMML [194], and SVG* [211]. The interoperability of GraphML with other file formats enables graphs built with GraphML to be easily translated (read) by most graph editors. This was a compelling reason for using GraphML in the development work of activity and attack graphs discussed in this research. The activity graph of network events is codified in GraphML file format, specification and primer as shown in definition 8.8.

Definition 8.8: A GraphML grammar header definition

   GraphML header definition

$\langle ?xml\ version = "1.0"\ encoding = "UTF-8"?\rangle$

$\langle !--Created\ by\ yFiles\ 2.4.2.1--\rangle$

$\langle graphml\ xmlns = "http://graphml.graphdrawing.org/xmlns/graphml"$

$xmlns:y = http://www.yworks.com/xml/graphml$

$xmlns:xsi = "http://www.w3.org/2001/XMLSchema-instance"$

$xsi:schemaLocation = "http://graphml.graphdrawing.org/xmlns/graphml$ (8.8)

$http://www.yworks.com/xml/schema/graphml/1.0/ygraphml.xsd"\rangle$

$\vdots$

      $/*\ insert\ graph\ definition\ in\ GraphML\ */$

$\langle/graphml\rangle$

Definition 8.8 shows the *GraphML header parameters*. The first line of the document is an *XML process instruction* which shows that the document adheres to the *XML 1.0* standard and that the encoding of the document is *UTF-8*, (8-bit unicode transformation format), the standard encoding for XML documents. Other encoding systems are possible for GraphML documents as discussed in [134]. The second line is a *"yFile"* statement that shows yEd [135] a *Java Graph Editor* as the visualisation editor to display the *graph*.

Definition 8.9: A simple graph definition in GraphML

$$
\begin{aligned}
&\textbf{Graph definition in GraphML} \\
&\langle graph\ id = 'G'\ edgedefault = 'directed'\rangle \\
&\quad \langle node\ id = n_0/\rangle \\
&\quad \langle node\ id = n_1/\rangle \\
&\quad \vdots \\
&\quad \langle node\ id = n_m/\rangle \\
&\quad \langle edge \quad source = n_0 \quad target = n_2/\rangle \\
&\quad \langle edge \quad source = n_1 \quad target = n_2/\rangle \\
&\quad \vdots \\
&\quad \langle edge \quad source = n_1 \quad target = n_m/\rangle \\
&\langle /graph\rangle
\end{aligned}
\tag{8.9}
$$

Definition 8.9 is a simple graph definition in GraphML format. It shows the generic graph nodes $n_0...n_m$ and their relationships (arcs) with each other. The variable (m) indicates the maximum node in the graph description.

8.4.7 Graph matching algorithm

8.4.7.1 Graph isomorphism

A graph matching problem is concerned with identifying similarities (or dissimilarities) in graph representations, as discussed in section 8.3.3. To identify similarity or dissimilarity between graphs, a graph matching algorithm is required. Algorithms for *graph isomorphism, subgraph isomorphism, maximum common subgraph, error-correcting graph matching* and *graph edit distance* exist and have been extensively reported [136, 130].

In this research, a graph isomorphism algorithm that exhaustively searches every possible occurrence of a template graph on the data graph is applied. Exhaustive graph matching algorithms aim to find every occurrence of a model graph in a data graph. The use of an exhaustive graph algorithm in this research is to obtain every instance of the template graph that may exist in the data graph of security events. It is important to note that exhaustive search algorithms may not perform so well in some computing systems due to their significant CPU, memory and storage requirements. Performance issues of graph matching algorithms, such as how fast a particular algorithm is, the physical requirements of the algorithm on a specific computing system, (for instance, memory, processor, page file, storage and program run-time requirements) needs to be estimated. However, performance complexity analysis of graph matching algorithms is beyond the scope of this book.

Note: template graph is constructed empirically by taking a sample of the events generated when an attack is launched on the network to construct a graph using the defined pattern activity graph. A template graph is constructed for each attack type demonstrated in Chapter 10. Generating a template graph for a specific attack is a one-time procedure that is done to obtain a model graph of that particular attack. Once this is completed, the template graph (model graph) then serves as a baseline for comparing the occurrence of a similar attack behaviour in the network. It is a recommended practice to generate template graphs while training the data in the network, so that template graph can be pre-loaded into the graph engine before data graphs are obtained.

Automatic graph generation is ideal for real-time monitoring, but it does not guarantee that attacks are accurately identified. Manual attack graph generation is useful for non-real-time or retrospective monitoring of the network. However, whichever method that is used (manual or automatic), an appropriate procedure for accurately detecting an attack is to compare template graphs to a data graph obtained whilst monitoring the network.

Algorithm 8.4 Graph isomorphism algorithm

Algorithm digraphMatcher:

Input: Digraphs G *and* H

Output: Correspondence between the two graphs, or no matching

$G \leftarrow$ template graph of known security threat signature

$H \leftarrow$ data graph generated from security events

if $(graphComparator\_isIsomorphic(G, H))$ **then** $print(G)$

end if

Algorithm 8.4 is an exhaustive search graph matching algorithm for comparing digraphs. It is used to compare template graphs and data graphs of security activities obtained from monitoring a testbed network.

8.4.7.2 Subgraph isomorphism

With subgraph isomorphism, the template graph is seen as a subgraph of the data graph, in which case the graph containing known attack signatures is matched against a graph containing security attack evidence. The algorithm employed to check similarity in graph data structures between the two is described.

Algorithm 8.5 Subgraph isomorphism algorithm

Algorithm SubgraphMatcher:

Input: graphs G *and* H

Output: Correspondence between the two graphs, or no matching

$G \leftarrow$ *template graph* of known security threat signature, a subgraph of H

$H \leftarrow$ *data graph* generated from security events data

if $(graphComparator\_subgraphIsomorphic(H, G))$ **then** $print(G)$

end if

Algorithm 8.5 is the subgraph isomorphism used to exhaustively search the data graph for exact matches of the subgraph. Note that exact graph matching at times is not possible, hence inexact graph matching technique may be utilised in comparing the template graph with the data graph.

8.5 Graph analysis

Mathematically, two data structures can be used to describe graphs, namely the *adjacency matrix* and *adjacency list*. The two data structures are compared in subsection 8.5.1, while graph centrality is discussed in subsection 8.5.2.

8.5.1 Graph data structure analysis

An adjacency list is a graph representation of all its edges or arcs as a list. One important advantage of using the *adjacency list* representation is that the amount of storage is proportionate to the size of the input, as shown in Table 8.2.

Table 8.2: Graph data structure analysis [139]

Representation	Space	Edge between V and W	Edge from V to anywhere	Enumerate all edges
Adjacency Matrix	$\Theta\left(V^2\right)$	$\Theta\left(1\right)$	$O\left(V\right)$	$\Theta\left(V^2\right)$
Adjacency List	$\Theta\left(E+V\right)$	$O\left(E\right)$	$\Theta\left(1\right)$	$\Theta\left(E+V\right)$

For example, given a graph G, the *amount of storage* depends on the *number of vertices* $V(G)$ and the *number of edges* $E(G)$. That is, $\Theta\left(E+V\right)$. This consideration is quite useful for sparse graphs. A graph is sparse if $|E(G)|$ is proportional to $|V(G)|$. That is, $G = (V, E)$ with $|E| = O(|V|)$, on the average, each vertex has a constant number of neighbours. Another graph representation is the *adjacency matrix*. The adjacency matrix is more efficient for locating edges in a graph, but is very constrained in its performance for dense graphs. A graph is dense if it has many edges, relatively speaking, if the number of edges is greater than twice the number of vertices. Suppose $G = (V, E)$ is a graph, then G is dense if $|E| = \Theta\left(|V|^2\right)$. The graph data structure used in the implementation is the adjacency list, because of its qualities in relation to space and efficiency when handling dense graphs.

In the real world, the amount of storage does not constitute a major performance issue with graph matching. Besides, the cost of storage devices is relatively afford-able. A significant performance issue with graph matching arises when one graph is exhaustively compared to another, by checking relationships between every ver-tex in one graph to another, especially, if one graph or both graphs are densely populated, which will be the case when solving most real world problems. This leads to a class of graph matching problem known to graph researchers as NP-complete (non-deterministic polynomial complete) type of problem. NP-complete type of problems are relatively difficult to resolve using traditional graph matching algorithms.

8.5.2 Graph centrality analysis

A graph centrality is a class of measurements that capture the relative structural importance of a vertex or an arc in a graph network. Graph centrality measures have been employed in diverse areas such as social networks to analysis graphs since the seminar work of Bavelas [132] in 1948. A graph centrality is a measure that is use to check which graph vertex or edge has significant structural influence in a graph. These measures are used in graph analysis to check which vertex or edge has the greatest impact in the graph (representation), in terms of the number of peer-contacts the vertex maintains, or its relationships to other vertices in the graph. The number of peer-contacts is the number of connections from a vertex to other vertices in the graph.

Measures of graph centrality include:

◆ *Connected edges* centrality, (degree centrality): This implies that important vertices are the ones with the most edges (connections) with other vertices.

◆ *Weight of connected edges* centrality, (cost centrality): This implies that important vertices are the ones with highest costs on their incident edges to other vertices.

◆ *Vertex betweenness* centrality: This implies that important vertices control information flow to other vertices, such that they fall on the shortest paths between pairs of vertices [132].

◆ *Edge betweenness* centrality: This implies that important edges are crucial information routes in the graph [144].

◆ *Closeness* centrality: This implies that important vertices maintain short distances to other vertices. Distance in this analysis means the number of hops between incident vertices. However, distance is a relative measure that means different things to different people. In most cases, it must be defined before its application. For example, a distance could be measured by the Cartesian metric between two points in a plane.

◆ *Eigenvector* centrality: This is similar to 'connected edges centrality', but works on the premise that not all connections are equal. Its mathematical underpinning is similar to that of the algorithm used by Google's PageRank algorithm [145].

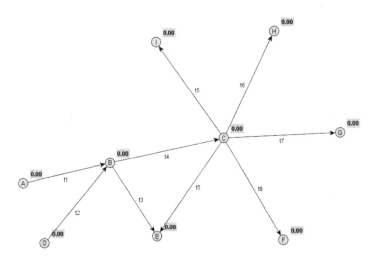

Figure 8.8: A representation of worm infection activity (centrality measure not applied)

In the analysis, *connected edges* centrality measure was employed, because the focus of the analysis was on evaluating which graph vertex had the most connections to other vertices. Knowing the vertex that has the most connections means this vertex can be isolated quickly to mitigate an incident. In evaluating the pattern activity graph, this centrality measure is used to determine which host has the greatest peer-contact to other hosts in the network, as shown in Figure 8.8. When this vertex (attacker) is removed from the network, the level of the attack/incident is lessened because the host generating most of the attacks has been removed from the network. For example, to mitigate a network worm outbreak, the system causing the most peer-to-peer contact to susceptible systems is removed from the network, whilst infected systems are quarantined.

Visualising the pattern activity graph of the worm infection as shown in Figure 8.8, by inspection, it is evident that *node C* is spreading the worm faster than the other nodes. This is because *node C* had the highest number of out-bound connections to other nodes in the network. In this respect, applying control measures on *node C*, such as quarantine, removal or repair, should significantly reduce the propagation of the worm incident. Thus, removing (disconnecting) *node C* from the network and applying quarantine patches should assist in reducing the scale of the incident.

Although manual inspection of activity graphs by a security administrator in order to detect an attack is promising, but this approach struggles in detecting widespread attacks swiftly, especially when the activity is dense and huge. Graph centrality measures are needed to swiftly isolate and identify vertices or edges in the graph of significant importance. Hence, connected edge centrality is applied to pattern activity graphs in order to automatically and swiftly detect attacks, especially widespread attacks in a dense and complex activity graph. A model of a pattern activity graph with graph centrality applied is shown in Figure 8.9.

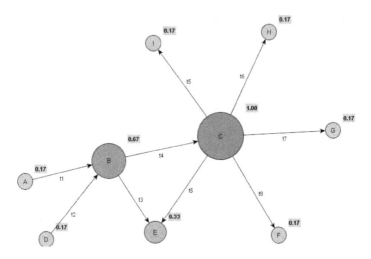

Figure 8.9: A representation of worm infection activity (connected-edge centrality measure applied)

Mathematically, *connected edges centrality measure* is computed as:

$$Edge_{centrality} = \frac{1}{\#E_{V_{max}}} \tag{8.10}$$

◆ $Edge_{centrality}$ denotes connected *edges centrality measure*

◆ V_{max} is the node with the highest number of connected edges

◆ $\#E_{V_{max}}$ is the number of edges for the V_{max} vertex. That is the sum of number of both inbound and outbound edges.

◆ Thus, $Edge_{centrality} = 1/6 = 0.1670 \cong 0.17$.

The size and colour of the nodes (as shown in Figure 8.9), are visible markers of the applied centrality measure. Red indicates the more influential nodes, and yellow the less influential nodes, while the size (the radius) of the node is proportional to its centrality value. The highest centrality value (for *connected edge* centrality) is 1. Hence, the node with the greatest influence has a measure of *centrality = 1*.

8.6 Summary

Analysis techniques employed to detect attacks to computer networks were discussed. These include graph theory, graph isomorphism, subgraph isomorphism and pattern activity graph.

First, it was explained why *graph theory and graph matching* were chosen as the analysis techniques; primarily to assist a security administrator in *visualising attack activities*, which in return provides insight into how best to mitigate perceived attacks. A graph model - *pattern activity graph* - was proposed to describe security attacks, in order to determine the nature of attacks perceived on the network. Algorithms for graph isomorphism and subgraph isomorphism were developed, and utilised to compare attack *graph templates* to *data graphs* constructed from security events gathered whilst monitoring the network.

Second, the different graph and subgraph matching algorithms used to analyse activity graphs to identify and detect attacks were explained. Third, the different graph data structures, such as adjacency list and adjacent matrix were discussed. Finally, to swiftly analyse dense and complex activity graphs, graph centrality measures were codified into several graph representations. This assists security administrators to swiftly identify and automatically isolate an attack node.

Chapter 9

Multisource data fusion

9.1 Introduction

To detect security threats or attacks, an approach is to monitor the network for suspicious network activities (security monitoring). In security monitoring, countermeasure systems, such as firewalls, IDSes, anti-viral, anti-malware are placed at different network points, and on individual hosts, to monitor and gather attack evidence perceived in the network. Network activities being monitored are suspicious activities, such as, changes in network behaviour, deviation in preset baselines, changes in traffic utilisation, and anomalous system behaviours. But gathering network activity logs, (for example, security events or audit trails) provides only symptomatic evidence, such as high CPU utilisation history, access-list violations, failed resource and attempted intrusion. Appropriate analysis of these collective symptomatic pieces of evidence is needed to conclusively detect security attacks.

Anomalous system behaviours are symptomatic system behaviour that often indicates an attack, such as failed user authentication, or recurrent system crashes. These symptomatic system behaviours are usually picked up by host-based intrusion detection systems. Suspicious network activities are reported by network-based intrusion detection systems. However, both network activities and anomalous system behaviours are often abrupt in nature, but provide only indicative pieces of evidence about potential attacks. Thus, network activities, or changes in network activity patterns, may not necessarily be due to security attacks. Changes in network activity patterns are not sufficient proof of network attacks. This is because changes in the network can be caused by other factors:

◆ genuine network behaviour with slight deviation in known patterns (normal).

◆ faults (inadvertent and accidental).

◆ mis-classified traffic (normal).

In a security monitoring environment, evidence about attacks from sensors is not always concrete, such as specific attack signatures. Unfortunately, some sensors are limited in the attacks they can detect, that is, they are unable to detect certain attacks. Hence, security evidence is often symptomatic, and based on changes in network behaviour, traffic utilisation or deviation from known network baselines. Such pieces of evidence are seen to be supportive, inconclusive, and at times contradictory [154].

Since no single source (for example, IDS, firewall, AV or anti-malware) is able to identify and detect all types of cyberspace attacks, it is imperative that multiple sources are used to gather attack evidence perceived in the network. But the gathering of network activity logs, for example, security events or audit trails provide only symptomatic evidence, such as (high CPU utilisation history, access-list violations, failed resource requests and attempted intrusion). Therefore, an important requirement to accurately identify and detect attacks perceived in most enterprise networks is to have an efficient and robust analysis unit. An analysis component that is able to synthesise collective symptomatic pieces of evidence gathered by the different sources distributed in the network, in order to conclusively identify and detect security attacks. In this respect, a multisource data fusion technique is sought to efficiently combine and analyse evidence from multiple sensors as shown in Figure 9.1.

We argue that a multisource data fusion approach is a step forward in accurately detecting varying threats and attacks perceived on computer networks compared with approaches that rely only on a single sensor, or the 'repeater effect' of using the same sensor but in multiple (different) network points.

9.2 Multisource data fusion

Multisource data fusion is a process carried on multi-source data towards detection, association, correlation, estimation and combination. It combines several data streams into one with a higher level of abstraction and greater meaning [82]. This encompasses theory, tools and techniques for exploiting the synergy in the information/evidence acquired from multiple sources, such as sensors, databases, intelligent sources and humans that helps us better understand a phenomenon and enhance intelligence [197]. In discussing multisource data fusion, the focus is on the collection of evidence from multiple sources in a live testbed network, discussed in section 10.5, and how to combine these pieces of evidence to determine if an attack is taking place on the network and the nature of the attack, which assists in determining appropriate measures to counter the attack.

Multisensor data fusion or *"distributed sensing"* seeks to combine data from multiple sensors in making inferences, which is not possible from a single sensor perspective, as shown in Figure 9.1.

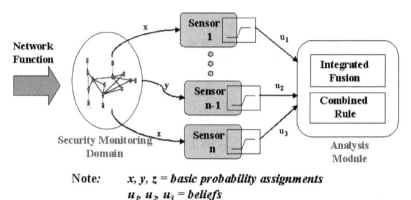

Note: x, y, z = basic probability assignments
u_1, u_2, u_3 = beliefs

Figure 9.1: A representation of multisensor data fusion

Figure 9.1 shows how sensors distributed across the network are used to monitor and gather security evidence, and communicate their belief to the analysis module where pieces of evidence are combined using the Dempster-Shafer theory of evidence.

9.3 Motivation for multisource data fusion

Intrusion detection systems (IDSes) are used together with firewalls to detect and control the level of security attacks targeting computer networks. Unfortunately, there is no single intrusion detection system that can detect every security attack [217, 179]. IDSes are limited in what they can detect. According to Hall and Mc-Mullen [109], 'there is simply no one perfect sensor'. That is, no single sensor or type of sensor can accurately detect, locate, and identify all types of cyber threats and attacks. According to Staniford et al. [181], specific sensors or specific intrusion detection systems are better at detecting a class of attacks than the other. Therefore, the use of a single sensor (or source) to detect cyber attacks is inherently insufficient in identifying emerging attacks perceived in enterprise networks today. Hence, we argue for a data fusion approach in detecting widespread and emerging attacks perceived in networks.

Multisensor data fusion has been shown to be the underpinning towards engineering of next generation intrusion detection systems [177]. It involves aggregating data from multiple sources such as sensors, databases, intelligent agents and humans toward detection, association, correlation, estimation and combination. Hence, data fusion enables several data streams to be combined into one with a higher level of accuracy and greater reliability than that obtained from a single source.

To combine evidence from different sources in data fusion, numerous techniques have been suggested in the literature such as traditional probability theorem, averaging, Bayesian probability, fuzzy logic, rough sets, and the Dempster-Shafer theory of evidence [109, 197]. These techniques are valuable in combining evidence from different sources and in making inferences that are plausible and beyond a single source perspective. Hence, a data fusion approach of combining pieces of attack evidence gathered by sensors assists to:

◆ reduce noise in security evidence gathered.

◆ eliminate inconsistencies in evidence, and therefore lowers the percentages of false positives and false negatives produced.

◆ accurately detect a wide variety of attacks, which are not possible with a single sensor or stand-alone countermeasure toolkit.

◆ accurately identify threats and attacks that would have gone undetected with most stand-alone independent toolkits.

Finally, techniques employed in the analysis such as graph, graph matching and multisensor data fusion assist security administrators to provide accurate detection of attacks, and consequently, security administrators are able to recommend effective responses to mitigate perceived attacks.

9.4 The application of multisource data fusion

Research on the application of data fusion to information security has attracted lots of attention recently, because of its relevance in solving real life problems. For instance, in alert correlation, current initiatives now employ multisource fusion techniques to accurately detect security attacks. They function on the premise that evidence from multiple sources combined to detect attacks provide better understanding of the attacks than a single sensor. According to Haines et al. [186], "previous results indicate that no single IDS can detect all cyber attacks. IDS research continues, but researchers have now turned their attention to higher-level correlation systems to gather and combine evidence from many *different* intrusion detection systems, and to make use of this broader evidence base for better attack detection". Among notable contributions, the following are relevant to this research.

Siraj and Vaughan [180] described an alert correlation technique using fuzzy cognitive modeling (FCM). FCM correlates multisensor alerts be describing causal relationships in alert data.

Haines et al. [186] used multiple correlators that combine pieces of evidence from various sensors to detect specific attacks and to identify attack targets. They argued that multi-sensor correlation focuses on taking diverse information from at least two sensors and combining it to form an integrated picture of an attacker's activity. This is important to an analyst because it improves and substantiates the accuracy of hypotheses regarding attacks. Tim Bass [177] argues that the future of next generation cyberspace intrusion detection systems depends on the fusion of data from myriad heterogeneous distributed network agents to effectively create cyberspace situational awareness.

Siaterlis and Maglaris [82] employed multiple sensors in detecting and mitigating denial of service attacks. Denial of service attacks are a type of attack that impacts the availability of computer networks. It clogs up systems and network resources leading to performance bottlenecks, such that computing resources become unavailable, or perform at unacceptable levels.

Yan et al. [156] demonstrated the application of multisource data fusion to oil monitoring, where multiple low-level oil monitors were used to detect defects, faults and failures in oil plants.

Finally, Hall and McMullen [109] illustrated various solutions of multi-sensor fusion in detecting military attacks, and warfare tracking for national security and defence intelligence.

9.5 Multisource data fusion techniques

To combine evidence from different sources in a data fusion, numerous techniques have been suggested in the literature, such as traditional probability theorem, averaging, Bayesian probability, fuzzy logic, rough sets, genetic algorithm, neural network and the Dempster-Shafer theory of evidence. These techniques are valuable in combining evidence from different sources and in making inferences that are plausible and beyond a single source perspective. In this research, the Dempster-Shafer theory of evidence was used to analyse security evidence gathered by sensors because of its relevance to the problem domain being resolved, as demonstrated in section 10.7. However, Bayesian theory and Bayesian inference are also discussed.

9.5.1 Dempster-Shafer theory of evidence

The Dempster-Shafer theory of evidence (D-S) was first introduced in 1976 by Glenn Shafer [152], as an extension of Arthur Dempster's probabilities [196] on multi-valued mapping. Since then, D-S has been applied to military applications such as automatic target recognition and battlefield situation analysis [109], and other areas, such as security monitoring, data fusion [82] and medical diagnosis [154].

The underlying principle behind D-S is the concept of a *belief function* as an adequate representation of ones degrees of belief, and the notions of doubt and plausibility, which are use to reason about and compute inconsistency in evidence, and to support belief in the quality of the evidence. D-S can combine a diverse variety of independent evidence through its rule of combination.

The rule of combination is a numerical procedure for combining independent pieces of evidence. Hence, Dempster's rule of combination is used to aggregate multiple sources of independent evidence to obtain a higher level of abstraction that is more accurate and reliable than that offered by a single source.

9.5.2 Bayesian theory

Bayesian theory is a statistical inference method based on traditional probability theorem. It was first introduced by the Reverend Thomas Bayes in 1763 [191], and since then Bayesian research has spawn many areas, such as Bayesian inference, Bayesian theorem, Bayesian networks, and used in diversified areas, such as medical diagnosis, belief networks, statistics and computer science. Bayesian theory relies on Bayesian inference. Bayesian inference uses numerical estimation to calculate belief, probability or score to determine the likelihood of a hypothesis, given a previous likelihood estimate and additional evidence (observation).

The Bayesian inference computes probabilities based on Bayesian theorem:

$$P(H \mid E) = \frac{P(E \mid H) P(H)}{P(E)} \tag{9.1}$$

Where:

◆ H represents a specific hypothesis or proposition.

◆ $P(H)$ is the prior probability of hypothesis H being true without having observed the evidence.

◆ $P(E \mid H)$ is the conditional probability of observing the evidence E, given that the hypothesis H is true. It is also called the *likelihood function* when it is considered as a function of H for fixed evidence E [182].

◆ $P(E)$ is the marginal probability of the evidence. That is the a prior probability of observing the evidence E under all circumstances (conditions) or hypothesis H.

◆ $P(H \mid E)$ is the posterior probability of the hypothesis H given evidence E.

9.6 Dempster-Shafer, Bayesian theory, traditional probability and other data fusion techniques

To analyse attack evidence gathered by myriad heterogeneous sensors deployed in the network, a data fusion analysis technique is required. It is always very difficult when making a selection of which technique to used over the other. A rule of thumb is to evaluate the problem domain and decide which technique is most appropriate. Sometimes it may require couple of techniques combined to analyse the evidence. However, it is very important that an unbiased technique is selected, irrespective of the area of expertise of the person implementing the framework. Hence, a thorough analysis of techniques used in data fusion to correlate, combine and aggregate pieces of evidence that are often incomplete, inconsistent, and contradictory (which is the case with evidence of network attacks gathered by sensors), are evaluated. And here are the reasons why the Dempster-Shafer theory of evidence is chosen as a correlation technique to analyse pieces of evidence gathered by security sensors used to monitor networks.

◆ Evidence of attacks gathered by sensors are indicative (*symptomatic*), such as high CPU usage, access-list violation or deviation in normal network utilisation. Because network changes possess a level of uncertainty, they are not sufficient to prove that a network is under attack. Because network activities are often abrupt, it is difficult to predict or determine prior incidents. For this reason, techniques that require "*a priori*" probabilities such as Bayesian networks were ignored.

◆ Evidence gathered by sensors often varies from one sensor to another, such that it can be contradictory at times, as shown in Row 13 of Table 10.3. To combine such pieces of evidence, physical techniques, such as the *Kalman filter* that requires knowledge of the state transition matrix [82] were not selected. The Kalman filter is an efficient recursive technique that estimates the state of a dynamic system from a series of incomplete and noisy measurements, developed by Rudolf Kalman [185]. The Kalman filter requires prior knowledge of the state transition matrix which makes it inappropriate for application in the problem domain under consideration.

◆ Techniques that require training of data, such as neural networks, were avoided because they are hard to obtain and time consuming to construct [82]. As a rough working guideline, techniques were chosen that are robust and fairly straightforward to implement, as against techniques that required rigorous setup time or training of data. Training of data requires down-time to first train the data and establish baselines (profiles). Although down-time is an issue, the main problem is that baselines change with new provisioning and

160

addition of new services. Consequently, data training techniques require re-training to establish new baselines.

♦ The deployment background is a security monitoring environment, where the expertise of the security administrators is important, and combined with sensor evidence to detect specific attacks. The objective here is to develop an *assistance framework* that takes advantage of a security administrator's expertise in analyzing threats and attacks. In this respect, fully automating responses was not necessary as it may significantly complicate the behaviour of the system.

♦ Evidence is not associated with only one possible event, but rather associated with multiple possible events; thus traditional probability theory that relies on the probability of one possible event was excluded.

♦ Bayesian theory cannot distinguish between lack of *belief* or *disbelief*, and thus, does not allow one to withhold belief from a proposition without assigning that belief to be a negation of the proposition [152]. That is, Bayesian theory computes the probability of a proposition (hypothesis), but D-S computes the probability that the evidence supports a proposition (hypothesis). So using Bayesian theory to fuse evidence from multiple sensors, as in this case, is not appropriate.

It is recognised that some techniques require rigorous setup time and training of data, such techniques are essential and useful for individual sensor implementation. However, this research is not aimed at individual sensors implementation, therefore, advantage was taken of the intelligence embedded in the individual sensors to gather evidence of specific attacks.

A significant achievement in this research is the use of a data fusion algorithm to develop an attack analysis mechanism that combines several pieces of attack evidence gathered by sensors under a clear mathematical framework using the Dempster-Shafer theory of evidence.

9.7 Mathematical formalism of the Dempster-Shafer theory of evidence

D-S is a mathematical technique for representing epistemic plausibility beyond subjective probability. This means that D-S goes beyond traditional probabilities by asserting belief in the quality of evidence it provides. It also supports its belief in evidence by demonstrating how plausible its stated belief is.

Let Θ be the *universal set*, often called the *frame of discernment*, assume the possible network states $A_1, A_2, \cdots, A_n \in \Theta$, are mutually exclusive and exhaustive (complete). The power set 2^Θ is the set of all possible subsets, including the empty set ϕ and the universal set Θ.

9.7.1 Basic probability assignments (bpa)

A *basic probability assignment (bpa)* is defined as a mass function m, which assigns beliefs in a hypothesis. Thus,

$$m \; : \; 2^\Theta \to [0,1] \tag{9.2}$$

Where $m(\phi) = 0$, and A a subset of Θ, that is, $A \subseteq \Theta$ such that $\sum_{A \subseteq \Theta} m(A) = 1$. The quantity $m(A)$ is defined as $A's$ *basic probability number*. It represents the strength of evidence of A. A is a hypothesis about the state of the network. That is, if the network is under attack, and if so, the nature of the attack. The value of the *bpa* for a given hypothesis A (represented as $m(A)$), expresses the proportion of all the relevant and available evidence that supports the claim in A, but not of particular subsets of A.

9.7.2 Belief function (Bel)

The belief $Bel(A)$ in a hypothesis A is defined as the sum of all the basic probability assignments (masses) of the proper subsets of the hypothesis A in the frame of discernment. Thus, $Bel(A)$ is given by

$$Bel(A) = \sum_{B \subseteq A} m(B) \tag{9.3}$$

$Bel(A)$ represents the exact belief in the proposition (hypothesis) represented by A, satisfying the following conditions.

◆ $Bel(\phi) = 0$, and $Bel(\Theta) = 1$

According to Xu et al. [121] a special case of belief arises when the basic probability assignment is same as the belief, this occurs when the following conditions are satisfied:

◆ When $A = A_i$ is a singleton, then $Bel(A) = Bel(A_i) = m(A_i)$.

◆ When $A = \Theta$, $Bel(\Theta) = 1$.

However, a collection of hypotheses, $A_1, A_2, \cdots, A_n$ subsets of Θ, is given as:

$$Bel\,(A_1 \cup \cdots \cup A_n) \geq \sum_{I \subseteq \{1,\cdots n\}, I \neq \phi} (-1)^{|I|+1}\, Bel\,(\cap_{i \in I} A_j) \tag{9.4}$$

According to O'Neill [155] equation 9.4 is the collective belief defined across a set of hypotheses in the same frame of discernment (Θ).

A belief function assigns to each subset of Θ a measure of the total belief in the hypothesis represented by the subset. Thus, a belief function is defined on the same *frame of discernment*, but is based on *independent* sources of evidence. The issue of independence is very significant when combining pieces of evidence with the D-S theory of evidence, because Dempster's rule of combination is a numerical procedure for combining beliefs acquired by *independent sources*. In the experiments conducted in this book, sensors distributed across the network to gather evidence of an attack do so independently. Sensors observe traffic and make their own independent judgment about the state of the network, and the type of attack perceived in the network. It is pertinent to note that sensors make their judgments about attacks independently, hence their beliefs about an attack are independent and mutually exclusive. In this respect, the D-S rule of combination becomes a naturalistic procedure for combining pieces of evidence gathered by sensors.

9.7.3 Plausibility (Pl) and doubt (Dou)

The *plausibility of a hypothesis* $A \subseteq \Theta$, is given as $Pl(A)$, such that,

$$Pl(A) = \sum_{B \cap A \neq \phi} m(B) \tag{9.5}$$

Thus, the *plausibility* $Pl(A)$ of a hypothesis A, is the assurance that the belief represented by the hypothesis A is possible based on the credibility of the evidence provided in favour of the hypothesis. The doubt in a hypothesis A, is given as $Dou(A)$, such that,

$$Dou(A) = Bel(A^c) \tag{9.6}$$

Plausibility is related to *doubt* and *belief* as follows:

$$Pl(A) = 1 - Dou(A) = 1 - Bel(A^c) \tag{9.7}$$

From equation 9.7, plausibility represents the lower bound of the belief that the proposition represented by A could possibly happen. Where:

◆ A^c is the hypothesis (not A).

◆ $Pl(A)$ is the plausibility of a hypothesis A based on available evidence.

◆ $Dou(A)$ is the doubt in the hypothesis A based on available evidence.

From equation 9.7, it is deduced that the less *doubt* in evidence, the more *plausible* the evidence. Thus, suppose, there is a 0.1% doubt in the evidence represented by A, it means that there is a 99.9% assurance (plausibility) that the exact belief in the evidence represented by A is correct. This implies that the true belief in A lies in the interval $[Bel(A), Pl(A)]$. That is, the amount of belief that directly supports a hypothesis at least in part, forms an upper bound. The degree of ignorance can be represented as $|Bel(A) - Pl(A)|$, that is, the difference between the belief in support of the evidence and the exact possibility that the belief is true.

It is important to note that the aim here is to detect attacks perceive on the entire network based on pieces of evidence $E_1, E_2, \cdots, E_n$ gathered and reported by sensors without having an explicit model of the system. In this case, an approach is needed to combine evidence $E_1, E_2, \cdots, E_n$ obtained by these sensors. Then D-S *rule of combination* for independent evidence becomes appealing.

9.7.4 D-S rule of combination

Dempster's rule of combination is a numerical procedure that is used to combine *independent* pieces of evidence or data. The purpose of aggregating pieces of evidence is to meaningfully summarise and simplify a corpus of data whether the data is coming from a single source or multiple sources [154]. Supposing m_1 and m_2 are basic probability assignments on the same frame of discernment Θ, the joint mass m of m_1 and m_2 is defined as:

$$m = m_1 \oplus m_2 \tag{9.8}$$

Where:

◆ $A \subseteq \Theta$, $B \subseteq \Theta$, $C \subseteq \Theta$ are any subsets.

◆ $m(\phi) = 0$, (ϕ denotes the empty set).

◆ $m(A) = \begin{cases} 0 & if\ A = \phi \\ \frac{1}{1-K} \sum_{B \cap C = A} m_1(B)m_2(C) & otherwise \end{cases}$

◆ $K = \sum_{B \cap C = \phi} m_1(B)m_2(C)$

K is a measure of the amount of conflict between the two mass sets. The function m is a basic probability assignment if $K^{-1} \neq 0$. *If* $K^{-1} = 0$, then, $m_1 \oplus m_2$ does not exist. Hence, m_1 and m_2 are said to be totally contradictory. K represents the basic probability mass associated with conflict [161]. $(1 - K)$ is a *normalisation factor*. It has the effect of completely ignoring conflict and attributing any probability mass associated with conflict to the null set (ϕ) [161].

To combine more than two masses we have:

$$m = m_1 \oplus \cdots \oplus m_k \tag{9.9}$$

Where:

◆ $m(\phi) = 0$,

◆ $A = \{A_i \,|\, i = 1, \cdots n\}$, if n=1, then $A = A_i$ is a singleton set.

- $B = \{B_i \,|\, i = 1, \cdots n\}$
- $C = \{C_i \,|\, i = 1, \cdots n\}$

$$m^k(A) = \frac{\sum\limits_{i,j;B_i \cap C_j = A} m_k(B_i) m_k(C_j)}{1 - \sum\limits_{i,j;B_i \cap C_j = \phi} m_k(B_i) m_k(C_j)} \qquad (9.10)$$

Note that Equation 9.9 is referred to as Dempster's rule of combination, and Equation 9.10 is Dempster's orthogonal sum. The later can be re-written as:

$$m(A) = K \sum_{\cap A_i = A} \prod_{1 \leq i \leq n} m_i(A_i) \qquad (9.11)$$

Thus:

$$K^{-1} = 1 - \sum_{\cap A_i = \phi} \prod_{1 \leq i \leq n} m_i(A_i) = \sum_{\cap A_i \neq \phi} \prod_{1 \leq i \leq n} m_i(A_i) \qquad (9.12)$$

Based on the *rule of combination*, as shown in Equations 9.11 and 9.12, evidence can be combined from sensors to deduce the level of attacks perceived on the entire network. This technique (Dempster-Shafer) makes a distinction between *uncertainty* and *ignorance* as is seen from Equations 9.6 and 9.7. Significantly though, it does not require *a priori* knowledge or *prior probability* distributions of the possible network states like the Bayesian approach.

Supposing the hypothesis A supported by each sensor is respectively $m_1(A)$, $m_2(A)$, ... $m_n(A)$, and the hypothesis A refuted by each sensor is respectively $m_1(\theta)$, $m_2(\theta)$, ... $m_n(\theta)$; where: θ is the hypothesis (*not* H), then:

$$\begin{aligned}
m_1(\theta) &= 1 - m_1(A) \\
m_2(\theta) &= 1 - m_2(A) \\
&\vdots \\
m_n(\theta) &= 1 - m_n(A)
\end{aligned} \qquad (9.13)$$

According to Beynon et al. [157] Equation 9.10 is given as:

$$m^k(A) = \frac{\sum\limits_{i,j;A_i \cap B_j = C} m^{k-1}(A_i) m_k(B_j)}{1 - \sum\limits_{i,j;A_i \cap B_j = \phi} m^{k-1}(A_i) m_k(B_j)}$$

$$= \tfrac{1}{1-\theta} \left[m^{k-1}(A) m_k(A) + m^{k-1}(A) m_k(\theta) + m^{k-1}(\theta) m_k(A) \right]$$

$$= m^{k-1}(A) + m^{k-1}(\theta) m_k(A)$$

$$= 1 - \prod_{i-1}^{k-1} m_i(\theta) + [1 - m_k(\theta)] \prod_{i-1}^{k-1} m_i(\theta)$$

$$m^k(A) = 1 - \prod_{i-1}^{k} m_i(\theta) \qquad (9.14)$$

Equation 9.14, is a generalised D-S rule of combination for k masses.

9.8 Summary

Multisource data fusion is used to analyse pieces of attack evidence gathered by myriad heterogeneous sources distributed across the enterprise.

It is evident that the use of a single sensor, for example, intrusion detection system, may not be sufficient in detecting a wide variety of emerging attacks launched in enterprise networks in the 21st century. A fundamental problem with this approach is that there is no single sensor or source that can detect all cyberspace attacks. Therefore, a step forward is to combine multiple heterogeneous sources in monitoring the network, for example, IDSes, firewalls, anti-viral systems, anti-malware systems, audit analysis systems etc. However, gathering attack evidence produced by these sources is one thing, the other is correlating and aggregating these pieces of attack evidence in order to make very high inferences that are reasonable, accurate, reliable and plausible.

In this respect, independent and cooperating *sensors* are deployed to detect specific attacks perceived on the network, and to evaluate the overall level of attacks identified in the entire network. To assist with the detection of attacks perceived in the entire network, *the Dempster-Shafer theory of evidence* was used to collectively aggregate pieces of evidence gathered by multiple heterogeneous sources, such as IDSes, firewalls, and anti-virus systems, about attacks, in order to determine beliefs about possible attacks, and to aggregate multiple sources of evidence to obtain a higher level of abstraction that is more accurate and reliable than that offered by a single source.

The decision why D-S is the most suitable technique for solving the problem under consideration was discussed. One way this was established, was by comparing D-S with other contending techniques, such as *traditional probability theory, Bayesian probabilities, and a Kalman filter* to show that D-S is the most appropriate technique for solving the defined problem. The crucial factors are that D-S is able to work on incomplete evidence, able to work on inconsistent evidence, and similarly, able to work on contradictory evidence, which is typical of network events and also, very often the case with evidence gathered by sensors. Finally, it was shown that D-S can be used to detect specific attacks perceived on the network by combining independent evidence from sensors using the D-S rule of combination.

Chapter 10

Experimentation

This chapter provides detailed discussion pertaining to the experiments conducted to validate the hypotheses of this research. The chapter demonstrates how security attacks were detected, and techniques employed to assist in detecting cyber attacks in a testbed network. In the next chapter, a conclusion to the work is provided.

10.1   Introduction

The experimentation was conducted using a testbed, for the purpose of collecting data to validate the research objectives. The research objectives validated were:

◆ to distribute host and network-based sensors across the testbed network to gather evidence of security attacks in real-time.

◆ to provide near real-time analysis of attack evidence communicated by sensors, by correlating and combining pieces of evidence from sensors, to obtain stronger belief in the evidence gathered about attacks.

◆ to provide visual representation of attack evidence perceived. The visual representation assists security administrators to visually inspect, identify and detect attacks, and consequently, able to mitigate the attacks.

10.2   Overview of the testbed

The testbed setup is simple, since the purpose is to investigate a proof-of-concept. In the testbed network, various sensors were placed on the network to monitor live Internet traffic, capturing both normal background traffic and attack data. Seven sensors were deployed in total in the network, together with an OSSIM monitoring server, as shown in Figure 10.1.

The testbed network was used to monitor various attacks that were conducted on the network. These include network worms, network scan, stealthy scans and policy violation attacks.

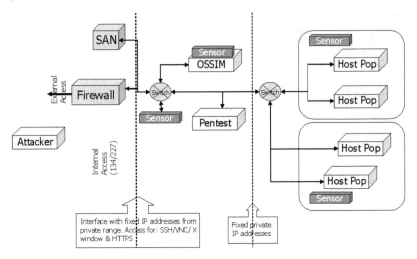

Figure 10.1: Testbed network for the experiment

Figure 10.1 shows the isolated testbed network used to gather both normal and attack data. Two systems (inside and outside) are setup to launch both manual and automated attacks on the monitored infrastructure. The system in the inside is labelled *pentest* (for penetration testing), while the outside is labelled *attacker*. Network exploration, hacking and file transfer tools, such as NMAP, NESSUS, FTP, and Telnet, were installed on both the pentest and attacker hosts. The pentest and attacker hosts were used to launch attacks for the experiment.

The fundamental reasons for selecting these attacks to be detected are as follows:

◆ existing attacks still cause significant harm to organisations leading to consequential financial losses.

◆ the ISAF framework proposed in this research is able to detect existing attacks that most stand-alone defence systems are able to detect.

◆ the ISAF framework is able to detect emerging attacks, which most stand-alone defence systems struggle to detect.

For example, network scans are precursors to attacks. They are predominantly used for information gathering prior to an attack. Most successful attacks start with reconnaissance. Network scans are a typical example of reconnaissance type threat, aimed at gathering information about a target (computer, network or service) for the purpose of using the information gathered to attack the target. Examples of network scans include: *port scan, host scan, vulnerability scan* and *distributed port scan.* According to Gates [86], "the success of an attack has a high correlation with the thoroughness of the reconnaissance". Scans are not necessarily harmful in themselves, but well crafted scans can go undetected, leading to attacks causing significant harm to computer networks, and consequently leading to financial losses to organisations. Panjwani et al. [162] claim that approximately 50% of attacks are preceded by some form of scanning activity, particularly vulnerability scanning. Similarly, *worms* are self-replicating, self-propagating malicious logic that are deliberately crafted to exploit known and specific vulnerabilities in certain applications. Worms are used as attack vectors for denial of service (DoS) and distributed denial of service (DDoS) attacks [10]. They cause harm to computer networks leading to significant financial losses. For example, *Code Red II (in 2001), Slammer (in 2003), MSBlast (in 2003)* and *Sasser (in 2004)* all caused significant financial losses to organisations.

We argue that an approach that demonstrates the capability to detect both existing and emerging security attacks is clearly a significant achievement.

10.3   Sensor selection

Sensors used in this experiment are independent, collaborating, and able to monitor network changes in real time. Sensor selection was driven by the need to *passively monitor network changes in real time.* Although network changes can be as a result of *slight deviation in normal behaviour, failed services/resource requests, attacks or a combination of these*; every indicator captured should be analysed. However, this can be time consuming, but the trade-off is in building a system that is very responsive and sensitive, as opposed to a system that misses obfuscated, crafted or motivated attacks due to selective monitoring. Note that analysing every indicator captured may not be feasible in most environments. There are varying constraints to this approach such as, storage capability for processing, retention or archiving data that results from monitoring and analysing events. The overall performance of the system may suffer (or deteriorate) because of the significant amount of data needed to be monitored, analysed and logged, so this approach of monitoring and analysing every indicator captured may not be suitable in every environment. In a small network, like the testbed network described in this research, it will be appropriate to analyse every indicator captured. However, in enterprise networks, selective (custom or bespoke) monitoring and analysis may be most appropriate.

The seven sensors carefully selected to gather security evidence about attacks are: SNORT, PADS, POF, NTOP, SPADE, ARPWATCH and TCPTRACK. It is important to note that, in a data fusion system, the use of two sensors is adequate to create statistics and make reliable inferences. However, the use of a good mix of sensors provides richer, stronger and more dispersed evidence for analysis, hence the need to deploy more than two heterogeneous sensors. The collection of sources used in this experiment are anomaly-based sensors such as SPADE and NTOP, signature-based sensors such as, SNORT, and low-level specialised monitors such as POF, ARPWATCH and TCPTRACK, and finally, an asset detection monitor such as PADS. The reason for choosing seven sensors is to be able to detect a wide variety of attacks based on the evidence provided by each sensor. The absolute number of sensors used (for example, six, seven or eight) is not important. What is important is that a good mix of sensors are used to gather attack evidence.

SNORT [127]: a lightweight open source network intrusion detection and prevention system utilising a rule driven language, which combines the benefits of signature, protocol and anomaly based inspection methods. It has the capability to combine different pre-processors for different types of intrusions, making SNORT adaptive, scalable, and robust. It is the most widely deployed open-source intrusion detection system in the industry.

PADS [147]: The passive asset detection system is a lightweight signature-based detection sensor, use to passively detect network assets. It is designed to complement IDSes by providing context to IDS alerts. It listens to a network and attempts to provide up-to-date statistics on hosts and services running on the network. In this experiment, PADS was used to identify assets in the network, and to detect threats or attacks targeting these assets.

POF [146]: The passive operating system fingerprint is a sensor that passively interrogates a remote system seeking connection to a website or corporate LAN, to determine the remote hosts operating systems, and implementation flaws that, although harmless, make certain systems quite unique. POF is use for collating evidence of OS profiling, penetration testing and for profiling information about external hosts seeking connections to the network.

NTOP [165]: a network sensor that detects network usage based on the *libpcap*, which enables traffic information to be analysed, and persistently stored in RRD format. NTOP assists in passively identifying host operating systems, anomalous network traffic based on overall network statistics, analysing IP traffic and sorting it according to source, destination and protocols, such as TCP, UDP, and DNS. It acts as a *netflow* or 'sFlow' collector for flows generated by switches or routers, for example, Cisco or Juniper routers and switches. NTOP produces RMON-like network traffic statistics, useful in evaluating anomalous traffic influx. Note: libpcap is a system-independent interface for user-level packet capture that provides a portable framework for low-level network monitoring, such as tcpdump. sFlow (switched flow or sampled flow) is a technique for monitoring traffic in data networks containing switches and routers [131].

SPADE [158]: The statistical packet anomaly detection engine is a SNORT IDS pre-processor plug-in, which is installed and enabled for detecting anomalous traffic. SPADE uses joint probability measurements to decide which packets are anomalous. SPADE has two kinds of components: an *anomaly sensor* and a *correlator*. The *anomaly sensor* captures packets (traffic) which are put in SNORT tables, and used to determine an anomalous score. The anomalous score is assigned by evaluating four traffic parameters: source IP, source port, destination IP, and destination port [181]. The *correlator* combines anomalous scores to determine which packet has the highest score.

ARPWATCH [149]: a sensor that monitors Ethernet activity, and maintains a 'flow' of ethernet to IP address pairings. It is useful in determining address spoofing and IP address changes to a MAC, and therefore helps to forge insider attacks that constantly change IP addresses in other to establish unlawful trust relationships.

TCPTRACK [150]: The transmission control protocol tracker - is a sensor that passively watches for connections on the network interface, keeps track of their state and displays a list of connections. TCPTRACK captures connection information such as source and destination addresses and ports, connection state, idle time, and bandwidth usage.

Note that sensors deployed in this research are *open source software agents*. This encourages researchers and practitioners to develop, extend and implement their variants, leveraging on the availability of their source codes.

In the experiments, the above-named security sensors were used to capture evidence about attacks perceived on the monitored LAN. Powerful and expressive analysis techniques were employed (discussed in Chapters 8 and 9) to analyse pieces of evidence collated by the sensors. Pieces of evidence about attacks obtained from each sensor were used in making inferences about the nature of the attack, and combined to provide better understanding of perceived attacks. To obtain insight in perceived attacks, pieces of evidence gathered were correlated based on a well-proven mathematical formalism - the Dempster-Shafer theory of evidence (discussed in Chapter 9).

10.4 Sensor placement

In the experiment, sensors were placed on network ingress points, and on individual hosts. It is most recommended to place sensors at strategic ingress points in the network, especially, at points where organisations interconnect with external organisation, such as points of interconnection with an ISP, or behind private peering points. However, for enterprises, sensors are recommended to be placed at both ingress and egress network points. For example, points of interconnection with partner organisations, ISPs, and large departments. Ingress is for inbound traffic, while egress is for outbound traffic.

10.5 Datasets

A dataset comprising of normal background data and attack data were captured using the testbed network, as described in section 10.3. Attack data were obtained through *normal* and *generated* attacks.

Generated attack data were obtained by launching specific attacks on the monitored LAN. Normal attack data were obtained by monitoring Internet traffic that were not specific attacks that were carried out during the experiments. Specific attacks launched were useful in evaluating sensor detection capabilities, and to characterise sensors. For example, SNORT pre-processors were enabled for portscan, stealthy network scans, policy violation, web and worm attacks.

The testbed provides an opportunity to obtain datasets that are natural, unbiased and that characterise real Internet behaviour. In contrast with simulated datasets, it is shown that simulated datasets obtained from a controlled environment do not often represent true network behaviours, and therefore produce datasets that do not closely reflect the reality of real Internet traffic [167].

The first large-scale datasets for evaluating intrusion detection systems were the DARPA datasets from MIT's Lincoln Laboratory [169] obtained in 1998, and further enriched in 1999. DARPA's datasets comprised both *simulated data* and real *background data*. According to McHugh [167] a major concern with the DARPA's datasets are that they do not reflect the reality of real life traffic. However, it is still argued by researchers that DARPA's dataset is still ideal for evaluating first-order IDS performance as a baseline [168]. DARPA's evaluation dataset is not discredited, but with concerns surrounding the dataset, it was thought wiser to use other datasets obtained through security monitoring of Internet traffic using a live testbed network, which does not contain simulated data.

10.6 Security log parser

To enable selected sensors to direct their evidence to a centralised database was challenging. Each sensor reports security events in different formats, for example, SNORT event format is different from ARPWATCH's event format. To direct logs from different sensors to a centralised database, a log parser was defined for each sensor.

With the log parser each sensor log is converted into a consistent format that is written to database table for persistent storage. To identify which sensor reported a given security event, (as discussed in section 7.6), a *unique identifier* is assigned to each sensor. This *unique identifier* is referred to as a *sensor id*. First, an identifier was assigned to each sensor. Second, a *log directory* was defined where events were forwarded, for example, the content of the environment variable *$LOGDIR*. Finally, an interface from where events were captured was specified. The interface information was necessary only if the monitoring system had at least a couple of network interfaces.

10.7 The application of the Dempster-Shafer theory of evidence to analyse security attacks

Each security attack consists of individual attack steps, and each attack step yields one or more corresponding sensor alerts. Based on the notion that each attack step is an observable event, sensor evidence was gathered that characterised attacks conducted. For example, when NMAP was used to launch a 'portscan attack', the SNORT flow portscan pre-processor sensed the attack, and reported a "(portscan) TCP Portscan" alert. Similarly, for the same attack, SPADE sensed and logged a "Closed dest port used" alert. NTOP sensed a "rrd_threshold: ntop host totCon-tactedRcvdPeers" alert. Note that four of the sensors used in this experiment had well-defined signatures for each attacks launched. With SNORT, its pre-processors were enabled for each attack launched on the network. Similarly, SPADE, NTOP and TCPTRACK have their different interpretations of each attack launched. Sensor outputs of attack characteristics were translated, as shown in Table 10.1. For example, a "(portscan) TCP Portscan" signature, was translated to "Abnormal in flow-portscan threshold". This is because the signature was detected by the flow-portscan pre-processor in SNORT.

The translation was done to provide an exact understanding of the attacks launched, and to deduce sensor interpretations of these attacks. Adding context into attack signatures was particularly important for interpreting or inferring meaning from the attack signatures detected.

Table 10.1: Translated attack evidence gathered by sensors

No.	Sensors	Scans	Worm	Policy Violation	Stealthy Scans	Web Attacks
1	SNORT	Abnormal in number of peer to peer contacts	Abnormal in number of peer to peer contacts		Abnormal in number of peer to peer contacts	Abnormal in number of peer to peer contacts
	SNORT Tag		Abnormal in rpc applications (ftp, chart, pcanywhere, vncserver)	Abnormal in rpc applications (ftp, chart, pcanywhere, vncserver)	Abnormal in sliding window factor, and increase in TCP, RST or ICMP un-reacheables	Abnormal in common commands used to exploit form variable vulnerabilities (ps, wget, tftp, python access attempt, httpd)
	Spp Portscan	Abnormal in flow-portscan threshold			Abnormal in flow-portscan threshold	
2	PADS	High service requests	Abnormal service requests for specific ports	Policy VNC server response	High service requests	High service requests
3	POF			High remote connections		High remote connections

Table 10.1: Translated attack evidence gathered by sensors						
4	NTOP	High peer to peer contact	Increase in anomalous network traffic for specific ports		High peer to peer contact; and High ntop host tot-Contacte-dRcvdPeers	High peer to peer contact
5	SPADE	Deviation in preset peer contact score; and Non-live dest used	Anomalous score, and Possible evasive RST detected	Abnormal Web activity detected	Non-live dest used; and Closed dest port used	Abnormal Web activity detected

Table 10.1 shows sensor interpretations of attack characteristics obtained by adding context, specifically for the attacks that were conducted, namely, *network scans, network worm, policy violation, stealthy scans* and *web attacks*. (Note that where no information is provided in the table, it means that that particular sensor provided no evidence about the attack.)

The Dempster-Shafer technique was used to correlate and combine sensor evidence (shown in Table 10.1) into evidence with a higher level of accuracy and greater reliability in detecting specific attacks launched on the monitored LAN. Thus, the goal of applying D-S in this experiment is to combine and analyse pieces of evidence from sensors about attacks. First, pieces of evidence about attacks from sensors were gathered, as shown in Table 10.1. Second, basic probability assignment (bpa) was generated for evidence gathered, as shown in Table 10.2. Third, beliefs in evidence gathered were combined using the D-S combination rule, as shown in Table 10.3.

As discussed in section 9.6, it is pertinent to compute basic probability assignment when using the D-S technique. The basic probability assignments for each sensor for a set of evidence leading to a hypothesis were acquired by training the sensors over a period of time in accurately classifying the attacks launched on the testbed LAN.

10.7.1 Basic probability assignment metrics

A conservative metric is used in generating basic probabilities as follows:

◆ A bpa of 0.5 is used when pieces of evidence match exactly to a known security attack.

◆ A bpa of 0.4 is used when pieces of evidence are strong but not exact match to a known attack.

◆ A bpa of 0.3 is used when pieces of evidence are less strongly matched to a known attack.

◆ A bpa of 0.2 is used when pieces of evidence are weakly matched to a known attack.

◆ A bpa of 0.1 is used for any intrusion as shown in Table 10.2.

A conservative metric was used in generating bpa's to evidence because of the inherent limitation that exists with sensors. Sensors are not able to identify every cyber attack, thus, their evidence possesses a degree of variance. Therefore assigning a high basic probability value above 0.5 to an evidence gathered by a sensor was deemed unrealistic.

No.	Evidence from Sensors	Scans	Worm	Policy Violation	Stealthy Scans	Web Attack
\[Table 10.2: Basic probability assignment based on sensor evidence about attacks\]						
1	Abnormal in flow-portscan threshold	0.3			0.3	
2	Abnormal in number of peer to peer contact	0.2	0.2		0.2	0.2
3	Abnormal in rpc applications (ftp, chart, pcanywhere, vncserver)		0.4	0.4		
4	Abnormal in sliding window factor, and increase in TCP, RST or ICMP unreacheables				0.5	
5	Abnormal in common commands used to exploit form variable vulnerabilities (ps, wget, tftp, python access attempt, httpd)					0.4

	Table 10.2: Basic probability assignment based on sensor evidence about attacks					
6	High service requests	0.1			0.1	0.1
7	Policy VNC server response			0.3		
8	Abnormal service requests for specific ports		0.3			
9	High remote connections			0.2		0.2
10	High peer to peer contact	0.2			0.2	0.2
11	Increase in anomalous network traffic for specific services (ports)		0.3			
12	High ntop host totContactedRcvdPeers				0.3	
13	Abnormal arp increase and withdrawals			0.2		
14	Deviation in preset peer contact score	0.2				
15	Anomalous score, possible evasive RST detected		0.2			
16	Abnormal web activity detected			0.3		0.3
17	Non-live dest used	0.2			0.2	
18	Abnormal increase in number of connections	0.2	0.2		0.2	0.2
19	Closed dest port used				0.4	

Table 10.2 shows the basic probability assignments (bpa) for each sensor to particular evidence leading to a hypothesis. For example, the bpa that a *network scan* occurred when a sensor produced an "abnormal in flow-portscan threshold" alert was assigned a mass of 0.3. This means that the measure of belief committed by the sensor in detecting a network scan exactly to a hypothesis - "abnormal in flow-portscan threshold" - was 0.3. Similarly, the bpa that a stealthy scan occurred when a sensor produced an "abnormal in sliding window factor, and an increase in TCP, RST or ICMP unreacheables" alerts was 0.5. Note that bpa assigns beliefs in a hypothesis. That is, the measure of belief that is committed exactly to a hypothesis. This is different from objective (aleatory) probability.

Another approach in obtaining bpa's for evidence is by the use of a simple linear sigmoid function. For example,

$$bpa = \int_0^1 f(x)dx$$

where $0 \le bpa \le 1$. The problem with this approach is that bpa's obtained using a sigmoid function are normally distributed (behave like the normal distribution curve) and based on some random occurrence instead of the accuracy of the evidence. It was decided not to use this approach (a linear sigmoid function) to compute basic probability assignments. This is because it would mean the assignment of basic probability values may not reflect the severity or correctness of the attack evidence described by each sensor, since they would be normally distributed. Instead, an empirical approach of using quantifiable metrics (described as basic probability assignment metrics, section 10.7.1) was adopted for obtaining bpa's based on the severity of attack evidence described by each sensor.

The Dempster-Shafer theory of evidence is able to analyse incomplete data in the face of uncertainties. This makes D-S appealing and appropriate when dealing with natural problems that often involve incomplete, complementary, and at time contradictory evidence. It is clearly evident from Table 10.2, that evidence obtained from sensors is incomplete, because the sum of each row is not equal to 1, that is: $\sum_{A \subseteq \Theta} m(A) \ne 1$. The missing evidence is for the hypothesis (*not A*), that is ($\neg A$), but since this evidence is not available, a basic probability could not be assigned to it. It is unlike traditional probabilities where the probability of the refuting hypothesis ($\neg A$) is $(1 - A)$. In Table 10.2, an empty cell meant that there was no evidence from a sensor for that particular attack, therefore, the basic probability assignment (mass) for that cell is zero. Hence, there was no committed belief in evidence.

Note that combined pieces of evidence from sensors were used to detect specific attacks perceived on the monitored LAN based on belief and plausibility values. In the same way, when new pieces of evidence become available as the network is being monitored, the combined belief of the system is updated to incorporated this new evidence.

10.7.2 Applying the D-S rule of combination

Using the D-S combination rule $m^k(A) = 1 - \prod_{i=1}^{k} m_i(\theta)$, according to the values in Table 10.2, evidence was combined to obtain a higher accuracy in identifying the attacks detected. For example, using *stealthy scans attack* to demonstrate the application of the D-S combination rule, from Table 10.2, the supporting bpa values computed by each sensor, SNORT, PADS, POF, NTOP, ARPWATCH, SPADE and TCPTRACK were presented. Using equation 9.14, that is: $m^k(A) = 1 - \prod_{i=1}^{k} m_i(\theta)$, where $k = 9$, and $1 \le i \le 9$, gives:

$$m_1(A) = 0.3; \quad m_1(\theta) = 0.7$$
$$m_2(A) = 0.2; \quad m_2(\theta) = 0.8$$
$$m_3(A) = 0.5; \quad m_3(\theta) = 0.5$$
$$m_4(A) = 0.1; \quad m_4(\theta) = 0.9$$
$$m_5(A) = 0.2; \quad m_5(\theta) = 0.8$$
$$m_6(A) = 0.3; \quad m_6(\theta) = 0.7$$
$$m_7(A) = 0.2; \quad m_7(\theta) = 0.8$$
$$m_8(A) = 0.2; \quad m_8(\theta) = 0.8$$
$$m_9(A) = 0.4; \quad m_9(\theta) = 0.6$$

$m^9(A) = 1 - \prod_{i=1}^{9} m_i(\theta) = 1 - 0.05419008 = 0.94580992$

This shows that by combining pieces of evidence from sensors (SNORT, PADS, POF, NTOP, ARPWATCH, SPADE and TCPTRACK) a 0.94580992 belief was obtained that a stealthy scan attack was conducted on the network.

Suppose one sensor's evidence listed in Table 10.2, is disregarded, then the combined belief obtained (using the combination rule) decreases. For example, suppose the belief in attack evidence from *TCPTRACK sensor* was ignored (that is, ignoring the last evidence, $m_9(A)$), then using the combination rule we have:

$$m^8(A) = 1 - 0.09031680 = 0.90968320$$

The computations above show that the more evidence collected, the higher the plausibility in detecting attacks targeting the enterprise. The combined belief of a collection of sensors in detecting security attacks targeting the enterprise is shown in Table 10.3. There were 128 possibilities (that is, by combination, $2^7 = 128$, since seven sensors were used). But no two identical sensors were combined (no duplication in sensor usage). Hence, the permutation reduced to 120 possibilities in the fusion system, as shown in Table 10.3.

To evaluate the reliability of the set of evidence gathered by sensors the Kth-value is calculated. K is a measure of conflict associated with evidence gathered by sensors. Recall that $K^{-1} = 1 - \sum_{\cap A_i = \phi} \prod_{1 \leq i \leq n} m_i(A_i) = \sum_{\cap A_i \neq \phi} \prod_{1 \leq i \leq n} m_i(A_i)$ as defined by equation 9.12 on page 165. Hence, using equation 9.12, and the values in Table 11.1 gives: K^{-1} = sum of ($\sum$Bel(network scan), $\sum$Bel(network worm), $\sum$Bel(Policy Violations), $\sum$Bel(Stealthy scans), $\sum$Bel(Web attack)). That is,

$$K^{-1} = (63.70196 + 71.04749 + 66.67296 + 85.59199 + 70.72141)$$

$$K^{-1} = 357.73581; \quad K = 0.00280$$

Since $K^{-1} \neq 0$, then pieces of evidence gathered by sensors are not contradictory.

After using D-S combination rule to computed beliefs of sensors about attacks, a higher degree of accuracy in the results of specific attacks perceived was obtained, compared to an inference based on a single sensor evidence, as shown in Table 10.3.

Table 10.3 shows the combined collection of sensors' beliefs about specific attacks, computed using the D-S combination rule. For example, combining seven sensors' beliefs, as shown on Row 120 of Table 10.3, gives a 79.4% belief that a *network scan attack* was detected, and 84.9% for a *worm attack*, 81.2% for a *policy violation attack*, 94.6% for a *stealthy scan*, and finally 84.5% for a *web attack*.

No.	Combined Sensor Belief (Evidence)	Scans	Network Worm	Policy Violation	Stealthy Scans	Web Attacks
1	SNORT; PADS	0.49600	0.664000	0.580000	0.748000	0.568000
2	SNORT; POF	0.440000	0.520000	0.520000	0.720000	0.61000
3	SNORT; NTOP	0.552000	0.664000	0.400000	0.843200	0.616000
4	SNORT; SPADE	0.641600	0.616000	0.580000	0.865600	0.664000
5	SNORT; ARPWATCH	0.440000	0.520000	0.520000	0.720000	0.520000
6	SNORT; TCPTRACK	0.552000	0.616000	0.400000	0.776000	0.616000
7	PADS; POF	0.100000	0.300000	0.440000	0.100000	0.280000
8	PADS; NTOP	0.280000	0.510000	0.300000	0.496000	0.280000
9	PADS; ARPWATCH	0.424000	0.440000	0.510000	0.568000	0.370000
10	PADS; ARPWATCH	0.100000	0.300000	0.440000	0.100000	0.10000
11	PADS; TCPTRACK	0.280000	0.440000	0.300000	0.280000	0.280000
12	POF; NTOP	0.200000	0.300000	0.200000	0.440000	0.360000
13	POF; ARPWATCH	0.000000	0.000000	0.360000	0.000000	0.200000
14	POF; SPADE	0.360000	0.200000	0.360000	0.520000	0.440000
15	POF; TCPTRACK	0.200000	0.200000	0.200000	0.200000	0.360000
16	NTOP; SPADE	0.488000	0.440000	0.300000	0.731200	0.440000
17	NTOP; ARPWATCH	0.200000	0.300000	0.200000	0.440000	0.200000
18	NTOP; TCPTRACK	0.36000	0.440000	0.000000	0.552000	0.360000
19	SPADE; ARPWATCH	0.360000	0.200000	0.440000	0.520000	0.300000
20	SPADE; TCPTRACK	0.488000	0.360000	0.300000	0.616000	0.440000
21	ARPWATCH; TCPTRACK	0.200000	0.200000	0.200000	0.200000	0.200000
22	SNORT; PADS; POF	0.496000	0.664000	0.664000	0.748000	0.654400
23	SNORT; PADS; NTOP	0.596800	0.764800	0.580000	0.858880	0.654400
24	SNORT; PADS; SPADE	0.677744	0.731200	0.706000	0.879040	0.697600
25	SNORT; PADS; ARPWATCH	0.496000	0.664000	0.664000	0.748000	0.568000

Table 10.3: Combined sensor beliefs about specific security attacks

	Table 10.3: Combined sensor beliefs about specific security attacks					
26	SNORT; PADS; TCPTRACK	0.596800	0.731200	0.580000	0.798400	0.654400
27	SNORT; POF; NTOP	0.552000	0.664000	0.520000	0.846200	0.692800
28	SNORT; POF; SPADE	0.641600	0.616000	0.664000	0.865600	0.731200
29	SNORT; POF; ARPWATCH	0.440000	0.520000	0.616000	0.720000	0.616000
30	SNORT; POF; TCPTRACK	0.552000	0.616000	0.520000	0.776000	0.692800
31	SNORT; NTOP; SPADE	0.713280	0.731200	0.580000	0.924736	0.731200
32	SNORT; NTOP; ARPWATCH	0.552000	0.664000	0.520000	0.843200	0.616000
33	SNORT; NTOP; TCPTRACK	0.641600	0.731200	0.400000	0.874560	0.692800
34	SNORT; SPADE; ARPWATCH	0.641600	0.616000	0.664000	0.865600	0.664000
35	SNORT; SPADE; TCPTRACK	0.713280	0.692800	0.580000	0.892480	0.731200
36	SNORT; ARPWATCH; TCPTRACK	0.552000	0.616000	0.520000	0.820800	0.616000
37	PADS; POF; NTOP	0.280000	0.510000	0.440000	0.496000	0.424000
38	PADS; POF; SPADE	0.424000	0.440000	0.608000	0.568000	0.496000
39	PADS; POF; ARPWATCH	0.100000	0.300000	0.552000	0.100000	0.280000
40	PADS; POF; TCPTRACK	0.280000	0.440000	0.440000	0.280000	0.424000
41	PADS; NTOP; SPADE	0.539200	0.608000	0.510000	0.654400	0.496000
42	PADS; NTOP; ARPWATCH	0.280000	0.510000	0.440000	0.280000	0.280000
43	PADS; NTOP; TCPTRACK	0.424000	0.608000	0.300000	0.424000	0.424000
44	PADS; SPADE; ARPWATCH	0.424000	0.440000	0.608000	0.568000	0.370000
45	PADS; SPADE; TCPTRACK	0.539200	0.552000	0.510000	0.654400	0.496000
46	PADS; ARPWATCH; TCPTRACK	0.280000	0.440000	0.300000	0.280000	0.280000
47	POF; NTOP; SPADE	0.488000	0.440000	0.440000	0.731200	0.552000
48	POF; NTOP; ARPWATCH	0.200000	0.300000	0.360000	0.440000	0.360000
49	POF; NTOP; TCPTRACK	0.360000	0.440000	0.200000	0.552000	0.488000
50	POF; SPADE; ARPWATCH	0.360000	0.200000	0.552000	0.520000	0.440000
51	POF; SPADE; TCPTRACK	0.488800	0.36000	0.440000	0.616000	0.552000
52	POF; ARPWATCH; TCPTRACK	0.200000	0.200000	0.360000	0.200000	0.360000
53	NTOP; SPADE; ARPWATCH	0.488000	0.440000	0.440000	0.731200	0.440000
54	NTOP; SPADE; ARPWATCH	0.590400	0.552000	0.300000	0.784960	0.552000
55	NTOP; SPADE; TCPTRACK	0.360000	0.440000	0.200000	0.440000	0.200000
56	SPADE; ARPWATCH; TCPTRACK	0.488000	0.360000	0.440000	0.616000	0.440000
57	SNORT; PADS; POF; NTOP	0.596800	0.764800	0.664000	0.858880	0.723520
58	SNORT; PADS; POF; SPADE	0.677440	0.731200	0.764800	0.879040	0.758080
59	SNORT; PADS; POF; ARPWATCH	0.496000	0.664000	0.731200	0.748000	0.654400
60	SNORT; PADS; POF; TCPTRACK	0.596800	0.731200	0.664000	0.798400	0.723520

	Table 10.3: Combined sensor beliefs about specific security attacks					
61	SNORT; PADS; NTOP; SPADE	0.741952	0.811840	0.706000	0.932262	0.758080
62	SNORT; PADS; NTOP; ARPWATCH	0.596800	0.764800	0.664000	0.858880	0.654400
63	SNORT; PADS; NTOP; TCPTRACK	0.677440	0.811840	0.580000	0.887104	0.723520
64	SNORT; PADS; SPADE; ARPWATCH	0.677440	0.731200	0.764800	0.879040	0.697600
65	SNORT; PADS; SPADE; TCPTRACK	0.741952	0.784960	0.706000	0.903232	0.758080
66	SNORT; PADS; ARPWATCH; TCPTRACK	0.596800	0.731200	0.664000	0.798400	0.654400
67	SNORT; POF; NTOP; SPADE	0.713280	0.731200	0.664000	0.924736	0.731200
68	SNORT; POF; NTOP; ARPWATCH	0.552000	0.664000	0.616000	0.843200	0.616000
69	SNORT; POF; NTOP; TCPTRACK	0.641600	0.731200	0.520000	0.874560	0.692800
70	SNORT; POF; SPADE; ARPWATCH	0.641600	0.616000	0.731200	0.865600	0.731200
71	SNORT; POF; SPADE; TCPTRACK	0.713280	0.692800	0.664000	0.892480	0.784960
72	SNORT; POF; ARPWATCH; TCPTRACK	0.641600	0.616000	0.616000	0.776000	0.692800
73	SNORT; NTOP; SPADE; ARPWATCH	0713280	0.731200	0.664000	0.924736	0.731200
74	SNORT; NTOP; SPADE; TCPTRACK	0.770624	0.784960	0.580000	0.939789	0.784960
75	SNORT; NTOP; ARPWATCH; TCPTRACK	0.641600	0.731200	0.520000	0.874560	0.692800
76	SNORT; SPADE; ARPWATCH; TCPTRACK	0.713280	0.692800	0.664000	0.892480	0.731200
77	PADS; POF; NTOP; SPADE	0.539200	0.608000	0.608000	0.806464	0.596800
78	PADS; POF; NTOP; ARPWATCH	0.280000	0.510000	0.552000	0.596800	0.424000
79	PADS; POF; NTOP; TCPTRACK	0.424000	0.608000	0.440000	0.677440	0.539200
80	PADS; POF; SPADE; ARPWATCH	0.424000	0.440000	0.686400	0.568000	0.496000
81	PADS; POF; SPADE; TCPTRACK	0.539200	0.552000	0.608000	0.654400	0.596800
82	PADS; POF; ARPWATCH; TCPTRACK	0.539200	0.608000	0.608000	0.758080	0.496000
83	PADS; NTOP; SPADE; ARPWATCH	0.631360	0.686400	0.510000	0.806464	0.596800

Table 10.3: Combined sensor beliefs about specific security attacks						
84	PADS; NTOP; SPADE; TCPTRACK	0.42400	0.608000	0.440000	0.596800	0.424000
85	PADS; NTOP; ARPWATCH; TCPTRACK	0.631360	0.552000	0.608000	0.654400	0.496000
86	PADS; SPADE; ARPWATCH; TCPTRACK	0.488000	0.440000	0.552000	0.731200	0.552000
87	POF; NTOP; SPADE; ARPWATCH	0.590400	0.552000	0.440000	0.784960	0.641600
88	POF; NTOP; SPADE; TCPTRACK	0360000	0440000	0.360000	0.552000	0.488000
89	POF; NTOP; ARPWATCH; TCPTRACK	0.360000	0.440000	0.360000	0.552000	0.488000
90	POF; SPADE; ARPWATCH; TCPTRACK	0.488000	0.360000	0.552000	0.616000	0.552000
91	NTOP; SPADE; ARPWATCH; TCPTRACK	0.590400	0.552000	0.440000	0.784960	0.552000
92	SNORT; PADS; POF; NTOP; SPADE	0.741952	0.811840	0.764800	0.932262	0.806464
93	SNORT; PADS; POF; NTOP; ARPWATCH	0.596800	0.764800	0.731200	0.858880	0.723520
94	SNORT; PADS; POF; NTOP; TCPTRACK	0.677440	0.811840	0.664000	0.887104	0.778816
95	SNORT; PADS; POF; SPADE; ARPWATCH	0.677440	0.731200	0.811840	0.879040	0.758080
96	SNORT; PADS; POF; SPADE; TCPTRACK	0.741952	0.784960	0.764800	0.903232	0.806464
97	SNORT; PADS; POF; ARPWATCH; TCPTRACK	0.596800	0.731200	0.731200	0.798400	0.723520
98	SNORT; PADS; NTOP; SPADE; ARPWATCH	0.741952	0.811840	0.764800	0.932262	0.758080
99	SNORT; PADS; NTOP; SPADE; TCPTRACK	0.793562	0.849472	0.706000	0.945819	0.806464
100	SNORT; PADS; NTOP; SPADE; TCPTRACK	0.677440	0.811840	0.664000	0.887104	0723520
101	SNORT; PADS; SPADE; ARPWATCH; TCPTRACK	0.741952	0.784960	0.764800	0.903232	0.758080
102	SNORT; POF; NTOP; SPADE; ARPWATCH	0.713280	0.731200	0.731200	0.924736	0.784960
103	SNORT; POF; NTOP; SPADE; TCPTRACK	0.770624	0.784960	0.664000	0.939789	0.827968

Table 10.3: Combined sensor beliefs about specific security attacks					
104 SNORT; POF; NTOP; ARPWATCH; TCPTRACK	0.641600	0.731200	0.616000	0.874560	0.754240
105 SNORT; POF; SPADE; ARPWATCH; TCPTRACK	0.713280	0.692800	0.731200	0.892480	0.784960
106 SNORT; NTOP; SPADE; ARPWATCH; TCPTRACK	0.770624	0.784960	0.664000	0.939789	0.784960
107 PADS; POF; NTOP; SPADE; ARPWATCH	0.539200	0.608000	0.686400	0.758080	0.596800
108 PADS; POF; NTOP; SPADE; TCPTRACK	0.631360	0.686400	0.608000	0.806464	0.677440
109 PADS; POF; NTOP; ARPWATCH; TCPTRACK	0.424000	0.608000	0.552000	0.596800	0.539200
110 PADS; POF; SPADE; ARPWATCH; TCPTRACK	0.539200	0.552000	0.686400	0.654400	0.596800
111 PADS; NTOP; SPADE; ARPWATCH; TCPTRACK	0.631360	0.686400	0.608000	0.806464	0.596800
112 POF; NTOP; SPADE; ARPWATCH; TCPTRACK	0.590400	0.552000	0.552000	0.784960	0.641600
113 SNORT; PADS; POF; NTOP; SPADE; ARPWATCH	0.741952	0.811840	0.811840	0.932262	0.806464
114 SNORT; PADS; POF; NTOP; SPADE; TCPTRACK	0.793562	0.849472	0.764800	0.945810	0.845171
115 SNORT; PADS; POF; NTOP; ARPWATCH; TCPTRACK	0.677440	0.811840	0.731200	0.887104	0.778816
116 SNORT; PADS; POF; SPADE; ARPWATCH; TCPTRACK	0.714952	0.784960	0.811840	0.903232	0.806464
117 SNORT; PADS; NTOP; SPADE; ARPWATCH; TCPTRACK	0.793562	0.849472	0.764800	0.945810	0.845171
118 SNORT; POF; NTOP; SPADE; ARPWATCH; TCPTRACK	0.770624	0.784960	0.731200	0.939789	0.827968
119 PADS; POF; NTOP; SPADE; ARPWATCH; TCPTRACK	0.631360	0.686400	0.686400	0.806464	0.677440
120 SNORT; PADS; POF; NTOP; SPADE; ARPWATCH; TCPTRACK	0.793562	0.849472	0.811840	0.945810	0.845171

10.7.3 Analysis of results

The use of multisensor fusion is promising because it detects most attacks that are not possible to detect with a single sensor. With a single sensor or an intrusion detection system, some attacks can go undetected, if that sensor is incapable of detecting those attacks. With multisensor fusion, there is a possibility that pieces of attack evidence will be detected based on the combined capability of multiple sensors. For example, see Row 13 of Table 10.3. Although *POF* and *ARPWATCH* sensors were unable to detect a stealthy scan attack, when evidence from these sensors was combined with *SNORT* (see Row 29), a *72% belief* in a stealthy scan attack on the network was obtained. A belief high enough to trigger any intrusion detection system to alert security administrators.

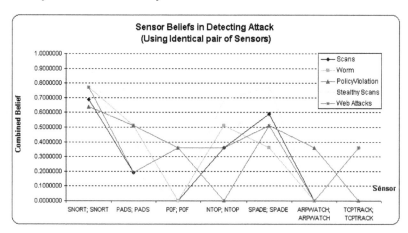

Figure 10.2: Sensor beliefs in detecting attacks based on a pair of identical sensors

Figure 10.2 shows the outcome of using a pair of identical sensors whose sets of evidence were combined to detect attacks launched on the network. It shows sensor beliefs in detecting specific attacks conducted on the monitored network by combining attack evidence from two identical sensors. As shown in the figure, policy violation was not detected when using a pair of NTOP sensors, network worm was not detected when using a pair of identical ARPWATCH sensors, similarly, policy violation and stealthy scans attack were not detected by TCPTRACK and POF sensors respectively. This helps to substantiate the hypothesis that sensors must be carefully selected, and the need to complement the capabilities of sensors when combining sensors in detecting attacks. In comparison, when a pair of heterogeneous sensors was used, some attacks were not detected, as shown in Figure 10.3. Attacks that were not detected have a zero intercept on the X and Y axes.

In contrast, with a pair of heterogeneous sensors the beliefs obtained were much better than those obtained using a pair of homogeneous sensors, as shown in

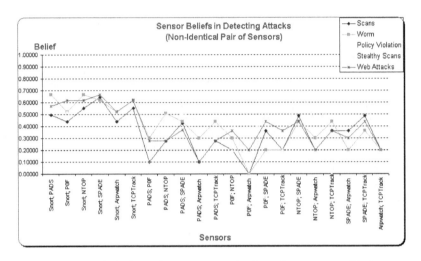

Figure 10.3: Sensor beliefs in detecting attacks based on a pair of heterogeneous sensors

Figure 10.3. The average belief obtained using a pair of heterogeneous sensors was in the neighbourhood of 65-68%. With more sensors, for example, six non-identical sensors, a higher degree of belief (in the region of 90-92%) was obtained and, remarkably, every attack conducted was detected, as shown in Figure 10.4.

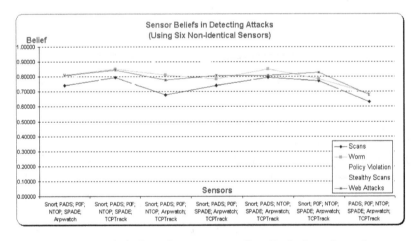

Figure 10.4: Sensor beliefs in detecting specific attacks based on six sensors

Based on security evidence gathered by sensors, together with using the D-S rule of combination, it is shown that the more evidence that can be gathered about attacks, the higher the accuracy in detecting specific attacks. Figure 10.5 shows sensor beliefs in detecting attacks perceived on the monitored LAN based on combined pieces of evidence from all (seven) sensors. Comparing Figure 10.3 (obtained with a pair of heterogeneous sensors) and Figure 10.5 (obtained using seven heterogeneous sensors). It is evident that beliefs based on the combined evidence of seven sensors were much stronger and accurate than beliefs computed from a pair of non-identical senors. Hence, the more pieces of evidence we can gathered about attacks, the more reliable (accurate) the results are.

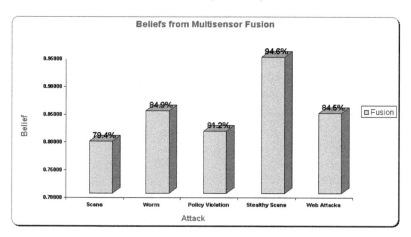

Figure 10.5: Sensor beliefs in detecting specific attacks based on all the sensors (seven)

10.7.4 Effect of choice of sensors

The choice of sensors is important in multisensor data fusion. For example, in Row 13 of Table 10.3, although pieces of evidence from two sensors were combined, it was not possible to detect *network scan, network worm* or *stealthy network scan* attacks. This is because the sensors (*POF and ARPWATCH*) utilised to gather attack evidence were unable to detect network scans, worm or stealthy scan attacks. Although multisensor data fusion is promising, the sensors must be carefully selected, as discussed in section 10.3 of this research. Hence, to detect security attacks in a multisensor fusion, the choice of sensors is as equally important as the technique used to combine and analyse pieces of attack evidence gathered by sensors. Sensors must be selected based on their abilities to detect certain attacks, so that when their pieces of evidence are combined, the resultant outcome provides a higher accuracy toward better understanding of specific attacks perceived.

10.8 Attack detection using pattern activity graphs

The objective here is to *construct activity graphs* of attacks perceived on the network. It is argued that activity graphs provide visual representations that assist security administrators to visualise and detect attacks, and consequently help them determine appropriate countermeasures.

A pattern activity graph (PAG) describes attack activities in relation to time of attack, attack source (the attacker), and the attack target, as discussed in section 8.4. The choice of attack attributes such as, *source IP address, target IP address, attack signature, and timestamp,* to represent an attack is dependent on what maybe interesting to the security administrator at a given time. It is argued that representing pattern activity graphs in terms of 'attacker' to 'attacked' model is useful for security administrators to quickly and swiftly recognise potential sources of attacks, which assists in providing timely response. A PAG is a flexible representation that allows for different visualisations.

For example, Figure 10.6 is a PAG of attacker to attacked model, relating to attack signatures and the timestamp of the attack. However, a PAG can be constructed using other attack parameters, such as the sensor that detected the attack, or the number of events generated by the attack.

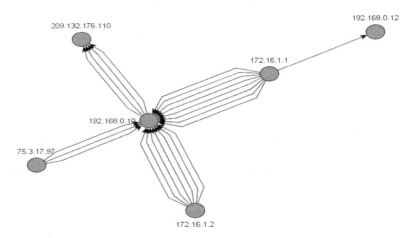

Figure 10.6: Attack description using a pattern activity graph model

Figure 10.6 is a visual representation of attacks perceived on the network, constructed using the activity graph model (discussed in section 8.3.2). The graph shows attackers and target systems being attacked. The *graph edge* represent the relationship, that reveals services being exploited in the attack, and the time the exploits were launched. In this figure, the adversary used three different hosts (75.3.17.97, 172.16.1.2 and 172.16.1.1) to conduct a port scan attack on the target (*host* 192.168.0.10). Although the adversary scanned *host* 192.168.0.12, this was done to introduce noise in the captured data. From the representation (Figure 10.6), host 192.168.0.10 contacted host 209.132.176.110, as deduced from the direction of the arc connecting the two hosts. What may be interesting at a given time, may be to investigate the time relation of these activities. It is shown that the port scanning activities from hosts 75.3.17.97, 172.16.1.2 and 172.16.1.1 to host 192.168.0.10 all happened at the same time, suggesting that the adversary may have used these hosts to launch a port scan attack on *host* 192.168.0.10.

10.8.1 Network scans

Here, the objective is to obtain a description of network scans using the PAG model in order to visualise network scan activities on the monitored LAN. Network scan activities detected are based on the capability of sensors deployed in the network. *Network scans*, such as *horizontal, vertical, strobe, block* and *stealthy port scans* were investigated. A *horizontal scan* occurs when a single port is scanned for a large population of hosts. For example, scanning several hosts on port 445 (Microsoft SMB over TCP). A *vertical scan* occurs when a several ports on a single host are scanned. For example, scanning a single host (192.168.0.1) for most open ports. A *strobe scan* is similar to a horizontal scan, but, it checks a few ports rather than a single port [181]. For example, scanning a couple of hosts for ftp, http and https ports is considered a strobe scan. A *block scan* combines both horizontal and vertical scans in one. For example, NMAP provides command line switches to assist in performing block scans. A *stealthy scan* is a scan that is conducted to avoid being detected, that is, a scan aimed not to be discovered. This occurs when the packet headers are modified to evade detection. For example, scanning using a spoofed address is considered a stealthy scan. Thus, stealthy scans modify TCP packets in order to go unnoticed [181, 86].

In this research both normal and stealthy scans were launched, and the classification includes: TCP Portscan, TCP Port-sweep, TCP Open port (half-open), UDP Portscan, ICMP Sweep, ICMP Ping NMAP. The algorithm described in section 8.4.5 was used to analyse the event database for portscan attacks, as shown in Figure 10.7.

Figure 10.7 shows portscan attacks detected on the network. It shows the host carrying out portscans, target hosts being scanned, and the times the scan activities were performed. For example, *host* (172.16.1.2) scanned the following *hosts* (*192.168.0.10, 192.168.0.11* and *192.168.0.12*). Further analysis is also possible with the graph. For instance, highlighting the *graph edge* reveals *the specific time* and *attack signature* the edge describes. In terms of mitigating the attack, that is, which hosts should be removed or blocked from the figure, it appears that blocking *host* 172.16.1.2 would significantly mitigate the attack.

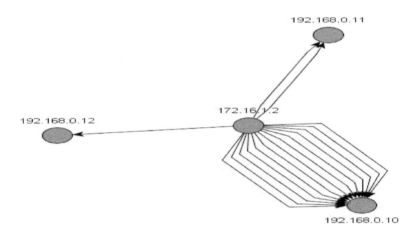

192.168.0.11

172.16.1.2

192.168.0.12

192.168.0.10

Figure 10.7: Graph description of network scan for a specified period of time

However, in a large-scale portscan attack, it will be difficult to manually single out a specific host causing the attack, so an automated technique for analysing graph networks may be required. In this case, a graph centrality measure, discussed in section 8.5.2 was employed. A graph centrality computes a measure to detect hosts causing the greatest (structural) impact on a graph network, in which case, isolating such hosts would lower the degree of impact.

For example, Figure 10.8, is a graph description of a network worm attack. It is straightforward for a security administrator to identify hosts causing significant harm in the network, as it is evident that *host* 8 is making the greatest peer contact. In a large-scale outbreak, although visual inspections are useful, because they assist security administrators to visualise attack outbreaks. Isolating a single host in a large-scale network by mere visual inspection can be challenging.

To address this issue, a graph centrality measure was encoded using the *edge connectedness centrality* (degree centrality) discussed in section 8.5.2. With *edge connectedness centrality*, the number of edges incident to a node depicts the level of influence that a node has on the overall graph network, as shown in Figure 10.9. The graph vertex with the highest number of connected edges is the node causing the greatest influence on the graph. When related to a network worm incident, it means that the graph vertex with the most number of incident edges is the one propagating the worm outbreak more than any other graph vertex in the network, because of the number of relationships it has with the other graph vertices in the representation, and therefore, this graph vertex is causing the greatest worm infection in the network.

The graph, as shown in Figure 10.9, is expressive and assists security administrators to easily visualise the most influential hosts in the network as per the

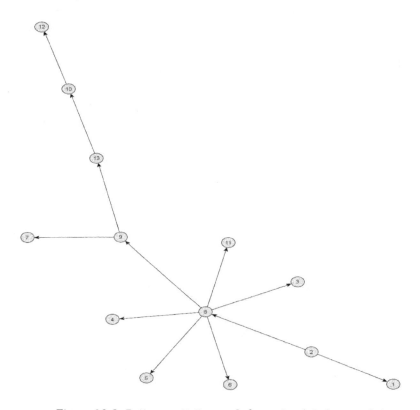

Figure 10.8: Pattern activity graph from simulated worm data

incident (worm outbreak). In this figure, it is straightforward to see that *host 8* was the most influential. Thus, disconnecting this host from the network would significantly lower the degree of propagation of the outbreak.

Figure 10.9 is a pattern activity graph of the simulated network worm with *edge connectedness centrality measure* applied. The applied centrality automatically encodes a measure to show which host in the graph network is most influential. The most influential host in a graph network using edge connected centrality is the host that has the highest number of edges to other hosts in the network. The most influential host is encoded to have the greatest radius, and its colour is red, while the least significant has the least radius, and its colour is yellow, as shown in Figure 10.9.

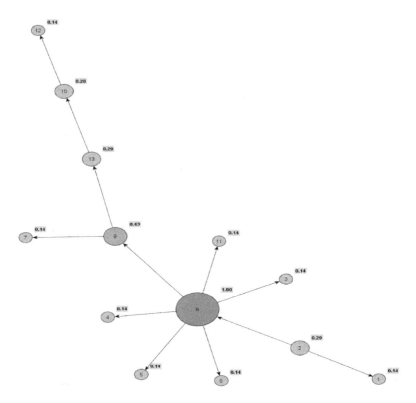

Figure 10.9: Pattern activity graph from simulated worm data with edge-connectedness centrality applied

10.9 Summary

A *testbed network* was designed as a proof of concept to demonstrate how sensors are used to sense and report attack evidence gathered, and to obtain datasets used to validate the hypothesis of the research.

Open-source, host and network-based sensors were distributed in the network to passively monitoring the network in real time. Sensor selection was driven by the need to *passively monitor network changes in real time.* The chosen sensors were configured to direct their evidence to a centralised database where evidence is stored persistently. Enabling sensors to direct their evidence to a centralised database is challenging, a log parser was used to accomplish this task. The log parser takes every event from a sensor and formats it into a consistent format that is written to a database table.

In the analysis, some techniques were employed to analyse sensor evidence, namely the Dempster-Shafer theory of evidence, graph theory and graph matching. The Dempster-Shafer theory of evidence was used to combine and analyse multiple pieces of evidence from sensors into evidence with a higher degree of belief, reliability and accuracy.

The D-S combination rule was used to combine pieces of independent attack evidence, and to compute sensor beliefs about network attacks, as shown in Table 10.3. This showed that the more evidence that can be gathered about attacks, the higher the accuracy in detecting both specific and widespread attacks. Combined beliefs obtained using the D-S rule of combination help provide a detailed understanding of attacks perceived on the monitored LAN. For example, it was shown that *stealthy scans* were the most conducted attacks on the monitored network based on combined sensor beliefs.

The beliefs obtained were 79.36% in accurately detecting network scans, 84.95% in detecting network worm attacks, 81.18% in detecting policy violation, 94.56% in detecting stealthy scans attacks, and finally, 84.52% in detecting web attacks.

Graph representation was then employed to further analyse and visualise security attacks perceived. Graph representations assist security administrators to detect, and visualise attacks assisting them to decide on how to respond to perceived attacks, as shown in Figures 10.6 and 10.7.

Chapter 11

Conclusion

This chapter provides a conclusion to the research, reaffirms the research's original hypothesis, and suggests the application of the framework to countering terrorism and organised crime as future work.

11.1 Summary of key contributions

The main achievements of this research is presented. These include a summary of key research investigations undertaken, an introduction to the theoretical framework for detecting widespread attacks in computer networks, the experimentation conducted to evaluate the research objectives, together with a discussion of the results obtained. A significant part of this work relates to its relevance to industry, which is well discussed, and finally, suggestion for future work is highlighted.

11.1.1 The theoretical framework

A security framework composed of *sensor*, *analysis* and *response* components is proposed and investigated. Sensors are responsible for gathering evidence of attacks perceived on the network, which are communicated to the analysis component. At the analysis unit, pieces of security evidence about attacks are combined, correlated and analysed. Responses to counter (mitigate) attacks are suggested based on the analysis outcome. Responses to attack could be both automated and manual. Automated responses are used to counter attacks of known security signatures, whereas manual responses are recommended for attacks whose signatures may not be exactly deduced, for example, freshly identified attacks. Manual responses to attacks are executed by security administrators. Hence, the expertise of security administrators may be required in furthering attack analysis, and also, in providing adequate response to perceived attacks.

A high level description of the framework is presented. This includes schematic representation of the framework, as shown in Figure 5.1, its application to both multisensor LAN, as shown in Figure 5.3, and integrated data fusion, in security monitoring, as shown in Figure 5.4.

The development paradigm leading to the framework includes the need for:

♦ a distributive security framework.

♦ an "assistance" security framework.

A distributive security framework divides the task of securing the network into separate functions for sensing, analysing and responding to attacks, as discussed in section 5.3. Security "assistance" in the framework is to incorporate human expertise (security administrators) in furthering responses to security attacks. The premise for a distributive approach is three fold:

♦ First, the analysis of information from the whole network is more pertinent than any individual countermeasure perspective.

♦ Second, a response that coordinates multiple countermeasures is potentially more effective than that which can be achieved by the sum of the responses of a set of standalone countermeasures.

♦ Third, frameworks that cooperate with human expertise in the analysis of perceived attacks are more flexible and subtle in decision-making than systems whose responses are fully automated. For example, fully automated systems can be easily lead to self-inflicted denial of service (DoS) by flooding the network with false positives.

Furthermore, the need for an assistance security framework is appealing because in network security, both security countermeasures and security threats are emerging. New vulnerabilities to computer networks are found continuously. Thus, fully automating responses to these newly identified vulnerabilities, or threats that exploit them, is not feasible. Hence, the need for frameworks that cooperate with human assistance in their analysis, especially, distributive frameworks that operate across the entire network.

Each component of the framework is discussed. This includes schematic, semantic and formalised description of each component of the framework, as shown in Figures 5.4, 5.5, 5.6, 5.7 and 7.5. It is pertinent to note that the components of the framework share security information (intelligence about attacks) via *security spaces*. A security space is a "tuple space", that allows information to be shared among the components of the framework, namely, sensor, analysis and response. Security spaces comprising of schematic, semantic and formal description are provided, as discussed in Chapter 7.

The *requirements for the framework* as a whole are explained. These comprise both the general and specific requirements of the framework. General requirements are the non-functional requirements of the framework such as scalability, responsiveness, robustness and resource sharing. In contrast, specific requirements are the functional requirements, such as requirements for sensor, analysis, signalling and response, as discussed in Chapters 8, 6, 7 and 9 respectively.

Sensor selection was driven by the need to *passively monitor network changes in real time*. Sensors were distributed across the network to collate pieces of security evidence about attacks on individual hosts, and on different parts of the network. Attack evidence gathered by sensors is communicated to the analysis component. In the analysis, pieces of attack evidence are combined to provide plausible understanding of the state of the entire network. The data obtained from synthesising this collective pieces of attack evidence together with the expertise offered by security administrators in monitoring the networks are combined to adequately detect security attacks.

The *analysis* component comprised of techniques that assist security administrators to combine multiple pieces of sensor evidence, and to provide visual descriptions of detected attacks. Analysis techniques employed to analyse the obtained datasets were graph theory, graph matching and the Dempster-Shafer theory of evidence. The justification for the selection of these analysis techniques was fully discussed (see sections 8.1, 8.3.1, 9.6, and 9.7). However, the main objective was to employ techniques that assist security administrators to evaluate, analyse and detect widespread security attacks, perceived at different points in the network, and on a population of hosts in the network. Graph theory and the Dempster-Shafer theory of evidence are favoured. The striking points to bear in mind are:

◆ graphs provide visual representation of security attacks perceived on a population of the network. This assists security administrators to visualise, inspect (analyse) and detect enterprise-wide attacks.

◆ graphs also provide a way of checking similarities (and dissimilarities) in graph representations in order to detect attacks, through graph matching of attack templates to data graphs representing attacks perceived in the network.

◆ D-S combines separate pieces of attack evidence based on belief functions and epistemic reasoning to compute errors, inconsistencies and contradictions in evidence.

◆ D-S does not require "a priori" knowledge of the network in order to identify, determine or detect threats and attacks perceived in the network, compared to say, Bayesian networks or traditional probability theory.

◆ D-S does not require training of data in order to draw network baselines. Training of data requires down-time, unfortunately, network baselines change continuously with the addition of new services or new provisioning. Although training of data is essential for the individual sensors in order to accurately characterise attack evidence perceived in the network; however, it is not a mandatory requirement for the overall fusion system.

◆ both graph and D-S are used to investigate known and unknown attack characteristics through heuristic and pattern matching analysis.

◆ both can be used to provide attack detection, and for forensic application to investigate security break-in retrospectively.

To detect security attacks, a requirement is to continuously monitor corporate assets for suspicious network activities, such as changes in network behaviour, deviation, changes in utilisation or attempted exploit. Network activities are often abrupt in nature, but provide only indicative pieces of evidence, which *may not always* be as a result of network attacks. Hence, network activities in relation to attacks consist of uncertainties, and a significant problem is to deduce which network activity is malicious or not, and which constitutes a fault or an attack.

In security monitoring, as discussed in section 9.2, evidence from sensors is not always concrete, such as exact attack signature. Also, not every sensor has the capability to detect all cyber attacks. Hence, evidence of attacks reported by sensors can be supportive, and at times incomplete or contradictory. To combine such divergent pieces of security evidence about attacks, in the face of uncertainties, the Dempster-Shafer theory of evidence was utilised. Thus, one of the key achievements in this research, is the use of a data fusion algorithm to develop an attack analysis mechanism that combines several pieces of independent evidence gathered by sensors under a clear mathematical framework using the Dempster-Shafer theory of evidence.

D-S is a evidential technique, that is applied in multisensor data fusion to combine pieces of independent evidence that seem to be supportive, inconclusive and at times contradictory. The reason why the Dempster-Shafer technique was used is because it is capable of analysing independent evidence of security events, by evaluating *beliefs* in evidence. The credibility of *beliefs* in evidence are evaluated by computing the *plausibility* and *doubt* in the evidence provided. This is beyond probability theory that deals with repetitive outcomes of events, or Bayesian network that requires both a *prior probability* and a *conditional probability* in order to compute a *posterior probability*. Further, D-S is also capable of analysing incomplete evidence, inconclusive or contradictory pieces of evidence. A thorough comparison of D-S and other techniques, including explanation to why D-S was used in the analysis was provided in section 9.6.

The Dempster-Shafer theory of evidence was used to formalise a novel correlation algorithm to combine beliefs from multiple sensors about attacks. The computed result showed a high accuracy in detecting specific security attacks launched on the monitored LAN, as shown in Table 10.3, Figures 10.3 and 10.5.

To assist a security administrator to visualise and detect security attacks, graph theory and graph matching were employed. With graphs, security attacks can be modelled as a visual representation. Graph representation assists security administrators to visualise and detect perceived attacks in the network, as shown in Figures 10.6 and 10.7.

To *respond* to attacks perceived in the network, both automated and human-assisted responses were offered. Response requirements, as discussed in section 6.7, include the need to:

◆ support both automated and human assisted responses in mitigating security attacks.

◆ support the combination of multiple responses (countermeasures) in mitigating attacks, such as automatic and adaptive reconfiguration, remediation, re-distribution and re-deployment of responses.

◆ be flexible and sufficiently open ended to accommodate a wide range of responses.

Automated responses: these are responses automatically deployed by responders to mitigate perceived attacks. These include responses recommended by fuzzy and generic responders, for attacks whose profile or signature are well known. *Human assisted responses:* are responses rendered by security administrators. Responses executed by security administrators are for freshly identified attacks whose signatures or attack profiles are vague, and often times unknown.

11.1.2 The experiments

Security attacks such as stealthy network scans, network worms, web attacks and policy violations were investigated. The experiments were conducted on a testbed network monitoring live Internet traffic, where network attacks, such as network scans, network worm attack, web attacks, policy violations and stealthy network scans were realised. In the testbed network, open source sensors were deployed to gather security evidence and communicate their belief about attacks. The dataset obtained from the testbed network was used to investigate the attacks launched in the network, and to evaluate the research objectives. In total, seven sensors were used to gather pieces of attack evidence launched on the testbed network. These sensors were SNORT, PADS, POF, NTOP, SPADE, ARPWATCH and TCPTRACK. A detailed description of each sensor is provided in Chapter 10.

Graph algorithms were used to construct and describe perceived attacks, as shown in Algorithms 8.1 to 8.5. Two graph matching algorithms, *graph isomorphism* and *subgraph isomorphism* were developed, and used to compare *template graphs* to *data graphs* in order to evaluate similarities between attack templates and evidence of attacks gathered.

Pattern activity graphs were used to describe (represent) the attack evidence gathered, which assist security administrators to visualise and detect attacks, and consequently assist them in deciding which response to apply in order to mitigate the attack, as shown in Figures 10.6 and 10.7. Graph representations are useful in analysing and visualising evidence gathered by sensors in order to characterise security attacks.

The Dempster-Shafer theory of evidence was used to combine sensor beliefs about attacks. The combined beliefs offered higher accuracy in detecting specific attacks conducted on the monitored LAN, compared with beliefs obtained from individual sensors. When evidence from a pair of non-identical sensors was combined, certain attacks on the network could not be detected, as shown on *Row 13* of Table 10.3. This means the use of a single countermeasure, such as a sensor, or an intrusion detection system, to detect every cyber attack is not possible. That is, it is not possible for a single sensor or an intrusion detection system to detect all cyber attacks. Hence, a single sensor is insufficient in detecting every attack perceived on different points in the network. This observation reaffirms the earlier point of view that countermeasures offered by *stand-alone* defence systems are insufficient, as discussed in section 1.2. For example, although pieces of attack evidence from two *non-identical sensors* were combined, it was not possible to detect a *network scan*, *worm* or *stealthy network scan attacks*. Imagine using a single sensor or relying only on an IDS to monitor an enterprise network.

Similarly, the use of identical sensors to gather attack evidence is not recommended, because sensor capabilities need to be complemented. For example, when a pair of identical sensors was used, it was evident that some attacks were not detected, as shown in Table 11.1, whose cells containing zero (0.0000), meaning that the combined belief (evidence) from these sensors is zero, hence they were unable to detect the attack.

Table 11.1: Combined belief about specific security attacks using a pair of identical sensors

No.	Combined Sensor Belief (Evidence)	Scans	Network Worms	Policy Violation	Stealthy Scans	Web Attacks
1	SNORT; SNORT	0.68640	0.76960	0.64000	0.92160	0.76960
2	PADS; PADS	0.19000	0.51000	0.51000	0.19000	0.19000
3	POF; POF	0.00000	0.00000	0.36000	0.00000	0.36000
4	NTOP; NTOP	0.36000	0.51000	0.00000	0.68640	0.36000
5	SPADE; SPADE	0.59040	0.36000	0.51000	0.76960	0.51000
6	ARPWATCH; ARPWATCH	0.00000	0.00000	0.36000	0.00000	0.00000
7	TCPTRACK; TCPTRACK	0.36000	0.36000	0.00000	0.36000	0.36000

Another reason why some attacks could not be detected when a pair of identical sensors was deployed in the fusion was because of the choice of sensors. Sensor selection is important. Hence, sensors need to be carefully selected. And because of this reason, we decided not to use the same type of (identical) sensors when detecting attacks in the network. Instead, a mix of heterogeneous sensors should be deployed at different places in the network to complement sensor detection capabilities. Even when heterogeneous sensors are used, their detection capabilities must complement each other. For example, signature-based sensors should be mixed with anomaly-based sensors. Packet-level sensors should be mixed with flow-based sensors. It is important to note that sensors or intrusion detection systems have limited capability towards attacks because they can not detect all cyber attacks. Certain IDSes are better at detecting certain types of attacks than others. For example, POF and ARPWATCH are specialised sensors for detecting specific threats (those they can interrogate their MAC address or operating system fingerprint), which is why they struggle in detecting threats outside their capabilities, as shown in Table 10.3.

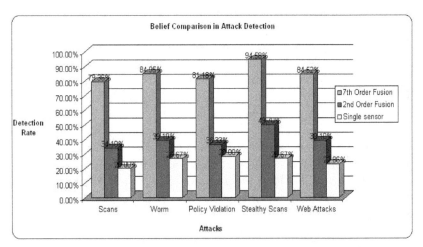

Figure 11.1: Comparing sensor beliefs in detecting attacks

With a single senor, it was not possible to detect most attacks, as shown in Table 10.2. The best combined detection averages for a single sensor were, 20.00% for scans, 26.67% for network worms, 28.00% for policy violation attacks, 26.67% for stealthy scans and 22.86% for web attacks, as shown in Figure 11.1.

This compares favourably with second order fusion (that is, when a pair of non-identical sensors were used), where on average, the belief provided were 34.10% detection for network scans, 39.19% for network worms, 36.33% for policy violations, 49.70% for stealthy scans, and 39.10% for web attacks. Thus, with a pair of heterogeneous sensors there was a less than 50% chance of detecting correctly certain network attacks.

With the fusion of sensor evidence, a variety of attacks targeting the enterprise were detected. Hence, data fusion of sensor evidence in detecting attacks is promising. For example, when attack evidence gathered by all sensors were combined, much improved beliefs were obtained, for instance, 79.4% confidence (belief) in detecting network scans, 84.95% in detecting network worms, 81.18% for policy violations, 94.58% for stealthy scans, and 84.52% for web attacks were achieved.

11.2 Discussion of results

The task of detecting enterprise-wide attacks, that is, attacks perceived on the entire network, is challenging. It requires collectively gathering pieces of security evidence about attacks on both individual hosts, and parts of the network into an integrated analysis unit where powerful and novel analysis techniques are applied to accurately detect specific attacks ongoing in the network.

Current approaches to detecting security attacks rely on the use of *stand-alone* countermeasures. These stand-alone but "localised" systems (for example, firewalls, or intrusion detection systems) are effective independent defence systems. They offer security protection in isolation and their evidence about attacks is not integrated. Each security system logs and analyses a session of traffic that passes through it, offering fragmented security evidence. Hence, these systems often struggle in detecting a variety of enterprise-wide attacks.

To detect enterprise-wide attacks, a novel approach to security defence was investigated. The approach relied on integrating the defences of multiple countermeasures, such that their independent pieces of evidence about attacks are combined to provide higher accuracy in detecting specific attacks perceived in the entire network.

Enterprise-wide attacks were detected by combining pieces of attack evidence based on the Dempster-Shafer theory of evidence. The application of the Dempster-Shafer technique in multisensor fusion was promising because of its capability in detecting a wide-range of attacks. Most importantly, this applies to attacks that would have ordinarily gone undetected with most existing stand-alone security countermeasures. It provided a *79.4% belief (confidence) in detecting network scans, 84.95% in detecting network worms, 81.18% for policy violations, 94.58% for stealthy scans, and 84.52% for web attacks*, as shown in Table 10.3 and Figure 11.1.

Using pattern activity graphs security attacks were characterised and visualised, as shown in Figure 10.8. Graph representation assists security administrators to visualise attacks and their patterns; hence, able to mitigate the attacks. In large-scale security attacks, a graph centrality measure was useful in analysing activity graphs, by showing the most influential node in the attack, such that isolating or removing that node would reduce the severity of the attack, as shown in Figure 10.9, in mitigating a network worm attack.

11.3   The relevance of this research to industry

The relevance of this work to industry is as follows:

◆ first, the research demonstrates an approach where security attacks that would have ordinarily gone undetected, can now be detected. This was achieved by combining and correlating pieces of attack evidence from multiple sensors.

◆ second, the approach guarantees that attacks to parts of an entire network can be detected. That is, it guarantees the detection of widespread attacks.

◆ third, it re-uses existing countermeasures, such as firewalls, intrusion detection systems and anti-virus systems. Hence, the approach minimises capital expenses in acquiring new hardware or different software. The foundation of this research relies on its ability to combine divergent pieces of independent security evidence gathered by different countermeasure systems to provide higher accuracy in detecting specific attacks targeting the network than those offered by stand-alone localised systems.

◆ finally, the approach provides elaborate representation of perceived attacks through graphs. Thus, graph representations assist security administrators in visualising chains of attacks exploiting their valued assets, and consequently able to offer effective response to these attacks.

The detection approach discussed in this research can be used for *near real-time attack detection* as well as for *forensic investigation* after an attack has happened. For forensic application, evidence of attacks that have happened can be analysed and visualised retrospectively.

11.4   Future work

11.4.1   Application of the security framework to countering terrorism and organised crime

Terrorism and organised crime are currently national issues for most countries in the world. Since the US 9/11 in 2001, terrorist attacks have also occurred in other countries. For example, in 2004, there was the Madrid train bombing attack (3/11); in 2005, the 7/7 attack in London, UK. Terrorism and organised crime are closely related. They appear to be similar in operation. They engage a collection of people who do separate and specialised functions among themselves. It is argued that if intelligence can be gathered about some of the individuals concerned in terrorism or organised crime, this intelligence could be combined (fused) to provide a higher-level of understanding of their activities, which may assist in detecting a terrorist or criminal network. To this end, the security framework could be deployed in criminal investigations, such as in the terrorism or organised crime arena to mine separate (or disparate) pieces of evidence gathered about each cell to obtain an epistemic reasoning of how they can be detected.

The relationship is to map *sensor* evidence to intelligence gathered on terrorist groups or organised crime. The *analysis* of sensor evidence being related to the analysis of intelligence (information) gathered about terrorists. Finally, the *response* to network attack, is related to responding to terrorist attacks.

11.5 Appendix:

11.5.1 Appendix A: Proof of correctness

Given D-S rule of combination as equation 11.1.

$$m^k(A) = \frac{\sum\limits_{i,j;B_i \cap C_j = A} m_k(B)m_k(C_j)}{1 - \sum\limits_{i,j;B_i \cap C_j = \phi} m_k(B_i)m_k(C_j)} \qquad (11.1)$$

Supposing the hypothesis A supported by each sensor is respectively $m_1(A)$, $m_2(A)$, $\cdots$, $m_n(A)$. The hypothesis A refuted by each sensor is respectively $m_1(\theta)$, $m_2(\theta)$, $\cdots$, $m_n(\theta)$

Where:

$$\begin{aligned} m_1(\theta) &= 1 - m_1(A) \\ m_2(\theta) &= 1 - m_2(A) \\ &\vdots \\ m_n(\theta) &= 1 - m_n(A) \end{aligned} \qquad (11.2)$$

By substitution, equation 11.1 becomes:

$$m^k(A) = \frac{\sum\limits_{i,j;B_i \cap C_j = A} m^{k-1}(B_i)m_k(C_j)}{1 - \sum\limits_{i,j;B_i \cap C_j = \phi} m^{k-1}(B_i)m_k(C_j)}$$

$$= \tfrac{1}{1-\theta}\left[m^{k-1}(A)m_k(A) + m^{k-1}(A)m_k(\theta) + m^{k-1}(\theta)m_k(A) \right]$$

$$= m^{k-1}(A) + m^{k-1}(\theta)m_k(A)$$

$$= 1 - \prod_{i=1}^{k-1} m_i(\theta) + [1 - m_k(\theta)] \prod_{i=1}^{k-1} m_i(\theta)$$

$$m^k(A) = 1 - \prod_{i=1}^{k} m_i(\theta) \qquad (11.3)$$

11.5.2 Appendix B: UML diagrams for the graph representation and graph matching algorithms

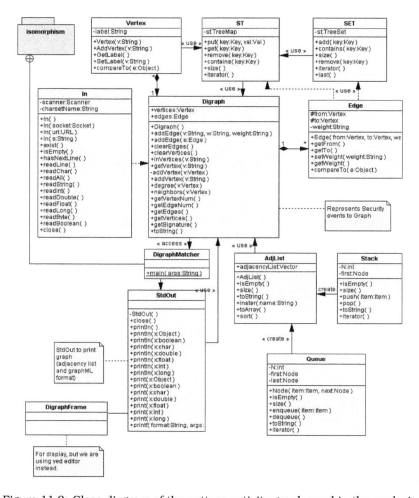

Figure 11.2: Class diagram of the pattern activity graph used in the analysis

Figures 11.2 and 11.3 show class diagrams of the algorithm used in the analysis to visualise and compare security events.

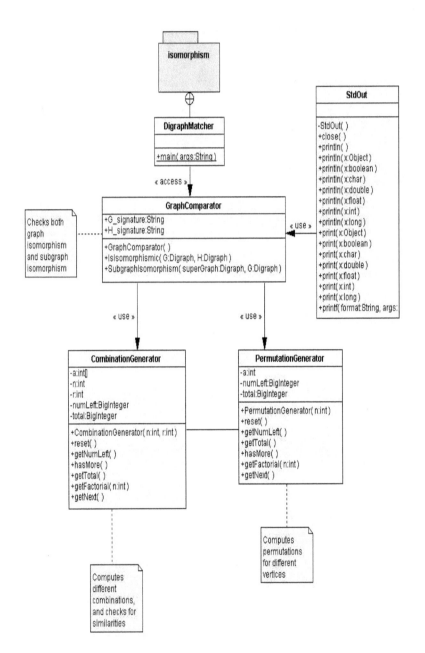

Figure 11.3: Class diagram of the pattern activity graph used in the analysis CONTD

206

Bibliography

[1] Computer Security Handbook: "The NIST Handbook", Special Publication 800-12, pp.62.

[2] M. E. Whitman, "Enemy at the Gate: Threats To Information Security", *Communications of the ACM, **Vol. 46, No. 8**, August 2003*.

[3] R. Power, "CSI/FBI Computer Crime and Security Survey", *Computer Security Issues & Trends, **Vol. 8, Issue 1, pp. 1-24**, 2002*.

[4] US-CERT, "Quarterly Trends and Analysis Report", **Vol. 1, Issue 2, pp. 1-6,** *November 28, 2006*.

[5] D. Yang , C. Hu, and Y. Chen, "A framework of Cooperating Intrusion Detection based on Clustering Analysis and Expert System", *Proceeding of the InfoSecu04, pp. 150-154, Pudong, China; ACM ISBN: 1-58113-955-1, Nov. 2004*.

[6] A. Eddaoui and A. Mezrioui, "An Active Network Approach for Security Management", *International Journal of Computer Science and network Security,* **Vol. 6, No. 5B,** *May, 2006*.

[7] A. K. Ghosh, "Code-Driven Attacks: The Evolving Internet Threat", *Proceeding of the 4th International Conference on Information Survivability Workshop, Boston, MA, October 2000*.

[8] D. Moore, C. Shannon, and J. Brown, "Code-Red: a case study on the spread and victims of an Internet Worm", *Proceeding of the ACM/USENIX Internet Measurement Workshop, France, November, 2002*.

[9] S. Braynov and M. Jadiwala, "Representation and Analysis of Coordinated Attacks", *Proceeding of FMSE03, Washington DC, October 2003*.

[10] C. Onwubiko, A. P. Lenaghan, L. Hebbes & R. Malyan, "The Representation and use of Relation Information for the Detection of Threats by Security Information Management Systems", *Proceeding of European Conference on Computer Network Defence, EC2ND 2005, University of Glamorgan, Wales UK, ISBN/ISSN 1-84628-311-6, Springer, December, 2005*.

[11] C. Onwubiko, A. Lenaghan, "Managing Security Threats and Vulnerabilities for Small to Medium Enterprises", *Proceeding of the IEEE International Conference on Intelligence and Security Informatics, IEEE ISI 2007, IEEE Press, Editors: Gheorghe Muresan, Tayfur Altiok, Benjamin Meland, Daniel Zeng, IEEE Catlog Number: 07EX1834, ISBN: 1-4244-1329-X, New Jersey, USA, May, 2007.*

[12] C. Onwubiko, A. Lenaghan, "Vulnerability Assessment: Towards an Integrated Security Infrastructure", *Proceeding of the 1st International Conference on Computer Science & Information Systems (ICCSIS 2005), Computer Science and Information System ATINER, June, Athens, Greece, ISBN/ISSN 960-88672-3-1, pp. 157-172. 2005.*

[13] A. Lenaghan, C. Onwubiko, L. Hebbes, R. Malyan, "Security Spaces for Protecting Users of Wireless Public Hotspots", *Proceeding of the IEEE International Conference, IEEE EUROCON 2005, Vol. 1, pp. 648 - 651, Serbia & Montenegro, Belgrade, November 2005.*

[14] C. Onwubiko, A. Lenaghan, and L. Hebbes, "An Integrated Security Framework for Assisting in the Defence of Computer Networks", *Proceeding of the Joint IST Workshop on Sensor Networks & Symposium on Trends in Communications, Bratislava, Slovakia, June, 2006.*

[15] C. Onwubiko and S Omosule, "An Information Systems Security Infrastructure to address Content Security Threats", *Proceeding of the International Conference on Advances in Information and Communications Engineering, AICE 2005, Ghana, ISBN/ISSN 9988643136, August 2005.*

[16] C. Onwubiko and A. Lenaghan, "Response Mechanism for Defending Computer Networks", *International Journal of Computer Science and Network Security', IJCSNS, **Vol. 6, No. 8A, pp. 36-42**, Computer Science, ISBN/ISSN 1738-7906, August 2006.*

[17] C. Onwubiko and A. Lenaghan, "Spatio-Temporal Relationships in the Analysis of Threats for Security Monitoring Systems", *Proceeding of the 2nd International Conference on Computer Science & Information Systems, Athens, Greece, Current Computing Developments in E-Commerce, Security, HCI, DB ATINER, ISBN/ISSN 960-6672-07-7, pp. 455-471. June 2006.*

[18] C. Onwubiko and A. Lenaghan, "An Evolutionary Approach in Threats Detection for Distributed Security Defence Systems", *Proceeding of the 4th IEEE International Conference on Intelligence and Security Informatics, Intelligence and Security Informatics, ISI 2006, Springer Berlin / Heidelberg, San Diego, CA, USA, ISBN/ISSN 3-540-34478-0, pp. 696 - 698. May 2006.*

[19] C. Onwubiko, A. Lenaghan, and L. Hebbes, "An Improved Worm Mitigation Model for Evaluating the Spread of Aggressive Network Worms", *Proceeding of the IEEE International Conference, IEEE EUROCON 2005, Vol. 2, pp. 1710-1713, Serbia & Montenegro, Belgrade, November 2005.*

[20] A. Avizienis, J. Laprie, B. Randell, C. Landwehr, "Basic concepts and Taxonomy of Dependable and Secure Computing", *IEEE Transactions on Dependable and Secure Computing, **Vol. 1, No.1**, Jan.-March 2004.*

[21] M T. Rose, "BEEP The Definitive Guide, Developing New Application for the Internet", O'Reilly & Associates, Inc. USA, ISBN: 0-596-00244-0, 2002.

[22] M. Bishop, "What is Computer Security", *IEEE Security & Privacy, **Vol. 1, No. 1, pp. 67-69,** Jan/Feb. 2003.*

[23] D. Gollman, "Computer Security", Chichester, England, John Wiley & Sons, 1999.

[24] M. Andrews and J. A. Whittaker, "Computer Security", *IEEE Security & Privacy, **Vol. 2, No. 5, pp. 68-71**, Sept./Oct. 2004.*

[25] U. Helmbrecht, President of the BSI, Germany National Security Agency [Online]: http://www.bsi.bund.de/english/index.htm [Accessed 10th Dec. 2006].

[26] T. Kelly, "The myth of the skytale", *Cryptologia,**Vol. 22, No. 3, pp. 244-260**, July 1998.*

[27] D. Kahn, "The Codebreakers: The Story of Secret Writing", ISBN: 0-684-83130-9, 1976.

[28] A. Ross, "Security Engineering: A Guide to Building Dependable Distributed Systems", John Wiley & Sons, ISBN: 0-471-38922-6, 2001.

[29] D. H. Hamer, G. Sullivan, F. Weierud, "Enigma Variations: an Extended Family of Machines", *Cryptologia, **Vol. 22, No. 3**, July 1998.*

[30] G. Whitson, "Computer Security: Theory, Process and Management", *Journal of Computing Sciences in Colleges, JCSC03, **Vol. 18, Issue 6, pp.57-66**, June 2003.*

[31] Bell and LaPadula, "Secure Computer System: Unified Exposition and Multics Interpretation", *ESD-TR-75-306, ESD/AFSC, Hanscom AFB, Bedford, MA, 1975.*

[32] F. J. Corbató, V. A. Vyssotsky, "Introduction and Overview of the Multics System", *(AFIPS 1965)* [Online]: http://www.multicians.org/fjcc1.html [Accessed 2nd Jan. 2007].

[33] Prof. Harold J. Highland, State University of New York, USA.

[34] D. L. Brinkley and R. R. Schell, "What is There to Worry About? An Introduction to the Computer Security Problem", *Information Security: An Integrated Collection of Essays,Essay 1, pp. 11-39, 1995.*

[35] W. Stallings, "Network Security Essentials, Applications and Standards", Prentice Hall, Upper Saddle River, New Jersey 07458, ISBN: 0-13-016093-8, 2002.

[36] Computers at Risk: Safe Computing in the Information Age, *Computer Science and Telecommunications Board (CSTB), pp. 49, 1991.*

[37] D. L. Pipkin, "Information Security Protecting the Global Enterprise", Hewlett-Packard Professional Books, ISBN: 0-13-017323-1 , Prentice Hall PTR, Upper Saddle River, NJ 07458, pp. 356, 2004.

[38] C. P. Pfleeger and S. L. Pfleeger, "Security in Computing", Third Edition, Prentice Hall, Professional Technical Reference, pp. 11, ISBN:-0-13-035548-8, Upper Saddle River, NJ 07458, 2003.

[39] National Computer Security Center, *Pub. NCSC-TG-004-88,* [Online]: http://www.fas.org/irp/nsa/rainbow/tg027.htm [Accessed 22nd Dec. 2006].

[40] R. C. Seacord and A. D. Householder, "A Structured Approach to Classifying Security Vulnerabilities", *Technical Note, CM/SEI-2005-TN-003, Survivable Systems, Carnegie Mellon Software Engineering Institute, Pittsburgh, PA 15213-3890, January 2005.*

[41] NIST, "International Standard ISO/IEC 17799:2000 Code of Practice for Information Security Management" Frequently Asked Questions, November 2002 [Online]: http://csrc.nist.gov/publications/secpubs/otherpubs/reviso-faq.pdf [Accessed 10th Dec. 2006].

[42] M. Siponen, "Information Security Standards Focus on the Existence of Process, Not Its Content", *Communications of The ACM, Technical Opinion, **Vol. 49, No. 8, pp. 97-100**, ACM 0001-0782/06/0800, August, 2006.*

[43] Common Criteria for Information Technology Security Evaluation, Part 1: Introduction and General Model, Version 3.1, Revision 1, CCMB-2006-09-001, September 2006.

[44] R. Courtney, "Computer System Security and Privacy Advisory Board", Annual Report (Gaithersburg, MD), pp. 18, March 1992.

[45] W. A. Arbaugh, W. L. Fithen, J. McHugh, "Windows of Vulnerability: A Case Study Analysis", *IEEE Computer*, **Vol. 33, No. 12, pp. 52-59,** *Dec. 2000.*

[46] B. Landreth, "Out of the Inner Circle: A Hackers Guide to Computer Security", *Phrack Magazine*, **Vol. 2, Issue 10, phile 9 of 9,** *1985.*

[47] M. Rogers, "Psychological theories of crime and hacking", [Online]: http://www.cbeji.com.br/br/downloads/secao/hackers.pdf (in french), [Accessed 15th April 2007].

[48] R. O. Hundley and E. H. Anderson, "Emerging Challenge: security and safety in cyberspace", *IEEE Technology and Society Magazine*, **Vol. 14, No. 4, pp. 19-28,** *1995*

[49] A. Avizienis, J. C. Laprie, and B. Randell, "Fundamental Concepts of Dependability", UCLA CSD Report no. 010028, LAAS Report no. 01-145, Newcastle University Report no. CS-TR-739, 2000.

[50] J. Mölsä, "Mitigation Denial of Service Attacks in Computer Networks", Doctoral Dissertation, TKK Dissertation 32, Helsinki University of Technology, Department of Electrical and Communications Engineering, Communications Laboratory, June 2006

[51] J. Mirkovic, J. Martin, and P. Reiher, "A Taxonomy of DDoS Attacks and DDoS Defense Mechanisms", UCLA, 2003.

[52] C. Patrikakis, M. Masikos, and O. Zouraraki, "Distributed Denial of Service Attacks", *The Internet Protocol Journal*, **Vol. 7, No. 4,** *2004.*

[53] E. Spafford, "The Internet Worm Program: An Analysis", *ACM Computer Communications Review*, **Vol. 19, pp. 17-57,** *January 1989.*

[54] C. Gates, "The Modeling and Detection of Distributed Port Scans: A book Proposal", Technical Report CS-2003-01, Faculty of Computer Science, 6050 University Ave. Halifax, Nova Scotia, B3H 1W5, Canada, 2003.

[55] R. G. Bace, "Intrusion Detection", Macmillan Technical Publishing, Indianapolis, USA, ISBN: 1-57870-185-6, 2000.

[56] S. Axelsson, "Intrusion Detection Systems: A Survey and Taxonomy", Department of Computer Engineering, Chalmers University of Technology Goteborg, Sweden, March 2000.

[57] B. G. Helmer, J. Wong, V. Honavar, and L. Miller, "Lightweight Agents for Intrusion Detection", *The Journal of Systems and Software, **Vol. 67, pp. 109-122**, 2003.*

[58] Cisco Systems Inc., "White paper; Cisco NAC: The Development of the Self-Defending Network", (22/7/05) [Online]: http://www.cisco.com/en/US/netsol/ns617/networking_solutions_sub_solution_home.html [Accessed 26th April 2007].

[59] Microsoft, "Network Access Protection (NAP)", [Online]: http://www.microsoft.com/technet/itsolutions/network/nap/default.mspx [Accessed 26th April 2007].

[60] Enterprise Security Management SIMS by ArcSight, [Online]: http://www.arcsight.com/ , [Accessed 30th April 2007].

[61] Security Information Management Systems, by Cisco Systems Inc., [Online]: http://www.cisco.com/en/US/products/sw/cscowork/ps5209/index.html [Accessed 30th April 2007].

[62] Unified Threat Management and Network Security Systems, by Checkpoint, [Online]: http://www.checkpoint.com/products/utm.html [Accessed 30th April 2007].

[63] OSSIM: Open Source Security Information Management Systems, [Online]: www.ossim.net/ [Accessed 2nd May 2007].

[64] OSSEC (2008), "Host-based Intrusion Detection System", [Online]: www.ossec.net

[65] B. Schneier, "SIMS: Solution, or Part of the Problem?", *IEEE Security & Privacy, **pp.88,** ISBN: 1540-7993, 2004.*

[66] A. T. Williams and J. Heiser, "Protect Your PCs and Servers from the Botnet Threat, Gartner Research", ID No. G00124737, December 29, 2004.

[67] Microsoft Security Bulletin MS03-026, Buffer Overrun In RPC Interface Could Allow Code Execution (823980), July 2003: [Online]: http://www.microsoft.com/technet/security/bulletin/MS03-026.mspx [Accessed 14th Dec. 2006].

[68] W32.Sasser.worm, discovered April 30 2004, [Online]: www.symantec.com/security response/writeup.jsp?docid=2004-050116-1831-99 [Accessed 14th Dec. 2006].

[69] CERT/CC, Microsoft Internet Information Server 4.0 (IIS) vulnerable to DoS when URL Redirecting is enabled, [Online]: http://www.kb.cert.org/vuls/id/544555 [Accessed 14th December 2006].

[70] CERT/CC W32/blaster worm advisory, [Online]: http://www.cert.org/advisories/CA-2003-20.html [Accessed 23rd August 2003].

[71] CERT ® Coordination Center, Overview of Attack Trends, [Online]: www.cert.org/archive/pdf/attack_trends.pdf [Accessed 5th May 2007].

[72] L. A. Gordon, M. P. Loeb, W. Lucyshyn and R. Richardson, "CSI/FBI Computer Crime and Security Survey 2006", *11th Annual CSI/FBI Computer Crime and Security Survey, 2006.*

[73] CERT/CC, Continuing Threats to Home Users, [Online]: http://www.cert.org/advisories/CA-2001-20.html [Accessed 8th May 2007].

[74] Jarmo Mölsä, "Mitigating denial of service attacks: A tutorial", *Journal of Computer Security*, **Vol. 13, No. 6, pp. 807-837**, 2005. © 2005 IOS Press.

[75] Arbor Peakflow Analyser, [Online]: http://www.arbornetworks.com/, [Accessed 30th April 2007].

[76] Cisco Guard [Online]: http://www.cisco.com/application/pdf/en/us/guest/netsol/ns480/c654/cdccont_0900aecd8032499e.pdf [Accessed 30th April 2007].

[77] P. Benjamin and S. Ramachandran, "Threat Response Management System (TRMS)", *International Conference on Integration of Knowledge Intensive Multi-Agent Systems, pp. 547-554, 30 Sept. 4 Oct. 2003.*

[78] M. Botha, R von Solms , K. Perry, E. Loubser and G. Yamoyany, "The Utilisation of Artificial Intelligence in a Hybrid Intrusion Detection System", *ACM proceedings of SAICSIT, pp. 149-155, 2002.*

[79] MIDAS: Monitoring, Intrusion Detection, Administration System, [Online]: http://midas-nms.sourceforge.net/screenshots.html [Accessed 30th April 2007].

[80] C. Gates, J. McNutt, J. B. Kadane and M. Kellner, "Detecting Scans at the ISP Level", Technical Report, CMU/SEI-2006-TR-005, ESC-TR-2006-05, 2006.

[81] SQUIL Event monitoring, [Online]: http://sguil.sourceforge.net/ [Accessed 20th April 2007].

[82] C. Siaterlis and V. Maglaris, "One Step ahead to Multisensor Data Fusion for DdoS Detection", *Journal of Computer Security*, **Vol. 13, Issue 5, pp. 1-26,** *September 2005* .

[83] S. Cheung, R. Crawford, M. Dilger, J. rank, J. Hoagland, K. Levitt, J. Rowe, S. Standiford-Chen, R. Yip and D. Zerkle, "The Design of GrIDS: A Graph-Based Intrusion Detection System", Department of Computer Science, University of California, Davis, CA 95616, January 1999.

[84] X. Yin, W. Yurick, M. Treaster, Y. Li, and K. Lakkaraju, "VisFlowConnect: Netflow Visualisations of Link Relationships for Security Situational Awareness", *Proceeding of the ACM Workshop on Visualisation and Data mining for computer Security, VizSEC/DMSEC 2004.*

[85] D. E. Denning, "An Intrusion Detection Model", *IEEE Transactions on Software Engineering*, **Vol. 13, No. 2, pp. 222-232,** *1987.*

[86] C. Gates, "Co-ordinated Port Scans: A Model, A Detector, and An Evaluation Methodology", PhD Thesis, Dalhousie University Halifax, Nova Scotia, February 2006.

[87] P. A. Porras and P. G. Neumann, "EMERALD: Event Monitoring Enabling Responses to Anomalous Live Disturbances", *Proceeding of the 20th National Information Systems Security Conference, pp. 353-365, Baltimore, Maryland, USA, Oct. 1997.*

[88] V. Paxon, "Bro: A System for Detecting Network Intruders in real-time", *in Proceedings of the 7th USENIX Security Symposium, San Antonio, TX, USA, Jan. 1998.*

[89] L. Me, "GASSATA: A Genetic Algorithm for Simplified Security Audit Trails Analysis", SUPELEC, B.P. 28, 35511 Cesson Sevigne Cedex, France, lme@supelec-rennes.fr.

[90] S. Kumar and E. H. Spafford, "A Pattern matching model for misuse intrusion detection", *Proceeding of the 17th National Computer Security Conference, pp. 11-21, Baltimore, MD, USA, 1994.*

[91] B. Mukherjee, L. T. Heberlein and K. N. Levitt, "Network Intrusion Detection", *IEEE Network*, **Vol. 8, No. 3, pp. 26-41**, *May/June 1994.*

[92] K. Lakkaraju, W. Yurick, R. Bearavolu, and A. J. Lee, "NVisionIP: An Interactive Network Flow Visualisation Tool for Security", *IEEE International Conference on Systems, Man, and Cybernetics, pp.2675-2680, October 2004.*

[93] J. McPherson, K-L. Ma, P. Krystosk, T. Bartoletti, and M. Christensen, "PortVis: A Tool for Port-Based detection of Security Events", *VizSEC/DMSEC 04: Proceedings ACM Workshop Visualisation and Data Mining for Computer Security, 2004.*

[94] SANS Institute: (SysAdmin, Audit, Network and Security) Institute, main page, [Online]: http://www.sans.org/resources/policies/, [Accessed 5th December 2006]

[95] J. Mirkovic, M. Robinson, P. Reiher and G. Kuenning, "Surviving threats: Alliance Formation for DdoS Defense", *Proceeding of the 2003 Workshop on New Security Paradigms, Ascona Switzerland, ACM 1-58113-880-6/04/04*

[96] A. Shnitko, "Practical and Theoretical Issues on Adaptive Security", *Workshop on Logical Foundations of an Adaptive Security Infrastructure (WOLFASI); A sub-workshop of the LICS Foundations of Computer Security (FCS04) Workshop, LICS 04, Turku, Finland, July 2004.*

[97] CERT, "Result of the Distributed-Systems Intruder tools Workshop", *CERT ® Coordination Center, Software Engineering Institute, Pittsburgh, Pennsylvania USA, November 1999.*

[98] D. Sterne, K. Djahandari, R. Balupari, W.Cholter, B. Babson, B. Wilson, P. Narasimham, A. Purtell, D. Schnackenberg and S. Linden, "Active network based DdoS Defense", *Proceeding of the DARPA Active Networks Conference and Exposition (DANCE 02), pp.193-203, San Francisco, CA, 2002.*

[99] T. Jaeger, X. Zhang and F. Cacheda, "Policy Management using Access Control Spaces"; *ACM Transactions on Information and System Security (TISSEC),* **Vol.6, Issue 3** *, ACM Press, August 2003*

[100] Matt Bishop, "Computer Security: Art and Science", Boston: Addison Wesley, 2003.

[101] D.E. Denning, "A Lattice Model of Secure Information Flow", *Communications of the ACM,* **Vol.19, Issue 5,** *ACM Press, 1976.*

[102] N. Li and M. V. Tripunitara, "Security Analysis in Role-Base Access Control", *Proceeding of Ninth ACM Symposium on Access Control Models and Technologies (SACMAT 2004), Yorktown Heights, NY, USA. pp. 126-135, ISBN: 1-58113-872-5, June 2004.*

[103] E. Casey, "Digital Evidence and Computer Crime", Elsevier Academic Press, London, UK, ISBN: 0121631044, 2004.

[104] V. Baryamureeba and F. Tushabe, "The Enhanced Digital Investigation Process Model", *Digital Forensic Research Workshop (DFRWS) 2004, Baltimore, MD, USA, August 2004*.

[105] G. Gupta, C. Mazumdar and M.S. Rao, "Digital Forensic Analysis of E-mails: A Trusted E-Mail Protocol", *International Journal of Digital Evidence, (IJDE 2004)*, **Vol.2, Issue 4, pp. 1-11**, *Spring 2004*.

[106] T. E. Uribe and S. Cheung, "Automatic Analysis of Firewall and Network Intrusion detection System Configurations", *Proceeding of the 2004 ACM Workshop on Formal Methods in Security Engineering (FMSE04), Washington D.C., USA, ACM 1-58113-971-3/04/0010, October 2004*.

[107] R. Bejtlich, "The Tao of Network Security Monitoring: Beyond Intrusion Detection", Addison-Wesley 2004, ISBN: 0-321-24677-2 (pbk), pp.25-43, 2004.

[108] R. A. Maxion, "Fault Prediction and Dynamic Error Analysis in Computer Systems", Presentation Abstract, *Proceeding of the Association for Computing Machinery Conference, ACM 81, November 1981*.

[109] D. L. Hall and S. A.H. McMullen, "Mathematical Techniques in Multisensor Data Fusion", Second Edition, ©Artech House, Inc., Norwood, MA 02062, ISBN: 1-58053-335-3, 2004.

[110] W. Emmerich, "Engineering Distributed Objects, Distributed System Requirements", pp. 9-10, London University, John Wiley & Sons Ltd, West Susses, England, 2000.

[111] E. Levy, "Worst-Case Scenario", *IEEE Security & Privacy, Attack Trends,* **Vol. 4, No. 5, pp.71-73**, *September/October 2006*.

[112] L. Marcus, "Introduction to Logical Foundations of an Adaptive Security Infrastructure", *Proceeding of the Workshop on Logical Foundations of an Adaptive Security Infrastructure (WOLFASI), A sub-workshop of the LICS Foundations of Computer Security (FCS'04) Workshop,(LICS '04), Turku, Finland, 2004*.

[113] K. J. Houle and G. M. Weaver, "Trends in Denial of Service", *Vol. 1.0, Report of the CERT/CC, October 2001*, [Online]: http://www.cert.org/archive/pdf/DoS_trends.pdf [Accessed 25th October 2006].

[114] W. Lee, W. Fan, M. Miller, S. J. Stolfo and E. Zadok, "Toward Cost-sensitive Modelling for Intrusion Detection and Response", *IEEE Journal of Computer Security*, **Vol. 10, No. 1-2**, *2002*.

[115] D. Gelernter and N. Carriero, "Coordination Languages and Their Significance", *Communications of the ACM*, **Vol. 35, Issue 2, pp. 97-107**, *ISSN:0001-0782, February 1992*.

[116] E. Freeman, S. Hupfer and K. Arnold, "Javaspaces TM Principles, Patterns and Practice The Jini Technology Series", Sun Microsystems Inc. 1999.

[117] A. L. Murphy, G. P. Picco and G. Roman, "LIME: A Coordination Model and Middleware Supporting Mobility of Hosts and Agents", *ACM Transactions on Software Engineering and Methodology (TOSEM)*, **Vol. 15, Issue 3**, *July 2006*.

[118] R. Presuhn, J. Case, K. McCloghrie, M. Rose and S. Waldbusser, "Version 2 of the Protocol Operations for the Simple Network Management Protocol (SNMP)", IETF RFC 3416, December 2002.

[119] C. Lonvick, "The BSD Syslog Protocol", IETF RFC 3164, August 2000.

[120] C. Katar, "Combining Multiple Techniques for intrusion Detection", *International Journal of Computer Science and Network Security*, **Vol. 6, No. 2B**, *February 2006*.

[121] L. Xu, A. Krzyzak, and C. Y. Suen, "Methods of Combining Multiple Classifiers and Their Applications to Handwriting Recognition", *IEEE Transactions on Systems, MAN, and Cybernetics*, *V***ol. 22, No. 3**, *May/June 1992*.

[122] R. Giugno, "Searching Algorithms and Data Structures for Combinatorial, Temporal and Probabilistic Databases", PhD book, Universita Degli Studi Di Catania, Catania, Italy, December 2002.

[123] Z. Shen, K.-L Ma, and T. Eliassi-Rad, "Visual Analysis of Large Heterogeneous Social Networks by Semantic and Structural Abstraction", *IEEE Transactions on Visualization and Computer Graphics*, **Vol. 12, No. 6, pp. 1427-1439**, *ISSN 1077-2626, November/December 2006*.

[124] D. Justice and A. Hero, "A Binary Linear Programming Formulation of Graph edit Distance", *IEEE Transactions on Pattern Analysis and Machine Intelligence*, **Vol. 28, No. 8, pp. 1200-1214**, *ISSN 0162-8828, August 2006*.

[125] S. Jha, O. Sheyner and J. Wing, "Two Formal Analyses of Attack Graphs", *Proceeding of the 15th IEEE Computer Security Foundations Workshop (CSFW02), 2002*.

[126] J. McPherson, K-L. Ma, P. Krystosk, T. Bartoletti, and M. Christensen (2004), "PortVis: A Tool for Port-Based detection of Security Events, VizSEC/DMSEC 04", *Proceeding ACM Workshop Visualisation and Data Mining for Computer Security, 2004.*

[127] What is Sort? [Online]: http://www.SNORT.org/ [Accessed 10th May 2007].

[128] X. Yin, W. Yurick, M. Treaster, Y. Li, and K. Lakkaraju (2004), "VisFlowConnect: Netflow Visualisations of Link Relationships for Security Situational Awareness", *Proceeding of the ACM Workshop on Visualisation and Data mining for computer Security, VizSEC/DMSEC 2004.*

[129] D. Justice and A. Hero, "A Binary Linear Programming Formulation of the Graph Edit Distance", *IEEE Transactions on Pattern Analysis and Machine Intelligence, **Vol. 28, No. 8 pp. 1200-1215,** August 2006.*

[130] H. Bunke, "Error Correcting Graph Matching: On the Influence of the Underlying Cost Function", *IEEE Transactions on Pattern Analysis and Machine Intelligence, **Vol. 21, No. 9, pp. 917-922**, September 1999.*

[131] sflow, "Sampled Flow", RFC 3176.

[132] L. C. Freeman, "A Set of Measures of Centrality Based on Betweenness", *Journal of Sociometry, **Vol. 40, No. 1, pp. 35-41,** March 1977.*

[133] GraphML, "The GraphML File Format", [Online]: http://graphml.graphdrawing.org/index.html [Accessed 4th April 2007].

[134] U. Brandes, M. Eiglsperger, I. Herman, M. Himsolt, and M.S. Marshall, "GraphML Progress Report: Structural Layer Proposal", *Proceedings of the 9th International Symposium on Graph Drawing (GD '01), LNCS 2265, pp. 501-512. ©Springer-Verlag, 2002.*

[135] yEd: Java Graph Editor from YWorks, [Online]: http://www.yworks.com/en/products_yed _about.htm [Accessed 9th April 2007].

[136] J. R. Ullman, "An Algorithm for Subgraph Isomorphism", *Journal of the Association for Computing Machinery, ACM, **Vol. 23, No.1, pp. 31-42,** 1976.*

[137] K. H. Rosen, "Discrete Mathematics and Its Applications", 2nd Edition, McGraw-Hill, NY, pp. 284-286, 1991.

[138] Wikipedia, [Online]: http://en.wikipedia.org/wiki/Graph_(mathematics) #Directed_graph, [Accessed 20th August 2008].

[139] R. Sedgewick, "Algorithms in Java, 3rd Edition", Addison-Wesley, Chapters 17-18, ISBN: 0-201-36120-5, 2004.

[140] NMAP, "Network Map, an Open Source Attack Tool for Network Exploration and Security Vulnerability Testing", [Online] http://nmap.org.

[141] DSCAN, "Distributed Port Scanner that scans from many hosts making it hard to detect", [Online] http://www.securiteam.com/tools/5AP0M1F4AE.html, [Accessed 8th Dec. 2008].

[142] R. Sedgewick, "Undirected graphs" [Online] http://www.cs.princeton.edu/courses/ archive/fall05/cos226/lectures/ undirected.pdf [Accessed 12th April 2007].

[143] Multics, "Multiplexed Information and Computing Service", [Online]: www.multicians.org.

[144] Centrality in Social Networks, [Online]: http://austria.phys.nd.edu/netwiki/ index.php/Centrality [Accessed 12th April 2007].

[145] M. E. J. Newman, "The Structure and Function of Complex Networks", *SIAM Review 45, 167-256, 2003.*

[146] M. Zalewski, "P0F Passive Operating System Fingerprinting", [Online]: http://www.stearns.org/p0f/README [Accessed 10th May 2007].

[147] M. Shelton, "Passive Asset Detection Systems (PADS)", [Online]: http://passive.sourceforge.net/about.php [Accessed 10th May 2007].

[148] RFC 2289, "One-Time Password, a timing-based authentication mechanism deployed in most authentication protocols", RFC 2289.

[149] ARPWATCH: ARP/IP changes watcher, [Online]: http://linux.maruhn.com/sec/arpwatch.html [Accessed 10th May 2007].

[150] TCPTRACK: TCP sniffer for LAN networks, [Online]: http://www.rhythm.cx/~steve/devel/TCPTRACK/ [Accessed 10th May 2007].

[151] D. E. Goldberg, "The Design of Innovation Lessons from and for Competent Genetic Algorithms"; Kluwer Academic Publishers, Reprint 2002.

[152] G. Shafer, "A Mathematical Theory of Evidence", Princeton University Press; Princeton 1976. [Online]: http://www.glennshafer.com/books/amte.html [Accessed 14/07/2006].

[153] SNMP, "Simple Network Management Protocol", RFC 1902.

[154] K. Sentz and S. Ferson, "Combination of Evidence in Dempster-Shafer Theory", SAND 2002-0835, Unlimited Release, Printed April 2002.

[155] Adrian O'Neill, "Dempster-Shafer Theory", [Online]: http://www.aonaware.com/ binaries/dempster.pdf [Accessed 12th April 2007].

[156] X. P. Yan, Y.B. Xie and H.L. Xiao, "Application of Dempster-Shafer Theory to Oil Monitoring", Wuhan Transportation University, China, 2005.

[157] M. Beynon, D. Cosker and D. Marshall, "An expert system for multi-criteria decision making using Dempster Shafer theory", *Expert Systems with Applications, **Vol. 20, pp. 357-367,** 2001.*

[158] SPADE: Statistical Packet Anomaly Detection Engine, [Online]: http://www.silicondefense.com/software/spice/ [Accessed 17th May 2007].

[159] G. Klir and M. J. Wierman, "Uncertainty-Based Information: Elements of Generalised Information Theory", Heidelberg, Physica-Verlag, 1998.

[160] L. Kitchen and A. Rosenfeld, "Discrete relaxation for matching relational structures", *IEEE Trans. System Man Cybernatics, **Vol 9, No. 2 pp. 869-874,** 1979.*

[161] R. Yager, "On the Dempster-Shafer Framework and New Combination Rules", *Information Sciences, **Vol. 41, Issue 2, pp. 93-137,** March 1987.*

[162] S. Panjwani, S. Tan, K. M. Jarrin, and M. Cukier, "An Experimental Evaluation to determine if Port Scans are Precursors to an Attack", *Proceeding of the International Conference on Dependable Systems and Networks, pp. 602-611, Japan, June 2005.*

[163] C. C. Zou, W. Gong, D. Towsley, "Code Red Worm Propagation Modelling and Analysis", *Proceeding of 9th ACM Conference on Computer and Communications Security, pp.138-147, November 2002.*

[164] D. Moore, V. Paxson, S. Savage, C. Shannon, and S. Staniford, "Slammer Worm Dissection. Inside the Slammer Worm", Cooperative Association for Internet Data Analysis and University of California, San Diego; *IEEE Security & Privacy, **Vol. 1 No. 4,** July - August 2003.*

[165] L. Deri, R. Carbone, S. Suin, "Monitoring Networks using NTOP", *IEEE/IFIP International Symposium on Integrated Network Management, pp. 199 -212, 2001.*

[166] ISO/IEC - International Standard Organisation 27001:2005(E) Guide for Information technology - Security techniques - Information security management systems - Requirements.

[167] J. McHugh, "Testing Intrusion Detection Systems: A critique of the 1998 and 1999 DARPA Intrusion Detection System Evaluations as performed by Lincoln Laboratory", *ACM Transactions on Information and System Security*, **Vol.3, No. 4, pp. 262-294**, *2000*.

[168] A. T. Brugger and J. Chow, "An Assessment of the DARPA IDS Evaluation Dataset Using SNORT", UCRL-CONF-214731, Department of Computer Science, University of California, Davis, CA 95616, USA, 2005.

[169] M. V. Mahoney and P. K. Chan, "An Analysis of the 1999 DARPA/Lincoln Laboratory Evaluation Datasets, Intrusion Detection Evaluation", *3rd International Conference in Recent Advances in Intrusion Detection, RAID'03, pp. 162-182, 2003.*

[170] K. M. Ali and T. J. Owens, "Selection of an EAP Authentication Method for WLAN", *International Journal of Information and Computer Security*, **Vol. 1, No. 1/2, pp. 210-233**, *2007*.

[171] AWCC - The Endace Applied Watch Command Center, [online]: http://www.endace.com/applied-watch.html [Accessed 28th October 2008].

[172] R. Anderson, "Security Engineering: A Guide to Building Dependable Distributed Systems", John Wiley & Sons, Inc. ISBN: 0-471-38922-6, 2001.

[173] L. T. Heberlein, G. Dias, K. Levitt, B. Mukherjee, J. Wood and D. Wolber, "A Network Security Monitor", *Proceeding of Symposium on Research in Security and Privacy, Oakland, CA, pp. 296-304, May 1990.*

[174] M. Crossbie, B. Dole, T. Ellis, I. Krsul and E. Spafford, "IDIOT - User Guide", Technical Report TR-96-050, Purdue University, COAST Laboratory, September 1996.

[175] D. Eppstein, "Subgraph Isomorphism in Planar Graphs and Related Problems", *Journal of Graph Algorithms and Applications*, **Vol. 3, No. 3, pp. 1-27**, *1999*.

[176] D. Ramanan, D. A. Forsyth, and A. Zisserman, "Tracking People by Learning Their Appearance", *IEEE Transaction on Pattern Analysis and Machine Intelligence*, **Vol. 29, No. 1, pp. 65-81**, *ISSN 0162-8828, January 2007.*

[177] T. Bass, *"Intrusion Detection Systems and Multisensor Data Fusion"*, Communications of the ACM, **Vol. 43, No. 4**, April 2000.

[178] ANI, "Animated Cursor Vulnerability, CVE-2007-1211", Microsoft Security Advisory (935423), Vulnerability in Windows Animated Cursor Handling; [Online] http://www.microsoft.com/technet/security/advisory/935423.mspx, March 31, 2007.

[179] T. M. Chen and V. Venkataramanan, "Dempster-Shafer Theory for Intrusion Detection in Ad Hoc Networks", *IEEE Internet Computing, pp. 36-41, November-December 2005.*

[180] A. Siraj and R. B. Vaughn, "A Cognitive Model for Alert Correlation in a Distributed Environment", *Proceeding of the IEEE Intelligence and Security Informatics Conference, pp. 218-230, Springer-Verlag Berlin Heidelberg, 2005.*

[181] S. Staniford, J. A. Hoagland and J. M. McAlerney, "Practical Automated Detection of Stealthy Port Scans", *IEEE Journal of Computer Security, **Vol. 10, pp. 105-136**, IOS Press, 2002.*

[182] Wikipedia, "Bayesian Inference", [Online]: http://en.wikipedia.org/wiki/Bayesian_inference (Accessed 6th Oct. 2008).

[183] IP Fragment, "Security considerations for IP fragment filtering", RFC 1858.

[184] GXL, "Graph eXchange Language," [Online] http://www.gupro.de/GXL/ [Accessed 4th Nov. 2008]

[185] R. E. Kalman, "A New Approach to Linear Filtering and Prediction Theory", *Transactions of the ASME - Journal of Basic Engineering, **Vol. 83, pp. 35-45**, 1960.*

[186] J. Haines, D. Ryder, L. Tinnel, and S. Taylor, "Validation of Sensor Alert Correlators", *IEEE Security and Privacy, **Vol. 1, No.1, pp. 46-56**, Jan-Feb. 2003.*

[187] K. Hwang, M. Cai, Y. Chen and M. Qin, "Hybrid Intrusion Detection with Weighted Signature Generation over Anomalous Internet Episodes", *IEEE Transactions on Dependable and Secure Computing, **Vol. 4, No. 1, pp. 41-55**, ISSN 1545-5971, January-March 2007.*

[188] J. Chirillo and S. Blaul, "Implementing Biometric Security", Wiley Publishing, Inc. ISBN: 0-7645-2502-6, 2003.

[189] RFC 3748, "EAP - Extensible Authentication Protocol - an authentication framework that supports multiple authentication methods", RFC 3748.

[190] B. Schneier, "Applied Cryptography", Second Edition, John Wiley & Sons, ISBN 0-471-11709-9, 1996.

[191] D. Hubbard, "How to Measure Anything: Finding the Value of Intangibles in Business", John Wiley & Sons, pp. 46, 2007.

[192] H. Debar, D. Curry and B. Feinstein, "The Intrusion Detection Message Exchange Format (IDMEF)", RFC 4765, 2007.

[193] GML, "Graph Modelling Language," Non-XML-based graph editor, [Online] http://dret.net/glossary/gml1 [Accessed 4th November 2008].

[194] XGMML, "eXtensible Graph Markup and Modelling Language," [Online] http://www.cs.rpi.edu/~puninj/XGMML/ [Accessed 4th November 2008].

[195] P. Costa, L. Mottola, A. L. Murphy and G. P. Picco (2007), "Programming Wireless Sensor Networks with the TeenyLIME Middleware", 8th ACM/IFIP/USENIX International Middleware Conference (Middleware 2007), Newport Beach, CA, USA.

[196] A. P. Dempster, "A generalization of Bayesian inference", *Journal of the Royal Statistical Society, **Series B, Vol. 30, pp. 205-247, 1968***.

[197] P. K. Varshney, "Distributed Detection and Data Fusion", Springer-Verlag, New York, Inc., ISBN: 0-387-94712-4, 1997.

[198] Safe Harbor, "European Commissions Directive on Data Protection Safe Harbor, 1998" [Online]: http://www.export.gov/safeharbor/SafeHarborInfo.htm, 1998.

[199] CEE, "Common Event Expression", [Online] http://cee.mitre.org

[200] Reliable Delivery for Syslog, RFC 3195, [Online], http://www.ietf.org/rfc/rfc3195.txt.

[201] B. Schneier, "Security vs. Privacy", [Online]: http://www.schneier.com /blog/archives/ 2008/01/security_vs_pri.html, [Accessed 20th August 2008], 2008.

[202] R. A. Wagner and M. J. Fischer, "The String-to-String Correction Problem," *Journal of ACM, **vol. 21, no. 1, pp. 168-173, 1974***.

[203] IDMEF, "Intrusion Detection Message Exchange Format", RFC 4765.

[204] IPSec, "Internet Protocol Security (IP security) Document Roadmap", RFC 2411.

[205] C. Alberts, "Viewing Security Management as a Business Practice", Part 3: Integrating Information Security with Business Management, 2002.

[206] World Trade Centre, New York City and the Pentagon, 9/11 terrorist attacks, 2001.

[207] K. Appleyard, "Raising the Bar", *Future of the Data Centre 2008 Conference, Information Age, 16th July 2008.*

[208] R. A. Caralli, J. H. Allen, J. F. Stevens, B. J. Willke and W. R. Wilson, "Managing for Enterprise Security", *Networked Systems Survivability Program, Software Engineering Institute, Carnegie Mellon, CMU/SEI-2004-TN-046, December, 2004.*

[209] Chamber 21st Century Dictionary (1996), [Online]: http://www.chambersharrap.co.uk/chambers/features/chref/chref.py/main?query=culture&title=21st

[210] DTI, "Information Security Breaches Survey 2004", Technical Report, PricewaterhouseCoopers, 2004.

[211] SVG, "Scalable Vector Graphics", XML Graphics for the Web, [Online] http://www.w3.org/Graphics/SVG/ [Accessed 4th november 2008].

[212] Gartner, "Organisations Underestimate the Challenges of Managing Security and Privacy in Global Outsourcing", *Gartner's Outsourcing & IT Services Summit, London, UK, 16-18th April, 2008.*

[213] B. C. George and D. R. Gaut, "Offshore Outsourcing to India by U.S. and E.U. Companies. Legal and Cross-Cultural Issues that Affect Data Privacy Regulation in Business Process Outsourcing", *Business Law Journal, University of California, Davis, School of Law, 2006*

[214] L. Goasduff and C. Swedemyr, "Organisations Underestimate the Challenges of Managing Security and Privacy in Global Outsourcing", 2007.

[215] B. Fraser, The Site Security Handbook, RFC 2196, 1997.

[216] M. E. Johnson and E. Goetz, "Embedding information Security into the Organisation", *IEEE Security & Privacy*, **Vol. 5, No. 3, pp. 16-24,** *May/June 2007.*

[217] C. Onwubiko, "Data Fusion in Security Evidence Analysis", *Proceedings of the 3rd Conference on Advances in Computer Security and Forensics, ACSF 2008, Liverpool, UK, ISBN: 978-1-902560-20-5, 2008.*

[218] C. Onwubiko and A. Lenaghan, "Challenges and Complexities of Managing Information Security", *International Journal of Electronic Security and Digital Forensics (IJESDF), ISSN 1751-9128,* **Vol. 3, No. 1,** *2009.*

Index

intrusion detection systems, 65, 68, 69
Intrusion Prevention Systems, 86
IP, 31, 171
IPP, 22
IPS, 31, 67, 86
IPS simulation mode, 86
IPSec, 31, 67
ISAF, 31, 93, 95, 96, 114–116
ISO 27001-2, 44, 49
ISP, 72
ITIL, 44

Java Programming Language, 143
JavaSpaces, 119
Juniper, 170
Juniper's cflowd, 71

Kalman filter, 160, 166
Kerberos, 39, 40

LAN, 171, 189, 193
Lattice model, 82
Legislation, 45, 54, 56
legislation, 53
LIME, 119
Linda, 117
Linked list, 143
Localised Countermeasure, 78
Localised defence systems, 76
Localised Security Approach, 77
localised systems, 23, 76, 91
log parser, 173
logical, 133
London, UK, 202

MAC, 171
Madrid train bombing attack, 202
Malicious codes, 22
Managing security, 20
Manipulation, 64
MARS, 31, 85
masters, 77
mathematical analysis, 25

Maximum common subgraph, 136, 138
MCS, 31, 138
Metaverses, 56
metropolitan area networks, 35
Microsoft, 79
military, 34
Modification, 20
Modularity of attack tools, 22
Monotonic responses, 108
MSBlast, 21
multisensor, 27, 70, 73, 123
Multisensor data fusion, 155, 156
multisensor fusion, 24, 70, 73, 185, 201
Multisource Data Fusion, 155
MySpace, 56

NAC, 65, 67, 83
NAP, 67, 83
national police, 34
Natural Disaster Threats, 58
Natural Disasters, 25, 58, 62
NDA, 49
NESSUS, 168
Netflow, 71
Network Access Protection, 65, 79
Network Admission Control, 65, 79
network scans, 27, 168, 175, 177, 189
Network Security, 33, 36
network security forensics, 87
network services, 83
network worm, 29, 168, 175
NIST, 31, 36, 38, 51, 58
NMAP, 21, 168, 173, 189
non-disclosure agreements, 49
non-functional requirements, 106
Normalisation, 85
Normalization factor, 164
NP-complete, 96, 149
NRT, 95
NSM, 31
NTOP, 103, 170, 173, 198

About the Author

Cyril Onwubiko, *PhD, MSc, BSc* (1ˢᵗ *Class Honours***)**

Dr. Onwubiko is a security consultant at British Telecommunications (BT). Prior to BT, he spent eight years at COLT Telecommunications, participating in several projects, whilst helping COLT develop its Pan-European IP VPN suite of services for managed customers, such as Enterprise-MPLS and IP Corporate VPNs.

Currently Dr. Onwubiko chairs the Intelligence and Security Assurance, E-Security Group at Research Series, London, UK. He is an IEEE member, a reviewer for various Information and Computer Network Security Journals, a guest speaker at various Conferences, and a visiting guest lecturer to a couple of Universities in the UK. He is the author of over 30 technical papers, reports, presentations and book chapter.

Dr. Onwubiko has a PhD in Computer Network Security from Kingston University, London, UK, an MSc in Internet Engineering from the University of East London, London, UK, and a BSc, *first class honours*, in Computer Science & Mathematics from Federal University of Technology, Owerri.

His research interests are in the field of Computer Network Security, Cyber Threat Analysis, Graph Theory, Intelligence & Security Informatics, Intrusion Detection Systems, and Data Fusion. He is also interested in the Mathematical Analysis of Security, and the application of Mathematics in solving real-life problems.

www.ingramcontent.com/pod-product-compliance
Lightning Source LLC
LaVergne TN
LVHW022308060326
832902LV00020B/3336